The Warrior's Manual
The Ancient Path of the Warrior King for the Warrior Bride

Dustin Carl-Lee Smith Hedrick

Second Edition

Copyright
THE HOLY BIBLE, NEW INTERNATIONAL VERSION®, NIV® Copyright © 1973, 1978, 1984, 2011 by Biblica, Inc.® Used by permission. All rights reserved worldwide.

Scripture taken from the New King James Version®. Copyright © 1982 by Thomas Nelson, Inc. Used by permission. All rights reserved.

Contemporary English Version®
Copyright © 1995 American Bible Society. All rights reserved.

The KJV is public domain in the United States.

First Edition Copyright © 2014 by Dustin CLS Hedrick
Copyright © 2016 by Dustin CLS Hedrick
All rights reserved. No part of this publication may be reproduced, distributed, or transmitted in any form or by any means, including photocopying, recording, or other electronic or mechanical methods, without the prior written permission of the publisher, except in the case of brief quotations embodied in critical reviews and certain other noncommercial uses permitted by copyright law. For permission requests, write to the publisher, addressed "Attention: Permissions Coordinator," at the address below.

Dustin Hedrick Publishing PO Box 601
Emmitsburg, MD 20 www.dustinhedrick.com

Ordering Information:
Quantity sales. Special discounts are available on quantity purchases by corporations, associations, and others. For details, contact the publisher at the address above.

Printed in the United States of America

Publisher's Cataloging-in-Publication data Hedrick, Dustin. The Warrior's Manual : The ancient path of the warrior king for the warrior bride / Dustin Carl-Lee Smith Hedrick.
ISBN 978-0990336952. The main category of the book —Non-fiction —Religion.

DEDICATION

This book is dedicated to my kids. The ones I know right now are Anna Elizabeth Hedrick, Lydia Grace Hedrick and Malachi Isaac Hedrick. There may be more to come, however, you three are the reason for my writing. And this book further goes out to any of my kids that are to be born or adopted, the grandkids and great grandkids that will be after and on.

And then I as well dedicate this book to all the kids (some of which are adults now) that have been in my youth ministries or churches or will yet to be.

Lastly, this book goes out to the kids that will grow up in a day where the days are shortened and the very elect are almost deceived. I leave this legacy to guide you. I pray it will decipher truth for you in a day when Holy Spirit may not be readily available. This book is for you, to help you find your way in the dark. HE can be found. Look to the LIGHT!

CONTENTS

	Forward	Pg vii
	Preface	Pg ix
1	The Warrior's Creed	1
2	The Warrior's Impetus	Pg 6
3	The Warrior's Path	Pg 10
4	The Maturing Warrior	Pg 23
5	The Warrior's Habits	Pg 39
6	The Warrior's Center	Pg 64
7	The Warrior's Ear	Pg 84
8	The Warrior's Gifts	Pg 92
9	The Warrior Bride	Pg 111
10	The War & Weapons	Pg 126
11	The Warrior's Bounty	Pg 156
12	The Warrior's Prayer	Pg 172
13	The Warrior's Comrades	Pg 186
14	The Warrior's King & Country	Pg 200
15	The Warrior's Strength	Pg 215
16	The Warrior's Heart	Pg 232
	Thank You's	Pg 245
	Appendix – Revival Timeline	Pg 246

FORWARD

My name means warrior. Thus, the name of the book. It's not original. It's just what burns in my gut. I have lived long enough and done enough years in ministry (20) that I can sincerely write this book and say what I am about to. There is no catch and I am very comfortable with who I am and who GOD is when I say this, so I say it with a clear conscience. After spending too many years concerned about what men thought, I just couldn't do it any longer. So, this book is straight forward and straight from the gut.

The real audience I intend this book for are immediately for my children and their kids. And later for those that come after who are more than church goers and actually may live in a time where there are no churches to go to that are not underground or owned by culture or are so pluralistic as to be false religions no longer saying Jesus is the Only way to the Father, the Only Truth and the Only Life. And if that is the case, then I hope this book really helps you. I meant it for you. Read on.

So, can I just say here that I really hope you do not read this book if you don't want to. It will not hurt my feelings, I promise. I hope you did not buy this book to do someone a favor and I hope it did not get given to you because it made some reading list.

If you don't like what you read, please put it down and walk away. I am not asking anyone to like the contents. As a matter of fact, there will be things that will make you uncomfortable and if I were able to do it, I would put some kind of warning on the cover that says, "Explicit Content."
I probably wouldn't like this book myself if I had not had Holy Spirit on my back stirring me up till it was done.

I wrote this book with a sense that it would be lost.

Before I wrote this work, I had been very ill and I knew that I needed to pass off my church as well as my way of life to another generation. This book is the sum of all the things that I live for. I wrote it all here for the next generation that was stirred for GOD.

And I wrote it here for my kids. I really do not mind if you do not read this book or if you do not like it. This book is meant to be sealed to the ones that are not to read it till the day when GOD opens the hearts and eyes so that it can be found again.

I have been obedient in life and ministry and now I have been obedient in writing down the things HE told me to. HE has led me to believe that later, after I am gone, this book will be important to a few.

I am writing this for you.

The few.

My hope is that as things grow darker, you will shine brighter. I have done my best to open the veil on my personal, intimate walk with Holy Spirit in a revealing way that I am uncomfortable with and I have attempted to share HIS heart as I hear it. I have not filtered this book and am not deleting or editing it. I wrote the entire contents in 10 days. And you can see it is a couple hundred pages. This book comes from a life lived. I am not telling you to do something I have not lived. I have lived the BIBLE and this book is what has come from it.

Again, please do not feel bad if you do not read this book. If you are my kid, YOU BETTER READ THIS BOOK! If you are not, don't worry about it. It will be revealed to the ones that must; by the burning in their inmost being and their response to Holy Spirit's drawing. So, if you burn now, read on.

PREACE

What we put in will be what we get out. If we sow into life, we will receive life and if we sow into death, we will reap death. Watch and be careful what you fill your time with, your heart will be filled with the fruit of what you consume.

"If you would be my followers, you must eat my flesh and drink my blood... Will you leave me too?" —Jesus

"Where would we go LORD? Only you have the WORDS of life..." -Peter (And all of us...)

Beginnings
The Warrior's Creed
Being Watchful
1. Keep an Eye out for things to Learn & Memorize.

2. Find ways to become founded.

3. Take moments throughout this chapter to take a look at your life and measure it to a new standard.

4. Then, ask Holy Spirit for help growing & changing.

5. Don't be afraid to dig deep.

6. Begin now with a prayer, "Holy Spirit, teach me. Let me know YOU. May I never be the same..."

1 The Warrior's Creed

There is really no way to start to share everything I want to share without first framing our faith. Today there is a sheer intolerance for intolerance, which seems to be a strange thing to say, but it is true. That being the case, no one likes the way real true Christian faith is seemingly intolerant and is not a club that has a low bar for membership. As a matter of fact, more and more in the Western church, the same old enemy is showing up. It is pluralism & universalism. For those that have not studied history of the church, this seems like a new thing. For those of us who have studied the history of this faith, we know that at almost every moment GOD has been about to move in revival power, this has been the case. These are not new things. We just think they are. It has always been a temptation to lower the bar for the church in order to grow or at least in order to keep from totally disappearing from the earth as our numbers dwindle. This is dangerous. We cannot lower the bar. We have no right to change anything that Jesus or Scripture has said.

In each season this has happened over the many generations of the church, the folks who are most easily swayed are the ones that do not found everything they are on Scripture. So, the first thing that I must do here is reaffirm what the Holy Spirit led through the early church Fathers and say that I agree with the canon of Scripture being the same as the one they came up with. I agree with the Pharisaic Torah and the New Testament without the Apocryphal writings (writings with false names or written by the wrong people with false information in them). Those 66 books are where I stand.

And I actually believe we should memorize as much of these as possible. What if you need them and do not have it on hand? What if they no longer exist? You may be the only Bible someone comes into contact with. Don't just memorize the names of the books, memorize the contents, the timeline, the stories, the exact words.

THE 66 BOOKS OF THE BIBLE ARE:
Old Testament:
Genesis | Exodus | Leviticus | Numbers | Deuteronomy | Joshua | Judges | Ruth | 1 Samuel | 2 Samuel | 1 Kings | 2 Kings | 1 Chronicles | 2 Chronicles | Ezra | Nehemiah | Esther | Job | Psalm | Proverbs | Ecclesiastes | Song of Solomon | Isaiah | Jeremiah | Lamentations | Ezekiel | Daniel | Hosea | Joel | Amos | Obadiah | Jonah | Micah | Nahum | Habakkuk | Zephaniah | Haggai | Zechariah | Malachi
New Testament:

Matthew | Mark | Luke | John | Acts | Romans | 1 Corinthians | 2 Corinthians | Galatians | Ephesians | Philippians | Colossians | 1 Thessalonians | 2 Thessalonians | 1 Timothy | 2 Timothy | Titus | Philemon | Hebrews | James | 1 Peter | 2 Peter | 1 John | 2 John | 3 John | Jude | Revelation

Secondly, we must agree with Jesus Christ being the one and only Messiah and LORD. GOD is three persons, yet one. This is in agreement with the Nicene Creed or Apostle's Creed, which is:

THE APOSLE'S CREED:
1. I believe in God the Father, Almighty, Maker of heaven and earth:
2. And in Jesus Christ, his only begotten Son, our Lord:
3. Who was conceived by the Holy Spirit, born of the Virgin Mary:
4. Suffered under Pontius Pilate; was crucified, died and buried: He descended into hell:
5. The third day he rose again from the dead:
6. He ascended into heaven, and sits at the right hand of God the Father Almighty:
7. From there he shall come to judge the quick and the dead:
8. I believe in the Holy Spirit:
9. I believe in the holy catholic church: the communion of saints:
10. The forgiveness of sins:
11. The resurrection of the body:
12. And the life everlasting. Amen.

(The reference to the catholic church in the Apostle's Creed is not the Roman Catholic church but meaning the church around the world as one body).

And Jesus is the only way to the Father. Which John 14:6 says that Jesus said in HIS own words that HE was THE way, THE truth and THE life. NO ONE CAN COME TO THE FATHER accept through HIM. So, if these are HIS words, we either agree with them or we don't. If we disagree, then we cannot say HE is Messiah and GOD. We have to say HE is a liar and a heretic. If we DO agree with HIM, then there are no other religions or works that can get us into heaven except HIS personal sacrifice on the Cross. HE is the ONLY way. So, if you have been looking for whatever it was that was missing in your life, "the empty spot," it is HIM!!!! And HE is not dead, HE is alive. So, when you accept HIM as LORD and Savior, the great news is no matter where you are or what you've done or how alone you feel, HE is now right there with you. Never will you be alone again. HIS Holy Spirit will now live inside your heart and will write the TRUTH of the law inside you. You will be FILLED with HIS Presence. And you have access to all of HIS legacy, inheritance and Person and Presence as a Son or Daughter of GOD. Now, as you learn about who HE is, you will learn who you are. It's a revealed thing.

And that's the key here. Christianity is NOT a head knowledge or studied religion. It is NOT a works religion. It is a revealed relationship. There is something mystical and otherworldly that happens as you come into contact with the Holy Spirit day by day and you should expect that. You are now something very different.

CLICK HERE TO WATCH DUSTIN'S VIDEO, "INTELLECT VERSUS ENCOUNTER: CHRISTIANITY IS A REVEALED RELIGION"

However, what if you are not different? What if you are not a believer yet? What if you have never stopped and asked Jesus Christ to come into your heart and for HIM to take your life and be ruler of it and be LORD of all of you? Well, then either all of this seems foolish and this book is causing you to become angry or you are hungry and desperate for something to change your life and you feel as if there are pins inside your body and pricking as at this very moment, something that you've never quite felt before since you were a kid is waking up. Some kind of stirring in your belly is making you hungry and desperate and you feel as if you are on the brink of something.

If the latter is the case, read on.

If the former is the case, put this book down and read no more. Actually, throw it away and run away. It is not for you. It may be later, but it is definitely not yet. Don't become bitter and angry by the words. Just walk away. What does it matter to you anyway?

But if you feel the pinpricks I am talking about, read on. You are about to wake up. As you read, ask the Holy Spirit to subtly come near you and change you. Ask HIM to open up your eyes right now and ask HIM to stir inside your belly. Ask HIM to make you feel an "aha" when new things spark understanding. And as you have light bulbs go off inside your mind and things begin to make sense, tell HIM, "Thank you, Holy Spirit… I am drawing near YOU… Draw near me…"

Ask for Him to give you the ability to receive learning and to receive rebuke. And get excited as things reveal where you fall short or you are weak. GOD chastens those whom HE loves like a Father chastens a child.

And if there are words you do not know, find the meaning. Stop and set this thing down and find the meanings and then come back. If you are blessed to have a Bible that you can read and understand, mark the verses you see in here in your Bible and reread them in the entire passage in which they are written. Don't just take my or any man's word at face value. There is only one book that matters in all the world. Only one book have men fought to destroy and men died to protect. The Bible.

I encourage my kids and youth to memorize the fruit, the books of the Bible, the Gifts, the armor of GOD and the Apostle's Creed so that they have a foundation to base their beliefs in the faith, they have something to call people to accountability with and they are able to utilize the tools they are given.

On top of that, it is impossible to use any Scripture GOD has in HIS Bible against the enemy if we are not reading it, meditating on it and finding the meaning of that Scripture for our daily lives, memorizing it and committing it to the core of who we are.

Psalm 119:11, "YOUR Word I have hidden in my heart so that I might not sin against YOU…"

Crawling

The Warrior's Impetus

Being Watchful

1. What is your first love? Be honest!
2. GOD spells love, "T.I.M.E."
3. What were you created for? What is your primary purpose?
4. What does it mean to abide in HIM?
5. Is there more to this life than what you are already experiencing?
6. Pray with me, "Father, is there something more to this life? Give me hope right now and begin to reveal to me by YOUR Holy Spirit who YOU say I am. In Jesus' name, Amen.

2 THE WARRIOR'S IMPETUS

Definition of Impetus:
"The force or energy with which a body moves."
What is our impetus? Is it duty? The older son would have told the prodigal this. No, it's love.

"You have forgotten your First Love…"

I don't think salvation can be discussed without understanding love. So many people out there do not discuss salvation any more because they really don't understand forgiveness, grace and GOD's love. I am convinced that this is an actual tactic of Satan. He knows the main thing we were created for in the beginning was to be a loving companion to GOD. GOD created an amazing world however HE mystically or scientifically did it.

And the one thing HE wanted in all of creation was someone like HIM that HE could relate to. Everything that had been made was made well including all life, animals, creation, stars, universe, angels or whatever. In the beginning, it was all good. Everything was united in love and the goodness of GOD. However, nothing, not even angels could have the capacity to truly love GOD. In order for that to happen, there had to be space for choice, error and redemption. Animals, ruled by internal behaviors based on survival and reproduction (which were inside of GOD's command to be fruitful and multiply. In other words, even this survival mechanism of Animal Behaviorism was created by GOD, on purpose), however, they could not LOVE GOD. The only thing they were able to do is be ruled by carnal base level desire.

Humans were created to have choice, be loving and therefore were allowed to make choices that were not for love relationship and were only for themselves. Thus, the need for redemption. And redemption was simply GOD buying back with the price required what HE had always wanted. This purchase is only ever made based on man's reciprocation of love back toward GOD.

We were made for a loving long walk in a garden. We have the opportunity to be redeemed into that love again. We must choose to turn away from our story, our desires and our plans and invite HIM to take over. We then join HIM in HIS story. HE takes control of our lives. We submit ourselves to HIS will, and we allow our plans to die as we follow HIS plan.

None of this is possible without a day in and day out constant conversation with GOD. And the person that is currently near us, always available for this conversation is the Holy Spirit. We must desire an all day, constant, abiding awareness of HIS nearness as we go through our days. We can be in a lifestyle of constant relationship as we are constantly talking back and forth with HIM all day long. I do this personally by immediately saying, "What are YOU doing, what are YOU doing?" every time I sense something is wrong, I see an issue or I have a good or bad uneasiness in my day to day life. All day long, I check in with HIM and say, "Hey Holy Spirit… I'm just checking in… Love you… Father, I love you…"

I do this kind of thing all day long. You don't have to do it just when you wake up or go to bed or at meals. Life is better having a constant long, hand holding walk with HIM. HE desires a relationship with you that is real and personal. This is legit.

So, how do you start this long walk? Well, a wise old preacher told me years ago that, "Son, sometimes you have to get people 'lost' before you can get them 'found.'"

This sounded like a weird thing to me but I realize now that oftentimes, we do not realize what we need. Often we go to doctors in real life in order to get someone who knows a little more to tell us what is wrong with us and if you play a sport, you get a coach who has been a bit further in the sport than you and who can see the whole field in a way you cannot to tell you what to do. The same is true here. Our hearts are deceitful beyond anything we can know. The Bible actually says that no man can even know HIS own heart. If that's the case, then the only way for me to help you see your need of Jesus' redeeming work in your life is to take you down a path of thinking I went down as well as many others have gone down years before me. These are not new thoughts or ideas and I do not take credit for them. I am putting them here because they are necessary now.

When I say to people that they need to be "saved." Often, they immediately say, "Saved from what?"

My response is that we need to be saved from ourselves. We need to be taken out of our story, our predicament, our daily death and into life. The Bible says that Jesus came to give life and life more abundantly. (Life overflowing), however it also says that Satan came to steal, kill and destroy. I believe that we are either daily waking up to a life that is overflowing in relationship to an amazing, loving GOD who wants to overflow us or we are waking up in our own personal version of Hell.

Just as much as Jesus came to give us life overflowing, Satan has come to give us a death that is overflowing and continuous. Satan loves that inward rot we feel. He loves the things that keep us up at night. Nothing brings him more pleasure than destroying the very things GOD loves so much. We were made to love and worship GOD and to have relationship with HIM every day and Satan wants to make sure that does not happen.

The great news is that GOD does not have to change anything in your current outward reality to bring you life overflowing. Right here, right now, no matter whether you live in a slum or a penthouse, right now, GOD can give you life overflowing. He can change your perception of where you are and make a dung-heap, a mansion. When GOD is there, inside of HIS very person is everything you've ever dreamed of. If you consider yourself someone that is seeking GOD, then let me tell you, when you find HIM (and you will), you are going to find joy and peace that opens your eyes to a real world so that you will see past everything that weighs you down. He doesn't necessarily change our circumstances. (Some would have you believe that HE immediately gives you riches and anything you command or desire, but this it not true). He changes our perception. He changes our worldview. HE allows us to see things the right way. HE makes sense of it all. All of a sudden, the world in it's purposeless mass and our lives in its purposeless state has meaning and purpose.

You were made for love...

So, let's walk an old path together as I introduce you to the one I am in love with. This is the one whom I wash HIS feet with my tears and hair daily. My Beloved is here in this text. You will discover HIM. You can be forgiven much, just as I have and feel freedom as I do. Here it comes...
Introducing... My Jesus...

Before you know HIM, let me show you how to approach HIM...

Baby Steps
The Warrior's Path
Being Watchful
1. How do we approach a King?
2. What is our only way into HIS Presence?
3. Why must we be saved?
4. What can we do to earn HIS grace?
5. Pray with me, "GOD, help me hear some tough things I do not wish to hear. Open my heart, mind and eyes today to YOUR desire for me. Draw me near to YOU. Grant me the gift of repentance, and move me into grace. In Jesus' name, Amen."

3 THE WARRIOR'S PATH

I learned years ago that it is not wise to give someone access to someone important unless they know first how to act. After walking with Kings, Princesses and Presidents as well as many other kinds of world leaders, I learned that saying or doing the wrong thing at the wrong time can get you into a ton of trouble. Seriously. That's a whole other series of stories. Why would it be any different with GOD? HE is King, isn't HE? Why do we walk into HIS buildings and HIS sacred places and act however we want? How is it that we treat HIS Bride however we want? How is it we have no reverence? How is it we treat HIM with disrespect? Anyone that acts like Jesus is his "homey" is only telling me that they don't know HIM very well. The beginning of wisdom starts with an ability to learn to walk in a Holy Fear and Reverence of GOD. This is not a fear from "not knowing" someone, this is a fear that is birthed out of sheer respect and a recognition of the great deeds, acts and power of the one we are coming into proximity to.

If saying the wrong thing to a king on this earth can get you killed, why does it not make sense to us that offering the wrong incense to GOD wouldn't get us killed as well?

And the truth is that we cannot even begin to know who we are until we begin to know who HE is. If we are finding our identity in being GOD's kids, then we ought to understand that first we have to know more and more about who HE is and what HE does and how HE acts and that will then shed light onto who HIS kids are...

So, on to the approach... How do we approach HIM? I mean, if you were standing outside heaven right now and GOD the Father came out in all HIS glory and asked you, "Why should I let you in?" What would your answer be?

I have heard it all. Tons of people have come to me over the years and they have told me many different things. I have heard people give me their personal "servanthood" resumes. Some cults from the Christian faith are big on this. They love to tell of the works they have done and how they have "earned" their entrance. There are others that tell me that their attending church or being a member does it... This also is saying that their actions deserve entrance. It's as if they believe they have "earned" a right to walk into GOD's throne room and do whatever they want. There are others that say they should be allowed because they are good persons inside. My response to those is that even if they have broken one part of the law, they have failed and are sinful. Jesus said that. He said that even if we have not committed adultery (breaking one of the 10 commands), if we thought with lust in our hearts, we have sinned and have fallen short of perfection. That's HIS words.

And think about it? How arrogant for any of us to think we should be able to walk up to a GOD who created everything and tell HIM what HE is going to do for us? How arrogant for us to think we can pay HIM back for sin.

And how disrespectful is it that we would say that anything less than the sacrifice Jesus made on the cross by dying and then being placed into a tomb for 3 days and then coming back to life by the power of the Holy Spirit is the correct price.

Put yourself in GOD's shoes for a minute. Stop and think, "If I were in GOD's shoes and someone was telling me why they deserved to get into heaven and why my sacrifice and my loss of my Son was worth so little, how would I feel?"

As a matter of fact, just do this. If you are a parent and someone told you that your kid had to die for millions of people you don't even know yet, to live, would you be excited about that? How would you feel if you had to sacrifice your child for others?

How would you feel if someone after the fact said, "oh sorry, there was another way… Our bad…"

Or, "Oh well, YOUR child was just one person. No big deal…"

Would you be ticked at the waste? What if after all was said and done, people just acted like it was no big deal? Was it a big deal to you? What did you lose? What did it cost you? What did it cost your child? Would you let your child be killed needlessly? If you were all knowing and there were another way, would you have found it?

Can you imagine how hurtful this is to GOD? And if you think HE cannot be hurt, remember Jesus said that the Holy Spirit could so get HIS feelings hurt that you would never be forgiven for it. GOD has feelings. HE HURTS. HE ACHES. HE LOVES. HE WEEPS.

…thus, the need for us to find the right way to approach HIM.
We must stop hurting the Holy Spirit right here and now. He is the one that

draws anyone to Jesus in the first place. If you have ever hurt HIM before and right now you know it, stop right here and pray a simple prayer, "Holy Spirit, please forgive me for hurting you. Forgive my arrogance. Please work inside me right now again and show me the way… The ancient path…" Let's look at what the Bible says about this and let's find the path to beginning a loving, life long, moment by moment long walk relationship with GOD.

Romans 3:23
"…for all have sinned and fallen short of the glory of GOD…"

How many made the mark? None. Only Jesus was ever perfect on the earth who wore human flesh. So, have you sinned? The only answer is yes. That is NOT a judgment. That is a reality. I am not judging you at all. I do not know you. I simply know that it is true that everyone has done something sinful at some time both knowingly and unknowingly.

As a matter of fact, right now in our era while I am living, people even believe that the 10 commands no longer are important even though so many great nations have used the basis of these commands to found themselves. They believe that all of the original Old Testament law is non-essential for Christian faith. They do not hold fast to the Tanach, the Law, the Prophets, the Writings or the Torah at all. I respond to them the following:

They say that after Jesus came, HE did away with the "Old Testament." And yet, it was Jesus HIMSELF that said, "I do not come to do away with the law, but to fulfill it. Not one mark will be lost from the text if I have anything to do with it." What did HE mean by "fulfill" it? He came to REVEAL IT. He came to make it full and final. He came to put an end cap on it. He made over 300 prophecies proved in one fell swoop. In just 33 years years, HE NAILED the lid on that coffin. HE did not come to do away with it. HE came to add an exclamation point at the end of Malachi called "The New Testament."

Booyah!
"It is finished…"
And it was!

1 - What Bible did Jesus read from, speak from, memorize and teach? Yep, that's right. The Pharisees kept the whole thing in tact for us even through Jesus' day and it is the one that we still use. The Old Testament. Tell Jesus that it's not important. Are you better than the master teacher? In

Luke 4, he even quoted Isaiah to explain how the overlap of Kingdoms had begun. He brought credence to it. HE revealed it. It was fun for HIM to go, "You wonder what that looks like? You're looking at it…"

HIS act was aggressive and HIS belief was intense. What do we believe?

2 - When Jesus spent time going over the 10 commandments in the New Testament, he didn't make them easier to deal with. He made them harder. Read Matthew 5-7. He said that it was not good enough to do the exact law any longer. HE said that GOD was going to judge every single underlying motive.

Do you know every motive of your own heart? My Animal Behaviorism professor from college would beg to differ if you said "yes."

You don't. Have you sinned? Yes.

Do you believe me? I don't mind if you don't. However, you cannot walk this path till you know that you do. And beware. This next series of steps will lead to brokenness and tears before they end. This ain't no cute thing. GOD has every right to decimate you. I mean seriously, what is Hell but GOD doing exactly what we asked for in this life and making sure that you don't have to spend an eternity stuck in HIS Presence. He is a gentleman. He is not going to force HIMSELF on you. If you don't want HIM now, you don't have to worry about HIM bothering you for eternity.

CLICK HERE FOR DUSTIN'S VIDEO "SIN SEPARATES"

Read on…

Romans 6:23
"…for the wages of sin is death, but the gift of GOD is eternal life through Christ Jesus, our LORD…"

Sin deserves death. It's that simple.

This is not something GOD desires for any human being just like the literal place of Hell is not something HE wanted for us. Hell was created to keep evil separate from GOD for eternity. Even right now, Satan is still going backwards and forth into GOD's Presence and accusing us. HE loves putting us down. Which, by the way, if you are hearing horrible voices or memories in your head over and over and it affects how you see yourself, that's not GOD's idea of a good time. That's Satan's.

So, just like in the real world there is an equal and opposite reaction to every action and force is not lost, there is balance in the Kingdom. It's called justice. And justice happens. It will come down to every single account on the final day and in that day, there is a price to pay for every law broken. We deserve what we get. Don't think it any different. There is a payment, a wage for sin. That debt cannot be undone.

However, Jesus paid the full cost in the debt for every single person in the world up front. It was the Cross, and thus, the power of GOD. The thing that seems to be utter foolishness to the world, "the cross," makes perfect sense here. There had to be a price paid. A perfect, sinless lamb could shed blood that would be placed on the doorposts of our heart houses and the Angel of death would Passover. Blood was shed for payment. A life for a life…

Price paid.

And then begins eternal life. That life starts now on this side. The great thing about eternal life in heaven is that it exists right here, right now in the space we live called "the Present." The fullness of eternal life is already available inside of us and it overflows. It literally changes us so much inside that in our worst trials, we can only see HIS beauty and nearness to HIM. (Oh so much more to say on this, but this is not the time…)

[CLICK HERE FOR DUSTIN'S VIDEO, "REPENTANCE IS A GIFT"](#)

Romans 5:8
"But GOD demonstrates HIS love for us in that while we were still yet sinners, Christ died for us..."

Jesus' death was proof of GOD's love. And it still is. This proof is so strange. I cannot fathom anyone dying for me. I maybe could see someone related to me dying for me like my wife or child as they threw themselves into harms' way for me. However, having a perfect stranger do it before I was even born makes no sense. It is utter non-sense. And seriously such a strange thing, isn't it? Why a cross? Why then? All of these answers are somewhat mysterious even though I can find some explanation through Scripture and history, it still makes so little sense.

And the truth is that this is part of why Christianity must be a "revealed" religion. It's the only one like it. It's the only religion where your "works" don't get you redemption at some level. It's the only one where a gift must be received to be forgiven. It's the only one that has the main deity dying for the dirtiest of all.

It is foolishness to those who are perishing. But to those who have accepted it, it becomes the very anchor on which they steady themselves, the epicenter of power from which they move and the hope of all of their futures and dreams. HE becomes cornerstone.

HE died for us. Wow.

And let's make it personal. HE died for you. Not just anyone and everyone out there, but you. HE died because you were on the line. HE cared about this moment. HE knew you would read this book. HE knew you before you were born as Psalms 139 says. And HE decided that you were worth it. You were worth the beatings, the blasphemy, the pain, the loss, the being a baby, the poo poo diapers, the utter humiliation of teen years, the submission to men and the cross. HE saw you way back there and way back then and thought to HIMSELF, "_____, is worth it…" (Fill in the blank with your name).

And you were.

You don't know this yet, but inside you is going to be the Hope of Glory. And the whole planet is waiting for your revelation with bated breath. So, right now it is time to admit, "I have sinned. I fell short of GOD's glory. Please forgive me GOD. I am turning away from the life I have lived and every sin in it. I want YOU!"

CLICK HERE TO WATCH DUSTIN'S VIDEO, "THROUGH JESUS CHRIST AND THE CROSS WE HAVE ACCESS TO THE FATHER"

Romans 10:9-10
"…that if you confess with your mouth that Jesus Christ is LORD and you believe in your heart that GOD raised HIM from the dead, you will be saved…"

So, let's get this literal. And let me say this clearly here. I do not believe this is a one time confession. I believe that you must confess and keep on confessing day in and day out. Right now may be the first time you confess and it may be behind closed doors all by yourself, but it is not to be the last time. And it should be in public as well as private. Confess Jesus!!!!!!

And what does it say here?

Does it say, "Confess Jesus as Savior?"

Heck no!!!!! It says, "Confess HIM as LORD." HE must be the owner of us. HE must be our King. HE must be the one that takes all our rights, plans and desires and gives us in its place, HIS desires, plans and authority.

We no longer own ourselves. Our own bodies are HIS. Our futures, our decisions, our actions, our work, our families, our everything.
LORD means LORD.

There are too many people that "profess salvation" and never "Confess Jesus Christ as LORD."

If you do this, you are done. And let me tell you. HE is either LORD of all or HE will not be LORD at all.

And then beyond that we have to believe a miracle. Don't say it if you don't mean it. Even if we don't understand it, we have to believe HE was raised from the dead. It was a miracle and it is the beginning of our obedience to belief. If you don't believe it, you don't get it. So, don't ascent to half of this. Confess and Believe ALL OF IT!

This is not some easy thing. And I am not begging you to do it. It is required.

CLICK HERE TO WATCH DUSTIN'S VIDEO, "LORDSHIP IS DIFFERENT THAN 'SAVED' AS THE CHURCH CALLS IT TODAY"

Ephesians 2:8-9
"...for it is by grace you are saved, through faith -and this is not from yourselves, it is the gift of GOD -not by works, so that no one can boast..."

Did you do anything worthy of this? Nope.

Back to the earlier question, if GOD asked you, "Why should I let you into MY heaven..." What would you say? The only answer is, "I received a gift from Jesus called grace. I repented of my sin. I accepted HIM. HE became

LORD. I confessed."

It's all about receiving what HE already gave. Our ability to come into heaven has nothing to do with anything we have done. We cannot earn nor can we deserve it. It's free!!!!

And isn't that the good news?

It's free!

HE already did it!!!!!

We can even stop here and say, "GOD, right here and now I want YOU. I feel YOUR Holy Spirit drawing me. I recognize my sin and my lack and how I am far from YOU and in need of YOUR salvation. Forgive me for my sin. Forgive me for all the evil things I have done and even thought. Make me clean inside. Wash my heart pure as snow. Thank you so much for the free gift of salvation. Please come into my heart right now and be my LORD and my GOD. I confess YOU, Jesus, as GOD, Christ and Messiah. I believe you died on the Cross and did not stay in the grave, but you came back to life and rose again. Father, thank YOU for giving such a gift and paying such a high price with YOUR Son. Thank you for salvation and becoming my LORD right now. Holy Spirit, come into my heart and fill me up. I want to be a disciple and follower of Jesus. Lead me into all truth. Thank YOU for the cross, thank YOU for YOUR SON, thank YOU for cleansing me from my sin and covering my iniquity. Help me to find other believers I can walk with and a church I can worship with. Help me to live for you every day. Help me to sell out to YOU completely, take everything I am, my desires, dreams, hopes and all. I only want YOU! I give everything I am for YOU and YOUR cause."

FREEZE!
Why not right now stop what you are doing and take the above written prayer and not just read it but pray for real if you never have prayed anything like that before? Now, this prayer is not an end point and it is NOT what I call, "Fire Insurance," (Meaning, it is not a way to avoid Hell). It is the agreement and covenant to walk in a relationship with GOD. Think about it like a marriage that you cannot get a divorce from. *I mean, you possibly could, but that is a whole other issue that is talked about in the book of Hebrews and there is no coming back from that.*

If you do pray this prayer and you mean it, then the Holy Spirit is coming inside you right now and this is Jesus' Spirit who will never leave you nor forsake you. HE is now your best friend and will be with you through anything. HE is the great teacher and counselor that Jesus promised in the book of John, (See John 13-17) and HE is writing the Law of GOD on your heart. This means that you are now growing into the likeness of GOD. You are becoming like HIM and HE is more than your "conscience." HE is literally infilling you and you can be refilled with more and more of HIM as you learn to live on less and less of your own will and self-desire. Thus, the long walk and journey has begun. It is a relationship and you now get to hold hands with HIM. You are now able to talk with HIM and HE with you and you will learn how that all works as you go on through this book and life. And even if you did not have this book, HE will teach and reveal all things to you. I hope this book helps. But don't hold this book even near to HIM nor the Bible, which are perfect!

Now, all of a sudden, you can see that approaching the right way makes sense. Doesn't this honor GOD? Seriously, like we said before, it was so dishonoring to even act like there could be another way to get in to heaven. Isn't it such a precious thing to come to GOD and say that we understand just how much HE gave and we now understand what it cost HIM. That HE is so amazing and we are so unworthy of such a gift.

We are unworthy. And yet HE loves us so much more than we can ever comprehend.

John 3:16
"…For GOD so loved the world that HE gave HIS one and only Son, that whoever believes in HIM will not perish but have eternal life…"

Love. It's that simple. HE loved us with a love that does not make sense. And it is so much bigger than us. It was for love that Jesus chose the cross. It was for love HE endured it all. Can't you see how much love HE has for you?

If you were wondering if GOD loves you or if HE could ever love someone like you and you are now reading these words, stop for a moment and let the reality of just how much HE did and how much it cost HIM and how HE felt that just you alone were worth it rush over you.

Take a moment and imagine what the whole crucifixion story must have been like. Let that rush over you as you realize HIS gift for you and then become aware and allow the Holy Spirit to give you an "aha" right now as you become aware of that love at this exact moment.

Doesn't that revelation make the story so beautiful? How could an execution become so beautiful?

It's because this death bridged the gap between man and GOD that sin had created and allowed that fellowship again.

Revelations 3:20
"…Here I am! I stand at the door and knock. If anyone hears MY voice and opens the door, I will come in and eat with him and he with me…"

HE wants to come in and eat with us. Eating with someone is intimate. And HE desires that face to face intimacy with each one of us. I want HIM to fellowship inside my being and my secret places and my heart and my thoughts. Come eat with us, Jesus…

Matthew 28
"…Therefore, go and make disciples of all nations, baptizing them in the name of the Father, and of the Son and of the Holy Spirit and teaching them to obey everything I have commanded you. And surely I am with you always, to the very end of the age."

We need to demonstrate our new found obedience to our new LORD. So, find a church where you can be baptized. I like doing it the way Jesus was baptized. John the Baptist in the Bible immersed him, so I was immersed as well. And then we have to learn and share what we've learned with others, helping them to grow up as mature believers.

And that is part of what this book is about as well.

Welcome to the Ancient Paths, Warrior. Today is a new day for you and you are new inside. Take a moment and thank GOD praying and just telling HIM about what you've read and what HE has revealed has made you feel better and cleaner inside. Take another moment and begin to write some of your first pages of a journal on what you've learned and read here.

Journaling needs to now become a daily part of your life. If GOD talks to you, do you think it might be important enough to write down? Then do it. Do it now and come back and read more after you are done. Don't forget to date it. Those writings will become high water marks in your life and you can go back to these "ancient landmarks" and remember what GOD taught you about HIS character in these moments. They really can pick you up when you are down and lift you higher when you are up.

Be sure to always treat moments and places where GOD speaks to you as "Holy Ground." Moses had to take his shoes off when GOD talked. Do you?

GOD reveals HIS person as we accomplish HIS purposes with HIM daily. So, write down daily what HE shows you about HIMSELF as you accomplish the moment-by-moment leadings HE shares.

<u>*WATCH DUSTIN'S VIDEO, "THE LOVE OF JESUS MAKES YOU SHINE"*</u>

Learning the Walk
The Maturing Warrior
Being Watchful
1. What is maturity?
2. How can we define it both in the church and in our larger world?
3. How do I get fruit of maturity?
4. What do I do if I am missing some fruit?
5. Should we place immature people in leadership because they are gifted?
6. Pray with me, "Father, draw me near YOU and fill me by YOUR Spirit. As I grow in YOUR Presence, please develop fruit of maturity in me. In Jesus' name, Amen."

4 THE MATURING WARRIOR

Maturity is more important than gifting or anything else.

We want to grow up before we grow old. So, with that said, it is important to begin to put together some kind of Biblical understanding of what maturity looks like.

After many years of ministry and much time in the Bible, I have found that maturity includes the following areas:

1 - Fruit
2 - Stewardship
3 - Purity
4 - Disciples

Please notice that I did not say, "Gifting or ability." Here is a truth. GOD is more interested in your availability than your ability. It is your greatest strengths that are truly your weaknesses.

FRUIT

The fruit of the Spirit are just that. They are fruit. Fruit comes from a branch that is in a constant, connected state to the vine it is drawing nutrients from. And we are to be connected to Jesus (the Vine, see John 15) and we are to continually bear fruit. If we are in a day to day, moment to moment relationship with Jesus through the Holy Spirit and we abide in the vine this way always training our minds back to being aware of HIS nearness, then we will have the result of fruit in our lives.

Fruit of the Spirit is a result. It's a side effect. It's an outcome and a benefit. We are not able to make ourselves fruitful, however, we become fruitful because of our nearness to HIM.

So, when we approach the list of fruit we are to have, we do not look at this as a checklist and say, "I have eight fruit, and I am missing one. I had better work harder at having that fruit…"

No!!!!!

When we notice there is a fruit we are missing, we slam on the breaks in our lives and stop everything. We slow down and listen. We take an internal audit and see where we have become calloused to Holy Spirit. Then, we apologize for the hardness of our hearts, we allow HIM to chasten us and teach us and then we ask HIM to reveal more of HIMSELF and Jesus to us. We commune with HIM and allow HIM to soak us inside. I turn on worship and turn off everything that distracts and get quiet and simply listen to HIM for a while till I can sense HIS nearness and I feel myself being refilled again. Sometimes I pull out the guitar and since I am daily reading the Bible, I will instead turn the Bible on on one of my recordings such as an app in my smartphone and listen to the Scripture and instead of studying it hard, I simply allow it to wash over me. As I do this, often times, HE simply refills me inside and the next thing I know, I can feel the fruit coming back on again.

The presence of fruit in our lives is sign of Holy Spirit abiding inside of us and our time spent daily in HIM.

The absence of fruit in our lives is proof of the flesh being in control and our being out of communion with the Holy Spirit.

When we or our mentors or accountability partners or spouses or friends notice that we are missing the fruit, we need to recognize what is happening and run back to relationship. If there is sin, we need to confess it. We need to open up the channels for communing with our beloved.

A long life of fruit filled living is a sign of maturity. The more someone is grafted into the vine and finding all their life resource from their being in HIS Presence, the more there is fruit. It is natural to have fruit when you are near GOD. And the more regular the fruit of the Spirit showing up over years in a person's life and the lack of fleshy fruit is real living proof of maturity.

So, we must stop giving people platforms and offices who are not mature in the fruit of the Spirit. We have made many mistakes in this era and the last revivals by calling people prophets who were not prophets and who were not showing long term fruit of the Spirit. We have to stop this. They may say something prophetically, but they are NOT A PROPHET without the fruit!!!!!!!!!

"Beware of the false prophets, who come to you in sheep's clothing, but inwardly are ravenous wolves. You will know them by their fruits. Grapes are not gathered from thorn bushes nor figs from thistles, are they? So every good tree bears good fruit, but the bad tree bears bad fruit."

-Jesus Christ (Matthew 7:15-17)

Does this make sense? Jesus is VERY clear that for someone to be a real, "Prophet" or anything else, they MUST BEAR FRUIT. And we are able to inspect someone else's fruit to discern whether or not they are false. We are expected by Jesus to be fruit inspectors. Jesus expects us to know who is false and who is true. This absolutely goes in the face of today's misuse of the idea that we are not to "judge anyone." You see, a mistaken verse about the lost world applied to the Body of Christ incorrectly makes everyone think that we are not to deal with issues of falseness in the Church. We are not only allowed to, but expected to…

In Ephesians 2:2-6, Jesus actually is even more tough on this whole topic. He says,

"…I know your deeds, your hard work and your perseverance. I know that you cannot tolerate wicked people, that you have tested those who claim to be apostles but are not, and have found them false. You have persevered and have endured hardships for my name, and have not grown weary.
⁴ Yet I hold this against you: You have forsaken the love you had at first.⁵ Consider how far you have fallen! Repent and do the things you did at first. If you do not repent, I will come to you and remove your lampstand from its place.⁶ But you have this in your favor: You hate the practices of the Nicolaitans, which I also hate."

Jesus wants us to "test" people? We should have a fruit test? Jesus "hates practices of people?" You see, it isn't me that is intolerant, it's Jesus. Jesus is the one that hates practices. Jesus is the one that doesn't "tolerate" wicked people. And seriously, there must actually be wicked people that exist if Jesus says so. So, not everyone is going to make it. Not everyone is "good," not every "way" is good like we mentioned before (John 14:6) and HE expects us to be serious about "testing." HE is testing us as to whether or not we "test" wicked people that try to penetrate the Body of Christ.

So, if we are to have a fruit test, let's define the fruit…

THE FRUIT OF THE SPIRIT:
Love
Joy
Peace
Patience
Kindness
Goodness or Meekness
Gentleness

Faithfulness
Self-Control

It would do us some good to spend time talking about what these fruit really are. So, let's define each one of them now as well.

LOVE
Love defined by the dictionaries is:
: a feeling of strong or constant affection for a person
: attraction that includes sexual desire : the strong affection felt by people who have a romantic relationship
: a person you love in a romantic way

However, I want to better define this. This definition is a good start, but it does not include all the Greek words for love, which in the Bible there are 3 used. Stergeo, Phileo, Agape. Natural affection, which we see above, is what is defined by our American English word, "love." It is "Natural Affections." Phileo is a love that is for brotherhood and Agape is GOD's Love. HIS love is otherworldly and far from Stergeo. HE is love. And if you look at the Bible, you find that HE IS LOVE. I encourage you to read John 14-17, 1 John and 1 Corinthians 13 for deeper understanding. And the 1 Corinthians passage is so right on that if you take the word, "love" out of it and inserted your own name, you would find where you are lacking compared to GOD's love.

GOD's love is perfectly inline with 1cor 13. It is the definition of GOD's "agape" love and who HE is in fullness. There is no real love apart from HIM. HE is the personification of love. All things looking like love are based in animalistic instinct and lust or personal desire or gain, not love. There is no true love apart from GOD.

And when we see we are lacking in a fruit, do we freak out and condemn ourselves? NO! We stop everything and run back to relationship and nearness to HIM. Our failings in fruit are a sign of emptiness and like I talk about in the chapter about the Warriors Strength, you need to run back for refills regularly, even daily.

One last thing, I think Satan's attack on love is best personified in lust and it's effects on those caught by it and the ones they affect. It ruins the core of what GOD designed for intimacy and twists GOD's perfect design in order to destroy intimacy. The direct enemy of true love and true intimacy is LUST! We must fight this enemy of lust! We must protect our hearts, eyes and children's hearts and eyes from this grand attempt to destroy us.

JOY
The Dictionaries of my time say:
: a feeling of great happiness
: a source or cause of great happiness : something or someone that gives joy to someone
: success in doing, finding, or getting something

However, let me redefine something for you here. Joy has NOTHING TO DO WITH HAPPINESS. You can have joy in the middle of great sadness. Joy is not understandable to its fullness by anyone that is not a believer. Since this is a fruit of course, having people write about it that do not have Holy Spirit in them causes us harm. And seriously, these words had different definitions when I was a kid till now. The dictionaries are ever changing, but the Biblical truth never changes. If you look at the dictionaries from the 1800's till now, you can see significant changes in the words and language in America. English in America is changing based on the people that are living now.

Joy is based inside of the Truth of who GOD is and is an outflow of the Holy Spirit. This is good news because when you are sad and things are going wrong, you can still have joy if you are in communion with HIM. It is an outflow of relationship. External reality has no bearing on it. We are not controlled by anything going on around us or the world. This world is not even the real world that we are governed by and citizen to as a child of GOD. Our joy comes from revelation as well. Sometimes in the middle of the struggle, GOD can reveal purpose or the next stage and joy comes even though there is great pain and not literal happiness in the flesh. I know this from experience. You can read my other book called, "A Warrior's Battle" about my dealing with sickness and pain and the joy GOD gave me in the midst of it.

So, the truth is that our emotions can be all over the place internally and externally, GOD can interact with us and have conversation and open up something otherworldly through joy. And we can even ask that when we are in the midst of our pain and unhappiness or loss that GOD reveal hope to us, which releases Faith and then that joy would come in the morning.

If I were dependent on my emotions and happiness to get up every day, I would have quit getting up during the season in life when the church split or I was kicked out or when I had to lead 5 small groups during the 10 year period of working two jobs when I averaged 80 work hours a week between church and IT and Finance.

Seriously, joy is based on who GOD is and HE can give us joy past the chemicals, mechanisms and more than are often battling us. We war against our very own bodies and we renew our minds with Scripture in order to stand during any obstacle or issue.

So, if you wake tomorrow in a sad state and a tough reality, ask GOD to reveal and give prophetic revelation so that you will live through the trial with joy!

PEACE
The Dictionaries say:
: a state in which there is no war or fighting
: an agreement to end a war
: a period of time when there is no war or fighting

I agree with these and add one more item. Patience as a spiritual gift must have a spiritual angle. There is a peace that comes from the Holy Spirit that is a fruit of HIS nearness, which I keep saying of the fruit of the Spirit. And it defies logic and understanding. It has the ability to give us rest in our soul in the face of great tragedy and adversity. I have seen this when GOD uses me in times of trial or tragedy. I have been a first responder a number of times at accidents over the years and I mean is has happened a lot. (Read my other book for stories).

And I am usually a pretty fired up and hyper person. When I am in the midst of a challenging situation, those that have seen me know that I do what I call, "Dialing it down." I take care of the issues and I get things down when the adrenaline kicks in. And instead of being hyper, very much against my own personal habits and style or personality, I am focused, direct and clear. That is a fruit of the Spirit. Especially when we exhibit personality traits that are different from our norm, we should give that credit to GOD.

PATIENCE
The Dictionaries say:
: able to remain calm and not become annoyed when waiting for a long time or when dealing with problems or difficult people
: done in a careful way over a long period of time without hurrying

I agree with this. However, there is a patience in man that is a human thing or an adapted response due to our evolving and learning survival techniques. (At the base level humans are animals and some stuff is innate, helping us eat, rest and procreate; all basic natural animal behaviorism). This patience goes past that. It has the natural patience that you see in this definition, and has the added patience that defies logic and defies animal behaviorism. There is a patience that does not work for protection, personal preservation or procreation. That's the stuff that comes from the Holy Spirit.

KINDNESS
The Dictionary says:
: having or showing a gentle nature and a desire to help others
: wanting and liking to do good things and to bring happiness to others

I agree with these as well. And I add the Holy Spirit has an added kindness that is totally altruistic in nature. It is not for what someone can receive back. And you cannot find that kind of kindness apart from the Holy Spirit inside someone. Remember, the heart is deceitful and even though we do not know it, built into all of our human kindness is some kind of expectation of reciprocation or reward even if it is for our kids and looks altruistic, we are programed to propagate our DNA and protect it. Therefore, when the added piece of true altruism is added to kindness and it is done with no expectation of reward and done in secret like Jesus talks about in Matthew 6 and 7 about acts of kindness and prayer, it is Holy Spirit. If you are doing kind acts and are angry because it did not have the results you wanted, you need to check your heart and run back to the closet and get into the Holy Spirit's presence till you are back in the middle of just doing HIS desires out of outflow.

GOODNESS OR MEEKNESS
The Dictionary says:
: having or showing a quiet and gentle nature : not wanting to fight or argue with other people

Good enough. I agree with this and I add to it that meekness is NOT WEAK! It is deep strength and it proves that someone is strong when they do not have to engage. Only fight the battles you have to and remember you are not fighting humans. You are fighting what's behind them. This revelation gives us compassion for the one fighting us and we then in humility begin to pray for them in hidden so that they will be released. Do not fight the human. Fight the real enemy that has captivated and captured them.

Like Jesus prayed, "Father, forgive them, they know not what they do…" However, we know that Satan behind those humans knew exactly what HE was doing! So, engage the right way.

GENTLENESS
The Dictionary says:
: having or showing a kind and quiet nature : not harsh or violent
: not hard or forceful

Again, I agree with the definition, and add that the Holy Spirit's added piece when this is a fruit is that this is not a feigned thing. It comes from being centered in the knowledge of WHO YOU ARE IN CHRIST! Therefore, it is impossible to truly be gentle from the right place and yet strong in the LORD unless you have revolutionary revelation of who GOD is which of course reveals who you are. Inside of that knowledge, we are settled and at rest and we do not respond the way we used to. When we lose this fruit, get in quiet and meditate on who GOD is and let Holy Spirit flow over you and fill you up on that as GOD refills into you who HE says you are. GRRRR!

FAITHFULNESS
The Dictionary says:
: having or showing true and constant support or loyalty
: deserving trust : keeping your promises or doing what you are supposed to do
: not having sex with someone who is not your wife or husband

In the Spiritual sense, this is not possible without the Holy Spirit being involved. The reason is Jesus upped the anty on these. To be faithful, it was not just an outward thing as this dictionary describes, it was something of the heart. So, you could not say your were faithful if you looked on someone with lust and you entertained thoughts that were not faithful from the enemy. Again, the thought is not the sin. We are all tempted just like Jesus. Jesus was flawless because HE fought the thought and did not entertain it by the Word and the Spirit. We must do the same. We cannot do this apart from the Spirit. So, there is a faithfulness that is human like an animal has such as a dog. However, in Christ, there is a deeper faithfulness that comes from HIS directing our eyes and covenant love relationship that makes us desire HIS ways. HE literally in relationship, writes the law on our hearts so that not one jot nor tittle is lost and we become truly faithful people.

SELF-CONTROL
The Dictionary says:
: restraint exercised over one's own impulses, emotions, or desires

I do not believe in any part of self-help when it comes to the Christian faith. So, I do not believe true deep self control from the right motives can even happen without the Holy Spirit revealing it to us. At the deepest breaking point, integrity is doing what you believe all the time even though no one may ever know. This kind of self-control cannot come from somewhere inside ourselves and even though as a wrestler in high school I was able to control my eating so that I ate a bite of corn, a cup of OJ and half a banana a day until I made weight, my heart was not in it. Once I made weight, I was gorging myself on whatever I could eat. We do not have self-control with the intent in the back of our hearts to not have to have it someday. So, this has to come from GOD as well. HE is the only one that can literally take the desires from us and make us shift into love that causes a response. In other words, when I began to fast more in college, I went on extended fasts that were really likely humanly impossible. I did it not because I could get something but out of a love response. Food tasted less important to me than being with HIM. I was so in love with HIS Presence I stopped being so hungry.

Some of us have had this happen in our relationships with a fiancé or before a wedding. It's the same kind of wooing that Jesus wants to do inside of us by the Holy Spirit that turns the light switch on in our inmost being and we respond with self-control which is really GOD control in us. But, HE does not control us like robots. Thus, we always have the ability to choose our own way, "self-control" with the impetus or unction of love.

DEALING WITH IMMATURITY
So, when someone is a leader and they are regularly not demonstrating the fruit of the Spirit but walk in fruit of the flesh, it is our duty to be fruit inspectors and judge their fruit and tell them. We need to stop them and make them step down. There have been many who have left the church who were younger believers who were hurt by fleshy, immature older church goers that lived in the fruit of the flesh and not the fruit of the Spirit and said that their being hard workers or being literalists in doctrine was more important than fruit showing in their lives and nothing in the world is further from the truth.

Jesus said that everyone will know that we are HIS followers by the love we have for one another. That is a fruit.

Also, the Bible says in Corinthians that every gift will cease when Jesus returns, but love will always remain. And look at that definition of love. I wonder if we could take every time the word "love" is mentioned in the text in 1 Corinthians 13, if we replaced it with our name, if the text would read true when it says, "_____, is patient. _____ is kind… _____ does not remember a wrong?"

It should if we are abiding in the Vine.

We will talk more about abiding in the vine later.

STOP RIGHT NOW AND WATCH OUR VIDEO ON THE FRUIT.

STEWARDSHIP

Jesus set the metric for what Stewardship was in his stories about the faithful steward and the deviant steward. In the story of faithful stewardship, Jesus shows that when we are faithful in small things, we receive responsibility for greater things. A faithful steward is put to the test when the master is not physically present.

And what did the stewardship look like? It was in money and talents. Today, we often look down on the days of small beginnings and we desire what I call microwave grace. However, if you have ever eaten something that is cooked on a stove top, it tastes much better than what we cook in a microwave even though it takes a bit longer to cook. As a matter of fact, things cooked in an oven often take even longer, but taste so much better than the former. My favorite meals are often made in a slow cooker or a crock pot. These things take the longest to prepare, but have the best results.

Slowly learning, growing and being steward over little things is the BEST! I have personally found that being faithful for many years in ministry that what to some would seem mundane has given me opportunity to have authority in higher and larger ways. It would seem hard to believe that stamping envelopes could put me in the same room with the President of the United States, but it did. And it would make no sense that staying in mud huts in the most rural edges of Kenya in danger would bring me into the leaders of the nation's homes for tea. But it did.

GOD always gives us small things to be obedient over before HE trusts us with the great things of the Kingdom. I prayed for hundreds before I saw the first person healed. You can too.

So, whatever it is that GOD has placed in front of you, do it with all your ability.

I have learned that obedience is what my wife defines as:

"Doing what your told, when you're told with the right attitude…"

I would agree.

We are just servants. We may not receive elevated status. That is not the goal. All we are after is hearing, "Well done my good and faithful servant…" I believe it is not the great ones that are speaking on TV and on the big pulpits around the world. It is the simple foot washing servant that is serving the dying day in and day out behind closed doors as Holy Spirit leads.

Do you have the ability to be a good steward with what GOD gives you?

What are we to be stewards over? It includes our finances, our abilities, our gifts, our time, our relationships, our business, our ministry, and everything else we are given. I believe that we must live in a sustainable way, not consumeristic and greedy and not living outside of our means, which many do today. And let me say here that debt is today's new modern form of human slavery. Fight it!!!!!! Be simple and prepare for tomorrow. Do not be in bondage to that slavery.

Can you be a steward? It requires your being in constant conversation every day with Holy Spirit. I am not telling the story here, but you can read it in my other book and the truth is that I remember being so careful with every penny GOD gave us and we had used so much of what we had to make the church happen. It was so scary to watch the market drop and one morning, March 9, 2009, GOD had me wake up that morning and put everything into the market at HIS leading. It was so hard to be a good steward, however, a long walk and a long conversation for many years had me do something I had been studying and praying about and guess what? That was the bottom of the market. The most experienced investors lost their shirts in that downturn and GOD had taken me and made me ruler over much. And remember, I had been faithful in small things for over 15 years at that point in ministry. So, slow and steady wins the race. If you want to read more about that story, get the book, A Warrior's Tale.

Lastly, long term stewardship is a sign of maturity.

I say stewardship is holding in your hand the gifts and blessings of GOD with an open hand. We simply allow ourselves to be a point where the blessings of GOD pass through. We do not have to believe that something we give will give a direct benefit and result in receiving. We give knowing that somehow, somewhere down the line that giving act opens up the Kingdom for receiving a reward later.

We do not do the giving in order to receive. We understand that we do it in order to bless Jesus. It's a real heart thing. GOD is all about the heart not simply the outward act. That's why in Matthew he says to do it in secret. I like to give quickly, then say a prayer giving the gift to GOD and its use and then trying to forget we ever did it. And for what I tell about in public, I have hoards of stories that no one ever hears behind closed doors and under the radar.

<u>**TAKE A MOMENT AND WATCH OUR VIDEO ON GIVING HERE**</u>.

PURITY

I actually believe a desire for purity comes as an outflow like fruit and that it is a kind of stewardship. Since Jesus says that adultery and the like are not just outward problems but are inward heart issues, then I believe that purity cannot simply start with being outwardly chaste, but is a heart thing and it begins in a prayer and relationship with Holy Spirit.

We have to do as Job did and make a covenant with our eyes and our hearts. Job said that he had made a covenant with his eyes not to even look upon a woman lustfully. So, it begins there. I actually took time when a teen to write out everything I wanted to become as a knight for Christ and made a creed that I put in a frame beside my bed and it became my covenant to GOD. I made a covenant to not lust or entertain lustful thoughts. I made a covenant to watch what I let go in my ears and my eyes. So, I literally threw away a hundred music albums, tapes and CD's. I stopped watching TV and movies or anything on a visual scale and literally would not sit where I could see a screen even at a restaurant.

One time I went to all the local grocery stores and asked that all magazines that had questionable covers were moved from where the children would see them. Many did it at my asking without an issue!!!!!

Now, this is a bit extreme, but I wanted to protect my heart and my life for the GOD who saved me and the wonderful powerful Presence that I had begun to see come in meetings where I spoke and I as well wanted to present myself to my wife someday as someone that was pure and had eyes for only her as well who had stayed sexually pure as I hoped she had for me.

This is what took place. Both of us had made some kind of list. I made one about the man I wanted to be for GOD and she did about the person she wanted to marry. And when we married, we were both virgins and had stayed chaste for our mate. Nobody does that! And nobody did that back then. We were weird. We were set apart.

Purity is our setting ourselves apart. I want to encourage you to make a covenant. Write out your list of what you want to set apart for GOD. Agree to it. Make a pledge to GOD to stay sexually and morally pure. As a matter of fact, people will say you are weird. Some people thought I was messed up mentally and I had friends pick on me for my choice, but no one is laughing now. We made a stand and you can too. So, take a pledge. Let it go something like this:

"LORD, I want to be this kind of person _____(fill in the blank with characteristics you want). Please set me apart for your use. I covenant with you today. I will stand for you. Please do the same in the person that is to be my future mate if I am to have one. I covenant to stay chaste till marriage night. I will wait for YOU. This is a demonstration of my heart as the Bride of Christ and it is a symbol of my waiting for you, Jesus to return."

I encourage you. You can do this. Don't have any kind of thing that takes your focus off GOD. And when you meet the person you are to marry, make sure to keep GOD number one in your life. DO NOT LET THEM TAKE HIS PLACE!

And if you have already made mistakes and you are no longer pure, I encourage you to make a covenant brand new today. Ask GOD to cleanse your heart and to purify you and stay chaste until the day you are married now.

YOU CAN DO THIS!

And when there is someone that walks in purity for a long time and it is demonstrated in their daily walk, then this is one more evidence of maturity. There are other points to purity, however, since our main battle today is against sexual immorality in all forms and its deviance from GOD's design, I think it is the easiest sign of maturity.

It all goes back to love. Just how much do we ache inside for Jesus. Are we loving brides waiting for the groom's return? Are we waiting with baited breath for the lover to come? Are we keeping our lamp wicks trimmed? Is the light burning for HIM? Do we have enough oil for the long wait? Will HE find us in bed with another lover? Are we prepared, mature and are we good stewards? MY HEART SAYS, COME QUICKLY LORD!

DISCIPLES

The last sign of maturity that I simply want to mention since I describe a disciple throughout this book (they are the warriors) is that a sign of maturity is "making disciples."

We have made the concept of making disciples to high and lofty and we as believers leave it for the ordained and trained to do.

Making disciples is a natural result of being a disciple. Jesus didn't ask us to do it. HE told us too. We are to make disciples. We are to simply teach someone else everything that Jesus teaches us through the Holy Spirit. I don't have a perfected way of doing it. It's just the fact that we are able to grab someone's hand and say, come with me as I learn.

Plants naturally reproduce plants and disciples of Jesus naturally produce disciples. A mature believer is naturally drawing at least one other person to grow into maturity in the Kingdom right behind them.

Every single thing in the world when it hits maturity reproduces. It's a natural thing.

Why do we make this so hard? We need to help someone else mature. It can be our kids and family, it can be another. We are commanded from the beginning to go be fruitful and multiply. And as Jesus said, "Go and make disciples." It's a fruit thing. It's a maturity thing.

So, guys, use these to discern if someone is mature. Let's grow up before we grow old.

<u>BEFORE MOVING ON, TAKE A MOMENT AND WATCH THE VIDEO ON CREATING A CULTURE OF DISCIPLESHIP</u>.

Building Stamina
The Warrior's Habits
Being Watchful
1. Where am I headed in life?
2. Am I purposeful in my direction?
3. Am I taking steps to get there and building habits in line with my goal?
4. Are there habits I need to replace?
5. What are habits I NEED in order to survive and thrive in my community, relationships, family work or school?
6. Pray with me before you start, "LORD, reveal to me where I am lacking. Direct me in what I can trade for better habits that will develop characteristics that are more like YOU by YOUR Spirit. In Jesus' name I pray, Amen."

5 THE WARRIOR'S HABITS

I am writing this chapter because I really hope that you are developing GODLY Habits that draw you into experiencing GOD deeper every day in your life. There are Phases of Worship that many of us never experience that happen really naturally if we will notice and allow GOD to move us through them. We often do not take time to cultivate our lives as we attempt to Encounter GOD, however look at what Henry Blackaby says are the key realities in experiencing GOD. He suggests as I agree that we must make significant adjustments in our lives and that we need to be obedient and join HIM in HIS work and that we need to accept HIS invitation. Each of these points require us to be proactive and be honestly and purposefully moving forward in this walk toward GOD.

In other words, you are going to go exactly where you prepare to go. If you prepare and plan to go nowhere and nowhere is your focus then you are going to get nowhere.

Take a moment right now and ask GOD to give you eyes to see and ears to hear what Holy Spirit is saying to you as you read on and prepare to make those significant changes.

Check out Blackaby's 7 realities in experiencing GOD here.

Those 7 realities are:

Reality 1: God is always at work around you.
Reality 2: God pursues a continuing love relationship with you that is real and personal.
Reality 3: God invites you to become involved with Him in His work.
Reality 4: God speaks by the Holy Spirit through the Bible, prayer, circumstances, and the church to reveal Himself, His purposes, and His ways.
Reality 5: God's invitation for you to work with Him always leads you to a crisis of belief that requires faith and action.
Reality 6: You must make major adjustments in your life to join God in what He is doing.
Reality 7: You come to know God by experience as you obey Him and He accomplishes His work through you.

Take a minute and let those sink in. Are you sure you want to go any further? However, if you stop here, you do realize that the next time you and GOD pick up in conversation, this is where HE will take you to first, right? So, why stop. Is it going to be easy? No. Is there risk involved? Yes. But, trust me. You will not regret the next part of this adventure. You can do it. I have done it before you. Just keep going.

If you have to put the book down because you are afraid of change, mark this place and do so and come back when hungry again. If you are hungry for more and you have been stirred inwardly at what I have been writing or maybe you got ahold of the other book I wrote called "A Warriors Tale" that I keep talking about and you are stirred with unction (that's an old word we do not use enough anymore), then keep reading. As you make the adjustments, HE will meet you. I mean seriously, this all started with me taking my Bible and setting it on the floor and reading it while on my knees in order to show reverence and then singing worship songs out loud in my dorm room with no music because I couldn't afford a CD player and weeping over these words in the Bible, stirred by the Presence. HE loves this desire. So, press on. HE is near!
So, I am not really going to develop these points from Blackaby. I am simply going to say that again, you need to get HIS book as well and read it. I have read it many times and I will read it again soon.

HIS way of describing how to "know and do the will of GOD" is one of the key lessons I learned. I have been a many year practitioner of Hearing GOD and I have cultivated the habits you are going to read about here in relation to knowing and doing the Will of GOD. So, HE wrote about doing it and these are the things GOD drew me into practically since I never read a book about them before until a few years after I already started doing them when I found Richard Foster's book, "A Celebration of Discipline."

Again, I believe that we humans primarily first and foremost exist to worship GOD, bring HIM glory, to be known by HIM, to know HIM and to be loved by HIM and know that love as well as to enjoy HIM and HE enjoy us. Since this is the case, everything I do as far as habits goes is focused in on that point and is anchored in that truth. If they become legalistic and rules or ritual versus a way for HIM to culturize me in the Kingdom and reveal HIMSELF to me as well as discipline me and grow me into a mature believer that is attached to the Vine and receiving life flow and nutrients from it which causes and outflow of fruitfulness in my life, then I am not going to do it. These are not works I "do for GOD." I only want to join HIM. So, be sure to get the love thing figured out first. HE showed HIS grace through the cross and has invited me to join HIM. What has HE invited me to join HIM in? Sometimes I do not know, but being invited first into relationship, I am cultivating that relationship the way HE likes and I know that these are some of the ways HE likes. And if that is the case, just like I learned a long time ago, I have to spend time listening to my wife and giving her hugs and responding to her for her to receive love and for our relationship to grow and for her to grow in love and life with me as well as we have to have shared dreams and visions. The same is true of Holy Spirit.

HE longs for a confidante, a companion, a friend, a lover, a believer, a listener, a learner, a worshiper and so much more. I want to be that person. I want to be closer to HIM than anyone else in the world. So, there are certain ways I cultivate that love relationship. All of a sudden, these habits are not something I have to do, they are something I "get to do."

And just like my wife, I have found that when I approach these with this attitude of "getting to" connect with HIM this way as a treat versus as doing this stuff out of obligation, not only is HE happy, but I come alive inside. How about that?

The same is true for your spouse. Don't believe me? Try it out. Do things that they love and invest in them. And it becomes easy to make them feel appreciated and fuller. Watch and see if they reciprocate and even if they don't immediately, don't you feel more awesome for doing it? That's how this love thing works for mature believers and lovers.

So, with that said… Here is some stuff you get to do!

GODLY HABITS

These are not the only GODLY HABITS there are, but I want to write about the ones I understand and personally do.

1 - Worship
2 - Prayer
3 - Bible Reading & Meditation
4 - Solitude
5 - Journaling
6 - Memorization of Scripture
7 - Giving
8 - Service
9 - Sharing Our Faith
10 - Fasting

There are more spiritual habits you can cultivate, but I want to focus on these for you to try. These I believe are my favorites for framing my personal habitual life of learning and discipleship. I spend regular and scheduled times of my life doing these habits in order to in-develop the activities and life of Jesus Christ in my life. I want to encourage you to put a number of these into place as daily activities done in a personal quiet time with GOD. Developing a daily habit of personal quiet time would cover the top 6 habits above. The next three are focused on our outflow from our daily time in GOD's Presence. And the last brings us into alignment further as we are seeking daily, weekly and monthly.

DAILY QUIET TIMES

As far as a quiet time goes, it is simple to plan 14 minutes a day when you can get away and get silence and focus on the first 6 items. Try doing the book of Proverbs and read a chapter a day, pray about the chapter before you start and invite the Holy Spirit to come and share with you what HE wants you to learn today. Stay quiet in solitude, write a page in your journal on what you hear as HE reveals the information to you. Date it. You want to remember what HE said and when HE said it. It's encouraging to go back and see over time how you have grown and what HE does.

Choose one verse from the passage and commit it to memory for the week.

When you close in your time, sing either out loud, in your heart or turn on music from an external source and agree with it and close by asking Holy Spirit to lead you that day in a way you can join the Father to do what HE is doing as HE is at work and ask HIM to reveal the passage you read that day through your day as you go. (See John 5:19 and John 15:5).

It's that simple.

Go to the end of this chapter for a worksheet on how to develop your personal devotional times.

STOP HERE AND WATCH OUR VIDEO ON HAVING DAILY QUIET TIMES.

WORSHIP

As you learn to worship, I want to draw from what I have learned from the early days of the Vineyard as well as what I've learned in fighting the battles we have faced more recently as the church is attempting to put "relevance to our culture" above the value of worshiping GOD fully and well. We have forgotten that we were made for love and GOD's love demonstrated alive and well is always relevant. We forget that we are not seeking the men who seek GOD, we are seeking the GOD who seeks men. And when HE comes in the room, seekers find what they've always have been looking for. My time in preparation for meetings is focused on not bringing performance, perfection or anything else. I am focused on the applause of ONE and the coming of ONE. WHEN HE COMES, clinic happens and nothing else matters. Remember this!!!!

The Kingdom is ALWAYS RELEVANT to those that encounter it!!!!!! WORDS OF KNOWLEDGE AND WORDS OF WISDOM come out of HIS person being in the building. They are relevant to the ones that receive them. Healing is always relevant to the sick and sight is always relevant to the Blind. Prisoners are always looking for the relevance of freedom and hope is always relevant to the broken. None of which is found in man nor in our abilities. Therefore, let's put our focus aright!!!!!!!!!!!!

Worship is the most important. His worship is our highest calling and the rest of this is a side effect of that worship. To put anything above this is truly lacking. There is nothing, no higher calling, not anything in the world we are called to do above this.

The Wimbers, used to talk about 5 Phases of Worship. They discovered these characteristics during the early days of the Quaker Friends small group meetings when Carol Wimber, Carl Tuttle and others were gathering to simply pray, worship and listen to GOD. They were stirred for something more and did not even have any idea what they were getting into.

In these early days, there were no methods and models or how to manuals on doing worship and prayer in a home group. And people did not largely separate worship and prayer as well as deeper Bible Study from the established church model that was centered on a building where people met weekly, bi-weekly or more often. Beyond this, as a simple college student, I personally started doing special worship as well as developing my own personal prayer closet at UNC at the "Green House."

I did not know anything about what these phases back then, but I personally, intimately learned these very specific characteristics about worship as it becomes more and more deep. So, when I learned what the Wimber's had experienced in their Quaker small groups, it further gave definition and I went deeper and deeper both in small groups and on my own.

YOU CAN TOO!!!! Start on your own and grab someone else or a small group that meets in your home or on your campus and try this yourself!

It was a really different thing to encourage people to worship together in homes with one or more people and as well to worship on your own.

So, as I discuss the 5 Phases of Worship, I am not sharing something that I came up with. It came from this place, however, I have been using these as a kind of help or tool NOT A METHOD OR MODEL as I have approached worship in homes with others as well as alone.

If this is not the way you experience GOD as well as demonstrate worship to GOD normally, I am not saying that your way is wrong. I am helping and sharing a tool that I learned over time and have more fully developed in my own personal worship times. So, if this helps you, that is great and if it is simply something that adds to your own personal worship style, that is awesome. However, I have noticed that as I worship, I open my heart up as well as Holy Spirit responds in very specific ways.

Here I want to use a definition for worship as we go forward. Let's say that; "Worship is the act of freely giving love to God."

In other words, worship is NOT about a building, a sacrament or a liturgy alone. Again, I did not say that any of those things are wrong. It's just that alone, they are not worship in and of themselves. They are ritual.

However, when these demonstrate or facilitate our giving love freely to GOD, then they are a part of our worship. Worship is sacrificing who we are and what we desire OUT OF A RESPONSE to GOD's love to us. In other words, our worship is an overflow of love toward GOD in response to an abundance of Love and forgiveness we have received. We CANNOT GIVE WHAT WE HAVE NOT RECEIVED! This is KEY!!!!!

Psalms is full of verses that describe our love for GOD like in Psalms 18:1.

Beyond this, worship is also an expression of awe, submission, and respect toward God (see Ps. 95:1-2; 96:1-3).

As believer's this is our primary purpose. If Jesus is right in saying that the most important thing is to "Love the LORD your GOD with all your heart, mind, soul and strength," and HE was stating this in reference to the first couple commandments from the 10 commandments which are, "Worship GOD alone and Have no graven images and idols," then we can easily say that worship of GOD is our response of love and is the first and most important command of GOD.

So, worship is NOT just a good idea and it is not something to simply "add" to our faith life, it is a requirement, it is a command, it is an expectation and it cannot come from ritual, rite or duty. It is LOVE driven, LOVE directed, LOVE drawn, LOVE deepened, LOVE developed, and LOVE demonstrated.

"Our heart's desire should be to worship God; we have been designed by God for this very purpose. If we don't worship God, we'll worship something or someone else." – John Wimber

So, that brings us to how we worship GOD. We know in the Psalms, that we can use various tools and instruments and there are many ways in which we can worship that the Bible either shows from history or actually COMMANDS us to do! Wow! That is strong stuff.

We can worship with song, hymn, new song, clapping, dancing, shouting, praising, bowing, silence, standing, arms raised, head bowed, spinning, jumping, with one voice or with our vocation in the Temple setting such as gold-smiths, artists and artisans in the Temple or even outside the Temple setting as Paul discusses that we should have an outflow of personal and corporate worship that goes into our daily lives as worshipers in ALL THAT WE DO! WOW! THAT IS HUGE!

Some actual means of worship in the church are:

- Confession, which is the acknowledgment of sin and guilt to a holy and righteous God.

- Thanksgiving, which is giving thanks to god for what he has done, especially for his works of creation and salvation. Again, these are demonstrated in the Psalms. Over and over we can read where David used terms of thanksgiving when communicating worship to GOD.

- Adoration, which is praising GOD for who HE is. We can use the Bible for this. It is full of descriptive terms about who GOD is as well as direct names from history that people have called GOD as they learned who HE is through daily activity.

Worship cannot simply be in our heads. It MUST involve more. It must include the body responding. We cannot worship GOD and lift HIM up if we will not demonstrate a lowering of self. I often call the church to get on our knees and bow to GOD. Nobody "likes" getting down on his or her knees and bowing to GOD. It is counter-intuitive. However, we MUST bow to GOD.

In our modern western culture worship is an action directed toward God and God alone. But this is not the case in the Hebrew Bible. The word "shehhah" is a common Hebrew word meaning to prostrate oneself before another in respect.

This being the case, we CANNOT truly worship GOD without prostrating ourselves to HIM. WOW!!!!!!

So, as you enter into this part of the worship discussion, go ahead and realize that you must lower your eyes and lower yourself when you approach the greatness of the KING OF HEAVEN who demands and requires our prostrated hearts. I personally feel that we must do this with our bodies regularly in order to keep HIM in HIS prospective place.

PHASES IN THE HEART DURING WORSHIP
(Try these both alone and with another person. Remember, we MUST keep worship and prayer personal and intimate alone which Jesus talked about when HE said in Matthew 6 and 7 that we should do our giving and prayer in secret as well as what was said in Hebrews when the writer said

that we should not forsake meeting together as well as what Jesus said when HE stated that HE was in the midst of us when 2 or more were gathered together. So, start at home on your own like I did in my room at college and then ask another person to join with you or start a small group. Don't wait for a church to do it. Be stirred and start one on your own).

PHASES IN THE HEART DURING WORSHIP

Let's discuss what actually takes place as we worship. It is important for us to realize what is taking place as we worship so we can purposefully ENGAGE GOD.

So often I feel like in churches today as well as in private lives, people are not fully ENGAGING GOD when they worship. I hear it in songs today. Many songs are written in the 3rd person or written about GOD rather than as a direct prayer and conversation TO GOD. There is a big difference in what we are doing with our imaginations as well as our minds, hearts, souls and strength when we are singing to others about GOD versus to GOD about HIMSELF, us and others.

For instance, songs that say, "Our GOD is a great GOD…" are singing about GOD. And think about who we are singing to when we are singing this song. Are we singing "to" GOD or "to" our neighbor? (This is not an actual song. I am just saying for instance). We are singing to our neighbor. If we were singing "to" GOD, we would be singing, "GOD, YOU are a great GOD…" And if we wanted to make it more personal, we would sing, "My GOD, YOU are a great GOD…"

Does this make sense? We need to be purposeful in our activity of singing worship. And you know, the same needs to be noted about liturgy and sacrament or rite. When we do any or each of these things and they are NOT directed toward GOD, we are doing them to the wrong place. Do we ever stop and ask ourselves why we worship and what it is we are doing when we worship? We need to. Also, it is important for us to start asking, "GOD, what do YOU desire when we worship? What songs do you want sung? What liturgy do YOU desire? What is YOUR direction?" We need to stop wondering what it is that will get a certain response from the people in the crowd. We need to worry about what Holy Spirit wants instead of the seekers.

We must realize that if we are only seeking seekers, we will never reach them. If we are seeking the GOD who seeks seekers, HE will be found like HE says and if we are intently aware of HIM and HIS desires and specifically careful with everything HE wants, not like Nadab and Abihu, (Aaron's sons that used the wrong incense and were burned up), HE will come and be found by us and people will find what they are looking for IN HIM!!!!!!

Understanding these phases of worship that we go through is helpful in our experience of God. And we need o keep in mind that as we pass through these phases we are headed toward one goal which is intimacy with God. Again, intimacy with GOD is purely not possible without forgiveness and love received. So, first, let's define intimacy. We can say that intimacy is revealing one's deepest nature and desire to another as well as belonging to that person. Characteristics of intimacy include presence or being present (this is a huge problem with people today. Many people are in rooms and are not "present"). Also, intimacy has close association and contact.

The phases of worship are:
1 - Drawing to Worship
2 - Engagement
3 - Expressing GOD's Love
4 - Visitation
5 - Generosity

PHASE 1 - DRAWING TO WORSHIP

This first phase is what I personally call the "Drawing to worship." We need to be called and drawn to worship in the first place. The Wimber's called this first phase, "the Call to worship" because In a worship service, a worship leader would be calling people to praise GOD and it is like the first Scripture shared, the first song or the buildup. In personal worship, this is a stirring that I often feel personally drawing me away from the things of the world to a time where I focus on GOD. There are times where this hits me in my gut and I literally get a stirring like butterflies in my stomach and all I can think is GOD is calling me away with HIM for a moment. These times are so heightened to me that I find myself racing home, running in the door and throwing everything to the side to dive into my prayer closet. Other times I cannot find a way to get home or a way to get to the Prayer Room and I find the nearest alone place like the 7th floor at my work which was always vacant and I would run in, dive in and prostrate myself and literally say, "I made it... I am here!!!! Here I am, LORD..." This is the "Drawing to worship."

The underlying thought of the call to worship is "Let's do it; let's worship now!"

I personally believe that if we are worshiping deeply all week long and we are flowing in relationship with Holy Spirit, abiding in HIS Presence, we build up all week long and Sundays end up being a big Crescendo where people have been building excitement all week and they are so stirred they get that drawing to be in GOD's Presence with others and as they come in the service, the drawing builds into the first song and this is explosive. I have been in revivals and renewals where this was the case. We were all so excited to see what GOD would do next. It was always exciting to be in the room because we knew that everyone wanted the same ONE THING and that it was about to get fun!!!!!

PHASE 2 - ENGAGEMENT

Engagement is the second phase and it is the exciting part. When we are in a group, you feel this dynamic of GOD's approval or HIS delight. This inside the personal worship experience is the same. Our worship expressions of praise, joy, love, petition, intercession, jubilation and all the dynamics of prayer are free flowing as an outflow and response to this "Engagement" of GOD. So many believers have never encountered GOD. They have never felt GOD engage them back. If the first step is our saying, "Let's do this," This would be GOD's response, "Yes, let's do this!" When the church is together in this moment, often we see the Manifest Presence of GOD and people often respond or GOD's power manifests in their body.

PHASE 3 - EXPRESSING GOD'S LOVE

As we are engaged by GOD, we find HIM revealing HIMSELF to us more clearly as well as sharing HIS thoughts, heart and more right in the middle of songs, liturgy, personal worship or whatever we are doing. Sometimes it is like HE is downloading information directly in my spirit about who HE is and who I am in relation. All of a sudden, Scripture makes sense as HIS revelatory power comes into the room with Holy Spirit. And as HE reveals who HE is, I realize how short I fall from coming near HIS holiness and glory. This isn't a bad thing. It is coupled with a continued chastening and the gift of repentance. This can often go from

Phase 2 through the rest of the Phases and is such a blessing. Just being able to see our own deceitful hearts as we realize just who HE is as HE reveals HIMSELF to us by HIS Spirit speaking through the WORD of GOD while we worship creates a flowing in and out of healing as well as revealing.

Then, we find ourselves no longer working up anything, as we see HIM as Father, we understand what is available as HIS kids. We don't have to strive for anything since it is already given.

We find ourselves using language that is more intimate and personal. It's kind of like when you first meet someone, you do not know what they really care about, so your conversation is light and is about something like the weather or the community you live in. However, as you learn more about the person, you find out your shared interests and loves, and likes. Once you do, you find yourself in a safe place where you can share your heart and there is common interest and common desire. This draws people into intimacy where there is a closeness and walls come down.

I have found that many people have a problem worshiping GOD because they are afraid of how HE feels about them or what they have done in the past and once they make it to this phase in worship, inhibitions go away and people find themselves face to face with LOVE revealed. As GOD moves closer and closer to revealing HIS heart and HE is drawing us deeper into letting down our walls, we find ourselves starting to really praise as well as to see our need for forgiveness. As HE comes closer to us, we find ourselves in need for HIS grace and mercy and forgiveness.

"Remember, worship is going on all the time in heaven, and when we worship we are joining that which is already happening, what has been called the communion of saints. Thus there is a powerful corporate dynamic." -John Wimber

PHASE 4 - VISITATION

This deepening of worship through revelation opens the doors of heaven. I know I cannot clearly state that there is causation and I would be wrong to turn this into a method here, however, I can see through Scripture that it is GOD's design and desire that HIS people become HOLY as HE is HOLY. So, as we become submitted and obedient in heart to HIM, we lower ourselves to HIS greatness, HE comes closer, we respond with opening up as I stated above and then we find it easier to receive rebuke as we understand who GOD is. If we believe GOD hates us, we cannot hear HIS words. We are afraid. Yet, as HE comes closer and we understand that HE is a loving Father like the Prodigal Son's father, we begin to desire HIS removing our dirty rags and changing our clothes. We then desire HIS embrace. VISITATION!

So, as we move into receiving the change of clothes or the receiving of HIS loving, fatherly rebuke and we embrace repentance, knowing it makes us more like HIM and it cleans the wounds in our souls and we love wisdom, we become HOLY like HIM. HE is moving us from glory to glory, revealing HIMSELF through us more and more as we are changed. We become like HIM as we allow HIM to reveal who HE is until finally, we are face to face.

This is the most intimate place with GOD. This intimacy causes us to meditate, thinking deeper about HIM even sometimes as we are singing or are engaged in some other act of worship. I have found myself in meetings or alone where I was mid-sentence in a song and I had to drop everything and jump right into journaling before I lost something. And let me tell you, when the GOD of all creation speaks, everything HE says is worth stopping everything for or dropping everything for and writing it down!!!!! Don't take any word of HIS for granted!!!!!

Here we find more where GOD is calling us to look deeply at every relationship, every thought, every motive and more to what HE desires and who HE is. Here in HIS Presence at the deepest place, sometimes I either imagine HIM on HIS throne or I find my heart and mind opened up to vision, revelation or dream (why lie. I have fallen asleep in the prayer room on the floor and had dreams right at this point).

At this point, physical demonstration in worship is a common occurrence. I believe that this is what was happening in David as he danced all the way into Jerusalem before the ark. And the literal Presence of GOD must have so visited so strongly because he did not even really notice that he danced his clothes off. What would have been an undigifying moment, was absolutely the greatest honor when you realize you are dancing to prepare the way for the fullness of the Presence of GOD to come back to the place where you are leader.

It was all in perspective. David's perspective was that HE preceded the greatest KING OF ALL as he danced and his understanding of the greatness of that KING was so much more than who he was that he planned to get even more undignified, thus demonstrating the vast distance between David's rule and GOD's rule.

Do we get it? I think not. However, in the middle of Visitation, you cannot help but "get it." HE is revealed.

Now, if people are working this up, it needs correction. If GOD is in the room, no one will notice the wild dancer in the corner. I PROMISE YOU THAT!

So, as expression has moved to the crescendo, we have fully expressed what is in our hearts and then we find ourselves lowering, slowing and listening. We stop talking and we wait. We begin to simply rest our minds and bodies as the greatness of GOD enters the room. We are in the midst of GREATNESS. Now, we LISTEN! ALMIGHTY GOD VISITS!!!!!!!

I find that this is where the gifts of the Spirit work the best. Again, this cannot be rushed and it cannot be worked up. And truthfully, any and all believers should know when it is wrong. When it is right, YOU KNOW! This is the fullness of what is best about revival and awakening. Visitation. "Remember, GOD dwells in the praises of HIS people." Does HE or does HE not. So, when HIS people are really praising, and they are together in HIS name, and we are even alone and at this point, then BOOM! HE COMES! "I will be found by you, when you seek ME with all your heart…" -GOD

And one last thing, if people want to see this in the church, then they need to be working on it in their hidden private closets. We should expect GOD to work in the midst of us alone and in the congregation. HE moves in different ways, but we see HIM move daily and often do not know it is HIM. Salvation, deliverance, healing, sanctification, and more as well as the gifts are signs of HIS nearness. However, in this phase, these become the norm and the room becomes charged with HIS sense of heaviness and nearness. There is an otherworldly sense about the room. I think people in church or personally do not even know what I mean here because HE largely does not come and we do not press HIM till this point.

I pray in a closet and in a room till people walk in and are overtaken by the heaviness of GOD's Presence. They become awesomely aware of HIS being real and present. This is something I have done over and over. It takes a lifestyle of doing this in the hidden with a cultivated relationship for this to be the norm in your life. The key to note here is that GOD is not our pet. HE is our KING, LORD, OWNER, FATHER, LOVER, BELOVED, GROOM, and MASTER. When we have this understanding, then we desire not to make HIM prove us or do tricks. We simply are available to HIS will, HIS purposes and HIS ways. At this phase in worship, this is our response. It is a moving away from self and our story and a moving into alignment with HIS.

PHASE 5 - GENEROSITY

The outflow of visitation is giving to HIS work, HIS will and HIS plans. We find ourselves not able to stop from giving. So many give out of duty and yet GOD desires to give out of love for HIM. And our giving must be something that costs us. It must come from somewhere in our guts. It must be moved by inward unction. It is a response of love again. Think about the woman that broke the jar of oil and poured it on Jesus or the sinful woman that washed HIS feet with costly oil. Think about what David said about the threshing floor? He said he would not take the floor for free for a altar for GOD. He said that he must pay "the full price…" David knew that if it did not include a heartfelt sacrifice, it was not the deepest worship to GOD. We give to GOD and others from this place of deep heartfelt desire to worship HIM. I believe this is what Jesus meant when HE said that when we do something small like give a cup of cold water in HIS name we will not lose the reward. Heartfelt worship that flows into worshipful giving is AWESOME! GOD LOVES THIS and it is the most mature outflow and result of worship.

Wimber used to say that "the church knows so little about giving, yet the Bible exhorts us to give to God. It is pathetic to see people preparing for ministry who don't know how to give." I always say that you have to "GIVE" to even release "RECEIVING." I believe it is more important to give when you are struggling than when you have much. If I hit a financially hard time, I find a way to give to GOD.

Wimber said, "We give our whole life; God should have ownership of everything. Remember, whatever we give God control of he can multiply and bless, not so we can amass goods, but so we can be more involved in his enterprise."

Don't think that this means GOD is going to make us rich and then we give. We have to be good stewards in the small things and then we become rulers of much. We have to love the days of small beginnings and make the best out of them. We have to be happy in having and happy in not. So, we give before we feel that we are safe to give. We do not give out of our abundance. We give out of our own need. Remember the widow with the two mite's? Jesus said that her gift was the best because she gave when it hurt.

Wimber says, "whatever I need to give, God inevitably first calls me to give it when I don't have any of it; whether it is money, love, hospitality, or information. Whatever God wants to give through us he first has to do to us."

"As we experience these phases of worship we experience intimacy with God, the highest and most fulfilling calling men and women may know." - John Wimber

<u>STOP HERE AND WATCH OUR VIDEO ON CREATING A CULTURE OF WORSHIP</u>.

THE NEXT HABITS
The phases of worship discussed above cover almost all of the depth I want to bring to the habits. However, I want to go on and say that habits happen when someone makes a commitment to do something purposefully daily for more than 21 days. A habit takes more than 21 times of repetition before it becomes ingrained.
The last habit I want to spend time on here is fasting.

FASTING
Jesus said in the Bible, "When you fast..." In other words, just as HE stated with prayer, fasting is an expectation, and an assumption, not a request.

However, what is fasting?

A lot of people say it is a lot of different things, but I go for the core belief that fasting is abstaining from something for a certain period of time in order to take the time that was devoted to that thing and apply it toward time focused on GOD.

The main kind of fasting I see in the Bible is abstaining from food. I suggest that if you have not fasted before, you start with a short fast like one that goes by the Jewish day which is sundown to sundown. You could say from 6pm to 6pm.

If you are comfortable fasting for a day at a time such as this, try doing a day from the time you wake up one morning until the following day. This is tougher because you do not eat for a full waking period.

When you have done this a few times and you want to go longer, try doing two separate days in the same week or two days back to back. And then if you have done this a while, you can go seven days.

There are people that have gone longer such as myself, (if you want to read more about some truly miraculous extended fasts, you can get my book, "A Warriors Tale."), however, I do not promote extended fasts.
Please keep in mind a few things that are important:

1 - fasting is ONLY to be led by Holy Spirit and is to be started at HIS leading and end at HIS leading.

2 - fasting in a very real way is killing the physical body. When you do not eat, your body is dying. As your physical body begins to fight for basic survival so your mind will often clear for some time and your "spirit" is able to hear better as it becomes stronger while your physical body is weaker. As Paul writes, we are at war with the "flesh." We of course cannot kill the body fully or we are no longer able to survive. So, there is a balance and we must stay led by the Spirit. But, truthfully, as the LORD leads and as we are able, we grow stronger every time we fast a little more, fighting against our natural urges. We are always trying to grow stronger against the fleshly desires and fasting definitely is a good way to gain control over our urges.

3 - What is the purpose of fasting? Nothing we do is to get GOD to do what we want. So, fasting as well has a purpose but it is not to get GOD to play tricks or to get HIM to give us what we want. If we knew who we were in Christ and our desires were left at the foot of the cross, we would

understand that when we are in alignment with HIS will, we can ask anything and it will be done for us. So, we don't have to fast and pray or do anything religious to have access to our Father's Kingdom and inheritance. So, stop trying to push HIM around. That is manipulation. So, why do we fast? We do it to come into alignment with HIS will. Just like when we start to pray, we desire to come into GOD's will. All we want is to know HIM more and to do HIS will. Everything we do needs to be centered in a deep-seated desire and longing for HIM and relationship to HIM. Fasting bends us. It molds us and makes us. We fast and we in the midst of it simply desire to know HIM and be known by HIM.

The result is that we are made more in HIS likeness. All of a sudden we realize that fasting does nothing for our gain except bring us near to HIM. We ache and long and hunger for our coming Groom. And we trade our hunger for food to ache for HIM.

The best way I have known it is time for fasting is like when I used to get excited for Lori to call me on the phone before we were married. Waiting on that call could sometimes make me totally lose my appetite. All I wanted was to hear from her. And I could forgo eating because of the butterflies in my gut.

It's the same thing I feel with the Holy Spirit about knowing Jesus more. There are times I just plain lose my appetite for food and I long to know HIM more and in the middle of that I just don't want food. And sometimes I get pulled into times where I trade that food and the hunger with it for hunger and aching and longing in HIS Presence. Sometimes that has drawn me into longer seasons of fasting. So be it. But, it isn't like it is a plan. It is a leading. It's as if HE is wooing me into an intimate quiet place where food matters little. I hunger for HIM and ache for HIM. And in those places and times, the flesh and the world become less real to me for a little while than HIS nearness. There is a more constant abiding awareness of HIM. And food loses its draw and taste.

This is a sacred intimate place. I love being drawn into it. And let me tell you, that says something because anyone that knows me knows that I may not be a glutton nor am I huge on food but I do like a good meal. So, these seasons are otherworldly and precious and we must stop everything for the Groom to woo HIS Bride.

Jesus said about the new and old wineskins that the problem with those who were caught up in the old way of doing the "seeking" and the habits and paths were mistaken about their approach only due to the fact that they lost the purpose. The purpose was going after HIM… The Groom. Get it?

It cannot be a program or just a "practice" as some call them. Our habits themselves are not a list. Just like the fruit, they come from relationship and they are a drawing. Get excited about being drawn into habits and seasons of wooing. When HE draws us away during these seasons, HE always reveals more of HIMSELF, HIS WILL and HIS WAYS. FUN!

DEVELOPING A DAILY DEVOTIONAL TIME WORKSHEET

Some people have asked me over the last while how I approach GOD, experience HIM and how do I daily and weekly prepare to teach, preach and/or do ministry. The funny thing is that when I was 9 years in some kind of more full time ministry or even in an established church, it was easier to focus and simply spend a whole week focus to develop my prayer life and/or the sermon I was preaching.

Now since I pastor a smaller church plant for the last 10 years (which has become a church that is self sustaining), I found it much more difficult with the addition of kids and a second full time job that is 40+ hours a week not to mention the 35 to 45+ hours I put in for the church sometimes through the night. And rather than becoming too busy to pray, I have become too busy NOT TO pray.

I have found that it is the most important thing for me to survive with praying and reading the word. I DRINK PRAYER & THE WORD now. I cannot survive without daily communion and when I go a day without hearing precious whispers, I feel my chest seize up, my back tighten, I get short with people, cannot breathe well and get overwhelmed. However, when I abide in HIM and stay in communion, listening and praying through the day, a habit developed from this discipline I outline hear, life no matter how difficult is VERY DOABLE!

And I find that instead of over the last 20 years of ministry that I am burning out, I am gaining maturity, patience, perspective and a larger capacity for life's challenges… Hey, I guess I am growing up before I grow old!!!!! Join me in this. Our capacity for dealing with life's issues or even our capacity to do ministry does not come from our ability. It comes from our relationship and its vibrancy with Holy Spirit, the Father & Jesus!

DEVELOPING THE FAITH LIFE

So, let's let our simple benchmark be making sure that we have specific concerted prayer for 15 minutes (literally forcing ourselves to stay still if we feel driven) every night. I think you are like me and are more of a night owl, so, let's say night instead of morning.

The catch is that I only know how to give you what I do. So, make this your own. However, the truth is that I have been going back to this old model since January (2011). I had changed my style of prayer ministry and Bible reading after I went to Blood n Fire and this is the way I used to do it in college. So, I am back to my old ways from college when GOD moved. I don't think it is the WAY or STYLE of the things we do that attract GOD, however, we know in Jeremiah that there are ancient paths that cause GOD's Presence to be drawn to us and us to be drawn to HIM. These are the Ancient Paths that I walked while the movement of revival stirred up.

WHEN YOU PRAY, TRY THIS:

1 – Start by making your thoughts, plans and will be placed at the cross. Literally state something like, "Jesus, here is this thing, this thing and this thing. They are yours. If you tell me to walk away from them or let them die, I will. I leave them at the cross. They are your problem now." (Even if you already do this, still do it here daily. It sets us up right to start the time with HIM). Actually, it is wise to run this routine in your mind before you start your day too.

2 – Then pray, "GOD, show me your will…"

3 – Then wait and listen and write down EVERYTHING HE says or that pops in your mind. (It could be anything from marketing to personal prayer plan to next steps tomorrow, etc.)

4 – Find one verse in the Bible you will meditate on all week. Place it on a card, write it on your hand or something that makes you see it over and over. (These verses usually go into my daily life-practice and end up being my sermon during the weekend. HE always teaches me something new before I preach).

This precedes my preaching, studying and planning.

Sometimes I even just take a Bible and open it up while I worship and read to GOD out loud as I worship and let the words soak into me.

5 – Worship on purpose. Make a five of these 15 minutes for worship. Where you FOCUS on the singing. YOU SINCERELY pray the lyrics.

Don't just blow through it.

For the morning and on during your day:

6 – Turn on the Bible as you get ready for the day. Let the WORD wash over you. It gets into your subconscious.

7 – Every time you hear Jesus say, "bow to me…" or "pray right now…" or "Stop what you are doing and do what I show you…" Do exactly what HE says right away. Try to do it in secret.

8 – It's time to designate a closet space for GOD. So, pray about taking a closet in your house even though it is going to steal space from your storage and devote it to the LORD. A room can be too big. I really draw from that passage where Jesus says, "Go into your closet…" And it feels like erecting an altar to HIM and making a Temple for HIM to come. I have a new closet that I don't know if I have ever shown you. It is hidden in my room. I am completing it this month and I am awaiting the Presence. (It's time to get SERIOUS and AGGRESSIVE about this). All my friends in college began to build their closets too after experiencing the closet at "the Green House" at UNC. That is where GOD first came.

<u>Check out a walk through of my current prayer closet here</u>.

Now, let's take a little bit of time to just talk a little bit more about the last few habits that are not explained in depth earlier before I close this book.

BIBLE READING AND MEDITATION
This is key to growth in Christ. We cannot expect to know how to follow the Holy Spirit, to discern the difference between GOD's voice and another or even to be able to know what is right or wrong unless we have studied the Bible. We have to put it into our lives. I have said it before, but

I am unable to go very long without reading the Bible now because it fills me up and gives me peace. It is healing inside me.

So, we take time to read it like I have explained and then to apply it to our lives throughout our day by saying simple things in prayer like, "Holy Spirit, help me do this today…" Then we think about that passage we read as we go through our day and this is a part of "meditation."

HERE ARE TWO VIDEOS ON BIBLE READING:
1- READING THE BIBLE, HOW TO START

2- THE BIBLE, IT'S AUTHORITY

SOLITUDE
Even though it is included in the topics before, I cannot stress enough how important it is to get time away from everyone and all the noise in our lives to simply be still and quiet and hear. This is solitude. You know it says over and over in the Gospels that Jesus had a habit of going off to solitary places and going off alone as well as to take the disciples away to do this as well. It even says this was HIS, "habit…"

We must get away! Sometimes, we should get away in nature. Some of my best times away with the LORD were on a prayer mountain set apart to meet with HIM.

JOURNALING

I believe journaling both our story and diary as well as our reading is important so we can go back and see what GOD has done. In our bad times, these journals become high water marks to remind ourselves that GOD has done it before and can do it again. We are able to press through hard times because we have learned who HE is and HIS character, will and ways while going through day to day life. I challenge you to take time to write in a journal that is set apart just for your daily life stuff as well as write your Bible reading down like I spoke about earlier. I even write in my Bibles and when one gets filled, I do another. These Bibles will leave a commentary for my kids to read after I am gone.

MEMORIZATION OF SCRIPTURE

"I hide YOUR words in my heart so that I might not sin against YOU." —Psalm 119:11

It's that simple. Hiding the Bible in our heart will keep us from sin. And more than that, it teaches us to live and fills us up. I love putting newly memorized Scripture in my heart. Years ago, I met a man named Dempsy Walker. He only studied the Bible all his life from 8 years old. And though he did not pass the 8th grade at school because the teacher said he had to read something else than the Bible and he wouldn't, when I met him at 21 years old, he was an old man at 93 and he had memorized the ENTIRE King James Version of the Bible!!!!!! You could ask him anything and he could quote Scripture, book, chapter and verse! I tested him thoroughly and that old preacher had the whole thing in there! WOW! And the presence of GOD that man held. It was amazing. Oh that we had this desire today!!!!!!

SERVICE

Service is a natural response to the great grace we have been given by Jesus in the cross. If anyone cannot serve, they cannot be HIS disciple. Jesus demonstrated it in washing the disciples feet and HE said we are to do this to each other for the rest of our days. It is that simple. Disciples of Jesus have certain habits built in and this is one of them!!!!! In my work, if someone cannot serve, they cannot lead. Leaders serve. So, humble yourself, see Jesus' face in each person you minister to and serve and get to some foot washing!

SHARING OUR FAITH

It's this simple. You have been redeemed and you have received grace as well as have a relationship with a person. HE is more real than all of the world and you have to tell others about it. Don't worry about sharing the exact way in detail that some great preacher does, just share your story. Your story is the second greatest story ever told! Tell what Jesus did in your and how you have changed. Others can see it.

For more on sharing the faith, if someone goes deeper and you don't know what to do, we have done some work to help you. If you have a cell phone, computer or anything that can show video, use our online tract and tools. You can learn the deep verses and thoughts. The link is below:

<u>**CLICK HERE FOR OUR OVERFLOWING LIFE RESOURCES IN SHARING YOUR FAITH**</u> **AND ONLINE TRACT.**

Building Endurance
The Warrior's Center
Being Watchful
1. Am I intimate with GOD?
2. Am I intimate with others beyond erotic love?
3. Do I cultivate relationships in a way that has deep, meaningful, conversation?
4. Are fear and lusts holding me back from deep, real, intimacy?
5. Are true love and intimacy possible to have with other people without GOD?
6. Pray with me, "Father, what needs to happen today for me to have deeper, more meaningful relationships? Do I fill YOU daily with the love I have for YOU? Do I need to walk in forgiveness for love to be released? How do I hurt you? Show me, please, In Jesus' name."

6 THE WARRIOR'S CENTER

May the grace of the Lord Jesus Christ, and the love of God, and the *fellowship **(GREEK: KOINONIA)*** of the Holy Spirit be with you all. -2 Corinthians 13:14

HAVING KOINONIA

Cultivating Koinonia (Becoming the kind of intimate person GOD stops everything to interact with. Mary, the woman with the issue of blood, and the sinful woman who washes Jesus' feet were the kinds of people that caught Jesus' attention).

Koinonia (definition):

Strong's Number: 2842, koy-nohn-ee'-ah
Official Greek Definition:

fellowship, association, community, communion, joint participation, intercourse the share which one has in anything, participation intercourse, fellowship, intimacy the right hand as a sign and pledge of fellowship (in fulfilling the apostolic office)

a gift jointly contributed, a collection, a contribution, as exhibiting an embodiment and proof of fellowship

So, let me say here about Koinonia some points about the definition from the Greek and what it means to the description of the Holy Spirit that Paul is using in the above Apostolic Prayer. He is doing something on purpose in the choice of the word. When these writers wrote these letters, they did not simply write what we see as literary documents, but their use of words described something that they experienced. Again, Christianity is a revealed, experiential religion that is focused on a real relationship with give and take and conversation.

The use of this word was literally "dirty talk" in these days when you think about how the Old Testament discussed anything sexual as "knowing." As in Adam "knew" Eve. There was a careful distance to these terms as well as to anything that could be seen as impure before the LORD. Not that sex is impure to GOD. He created it and it is not impure. But the conversation of these kinds of things was not in the vernacular of the era. As a matter of fact, theologians say that the Song of Songs by Solomon in

Pharisaic oversight as a scroll was considered so risqué that it was not even available to be read by anyone that was under a certain age.

So, Paul using a term that was used in a sexual manner describing intercourse had to be both purposeful as well as had to carry some kind of experiential meaning that warranted it.

The Greek above says that this word was used by Apostolic leaders in relation to the Apostolic office. Why would they use something as their term of choice about the Holy Spirit and their close union as a brotherhood that could be taken so badly or seen as heretical?

There had to be something more to it. There had to be a deeper relationship and a more intimate union here. As a matter of fact, looking at all the English words that are embedded in this one explosive word, we see that the church in Corinth as well as future churches were having prayed over them by Paul that they would:

1 - have close fellowship.
2 - have deep community and communion.
3 - would have an element of participation.
4 - there would be sharing of both ownership as well as in activity.
5 - there would be joint contribution.
6 - there would be a unity that is collecting them together in one accord.
7 - their union would be an embodiment and proof of fellowship. (They would "be" the Body of Christ).
8 - It would be more intimate or at least as intimate as when a man and a woman become one flesh.

This is interesting. Close fellowship with Holy Spirit, deep communion with HIM where we want to know HIS loves, hates, hurts, likes, thoughts, feelings and emotions. There is an element of listening and not just telling. This communion is something that we can see is missing in believers because they are unable to demonstrate it with others even their spouses. However, out of the overflow of this communion with Holy Spirit, they can enjoy it with their spouse and others.

The believer is being invited through this prayer to be a participant. There is joint contribution as seen as well and there is joint ownership. This is exciting. Holy Spirit is inviting us into joint participation in the work and life of the Kingdom and this is intimate. When we are working in GOD's Kingdom work, we are not off on our own doing the work of GOD "for" HIM. This would be like the older brother's mindset where in the prodigal son story Jesus told, he said to the father, "…how many years have I slaved for you?" This statement proved the older son may have stayed in the father's house, but he still did not understand the love the father had for him nor did he understand the intimate nearness that was always available as the father responded, "Everything I have is yours…" How many of us are the older brother in the house? We have lived in the Kingdom for a number of years and we do not know what is available for us without charge and freely within the Father's desire?

Intimacy in participation isn't doing the work "for" GOD, but it is knowing HE is always at work and waking up daily and going through life looking to see where HE is already at work (John 5:19) and asking where we can join HIM.

Holy Spirit wants to draw us into oneness and as well through HIM being in the center of us, HE wants to draw all of us into oneness with each other. This is NOT something where we lose our own unique place and identity. Actually, this is where HE brings us into agreement with our unique role, place and identity in the Body. "…is everyone a hand?" We are all placed in the Body of Christ and instead of being lost in oneness; we are empowered and released in it. We all are brought into the maturity of the faith as every part uses the gifts given to bring the Body nourishment and encouragement as well as edification. We need each other. The Holy Spirit intimacy that we are to enjoy makes this even more apparent as well as through HIM is the only possible way it will work. (See John 14-17).

Lastly, this intimacy should be a closer union than anything we even have with our spouses. The truth is that in Heaven, no one will be given in marriage and we will all be married to one, "Jesus Christ." With that said, we need to put HIS Spirit first and love and intimacy of HIM first. The first and greatest command Jesus said was, "…to love the LORD your GOD with all your heart, all your soul, all your mind and all your strength."

We are unable to do this in our own power.

This is not something we can earn.

This is not something we can learn.

We must begin to ask for revelation as we pray. We need to ask Holy Spirit to come and invite HIM to reveal the depth of intimacy in this term and to invite us into the depths of HIS heart and secret keeping (I reveal all MY secrets to my prophets…) And we need to ask for this intimacy to draw us into activity with HIM as well as into further communion with others.

Koinonia comes from somewhere.
It is the result of something.
It has results.
It is not head "knowledge." Jesus never asks if we knew HIM. He asks in the last day of judgment whether or not we will enter eternity based on whether or not HE KNOWS US!!!!

"…Enter into my rest you good and faithful servant…" "…depart from me you worker of inquiry because I never 'knew' you…"

We need to work out our being known by HIM through the Holy Spirit with fear and trembling. Instead of praying a one time "sinner's prayer," we may want to begin a long walk and a long talk with the ONE that must know us. I want HIM to know me. I will not deny HIM on this earth before men. I cannot wait till HE embraces me in the life to come!!!!!

GETTING BUSY OR BEING OBEDIENT

In the story of Mary and Martha, Jesus said of Mary who seemed to be the lazy one in Martha's perspective and instead of getting the house in order and getting the work done which was the correct role of the female in the household of that day, Mary chose to sit at Jesus' feet and listen to HIS every word.

When Martha got angry and wanted Jesus to reprimand her sister and get her busy since obviously due to culture and norms, the only thing she should be doing is working in the house, Jesus responds with an anti-cultural message as well as something that was shocking to all involved since it went against the norm of the day and said, "Mary chose what was better…"

So, what does this mean? Jesus desired not food and preparations but HE wanted nearness and their relationship. HE loved the fact that everything came secondary in Mary's heart to HIM. He knew her heart. HE knew that deeper inside there, she was truly not lazy and she did not intend to break the rules, she just couldn't help herself. She was so drawn by HIM. She was so loved by HIM. She was so amazed by HIM. She had HIM in such high esteem in the right way in the right place that everything else became a distraction. She just couldn't drag herself away from HIS feet. HE was worth the waste and the time.

Speaking of wastes…

What about the sinful woman who washed Jesus' feet with her hair, tears and perfume? -Luke 7:38 (I mean, think about tears and hair). What a waste of dignity and finance in the colossal cost of the perfume? This lovesick heart was proof and demonstration of received forgiveness. And was it really a waste? That was likely the best investment she ever made! Only deep intimacy that comes from forgiveness could have pulled that love.

And did you catch what Jesus said the the Pharisees that were there? He said, that she loved much because she had been forgiven much. If you have a love problem and an intimacy problem, the first step to a solution is admitting sin, asking for Holy Spirit to reveal what still needs forgiveness and then quickly repenting; deep repentance that pulls thankfulness for freedom and deliverance. And then, the result is this kind of lovesick intimacy that causes beautiful waste. This woman was so overcome by the depth of forgiveness that she wasted a year's worth of wages possibly on a jar of expensive perfume and poured out all the gain from all of the men that misused her, all of what she sold of herself was wrapped up in that jar and she decided that instead of allowing one more man to take her dignity, she would pour it out on the ONLY MAN THAT EVER MATTERED! And what a great choice!!!!! This waste on the ONE! When we get to Heaven in the end of things, this will be seen as not a waste, but the best gift. What would you give/ Would you give your all? Would you give the very thing that had become your idol? What does it take in a person to do this? Lovesickness.

Are you lovesick for Jesus?

If not, maybe this is a good moment to ask Holy Spirit to reveal what lovesickness looks like. Now, be aware, the kinds of prayers that take a long time for GOD to reveal are the ones that are selfish. These kinds of prayers are not selfish and HE will begin to reveal it right away. So, be careful. You will get what you ask for in this. I Still encourage you to ask right now, "Holy Spirit, teach me of forgiveness and cleansing that leads to this kind of lovesick heart."

Lastly, I add Mary Magdalene. Jesus had died and had been in the grave 3 days. He had just arisen and had not yet gone to the Father so that HE was truly "touchable." And we find Mary outside the grave so stricken with pain and loss that Jesus comes to her right then and there and consoles her.

This struck me because of the story where Jesus comes to resurrect Lazarus. In that story, Jesus even had just said that HE knew Lazarus was dead and that HE was glad of it so that the disciples would know the power of the Father when HE arose. And yet when HE sees Mary, Lazarus' sister (another, different Mary), "Jesus wept." And the word for wept there means something along the lines of "groaned deeply within HIS bowels." Jesus didn't just shed a tear, HE was inwardly twisted and in pain and anguish wept with Mary. Did HE weep because Lazarus died? I do not know, but I don't think so since HE knew HE was about to raise HIM from the dead? Then what happened? I think Mary was so intimate with Jesus in a very special, spiritual way that all of us have been invited into through Holy Spirit that Jesus felt her pain and had compassion on her. HE was so moved it stirred HIM into HIS inmost being. What a friend she must have been? What a close connection?!

And here is Mary Magdalene outside the tomb and Jesus stops everything in that moment and appears to her to console her. What kind of person gets this kind of attention? From what we see in the Greek, Jesus had stopped from going to the Father where HE had not yet been received and HE was then afterwards going to go and reveal HIMSELF to the believers at large and yet HE stopped because at that moment, the Father wanted to console an intimate follower. HE CARED! SHE CARED SO MUCH FROM THE DEEP CARE HE HAD GIVEN HER THAT SHE DREW THAT RESPONSE from the Father!!!! I want to be that kind of person. I want to be that intimate!!!!!! Don't you?????

And the kicker is that Jesus does not desire for that story to be the exception, HE DESIRES IT TO BE THE NORM! HE desires a love relationship with you that is real and personal and just for you! John even illustrates this as HE describes the various disciples as a rock, a doubter, a thief, etc and then he says that he was the one whom the LORD loved.

Be "a one whom the LORD loves…" Lay your head on HIS chest the way John did at the last supper. Sit at HIS feet like Mary. Anoint HIS feet with oil, tears and hair like the sinful woman. Weep outside the tomb. Don't be caught asleep in the garden. Be "a one."

HE desires a real relationship that is intimate and personal with your own stories of intimacy and your own love language and your own times together. I am serious, there have been times I have so felt the deep longing of the Presence of GOD that I ached inwardly so that I ran into a stairwell and wept on my knees in an office building, I ran back from class over a mile to my house because I could not wait for the bus and dove into my prayer closet, where I dove under my desk at work and prayed where no one could see me or I ran out and prayed in my truck with the windows up and the heat blazing down. I love it when I am so stirred this way in that personal, intimate wooing of Holy Spirit.

Start your relationship today. Tell HIM, "If YOU will whisper, I will drop everything and run after YOU. Can YOU draw me away and reveal Jesus to me all day?"

All of these stories from these Biblical seekers are all signs of intimacy with Jesus and I believe they are models we can use today as we approach Jesus' Spirit and we desire HIM to draw us away and prepare us for our wedding day with Jesus to come.

I believe this life of desire from Holy Spirit that draws us into the alignment we must have with HIM so we can reciprocate love and intimacy and makes us healthy as well as begins to bring us into purity and unity from glory to glory leads into a divine harmony.

HARMONICS

Cultivating FOCUSED Harmony (Intimacy with the Holy Spirit & Prayer and Ministering to GOD through Scripture)

John 4 - the harmony between Spirit and WORD of GOD.

In John 4, the woman at the well tries to get Jesus off topic and get HIM caught up in the battle of the day which is whether or not worship is done in the right place. We seem to have the same kinds of distracting theological arguments and control issues today. Is our style better or theirs? Is our location better or theirs? Is our performance better or theirs?

Jesus doesn't even deal in that exchange. HE speaks over the top of it and says that the place and location and style do not matter. All that matters is the heart worshiping GOD in Spirit and Truth. Jesus wanted people founded in the fullness of the Truth of the Bible and then open to the Spirit to bring the fullness of this Truth into a written on the heart place where the worshiper has such a deep desire on GOD with all their heart, mind, soul and strength that they find it hard to sin. They cannot draw themselves into civilian distractions, they are too hungry and too intensely focused on the groom. They cannot be distracted. I have been in a place where the reality of the nearness of the Presence of GOD is so evident and so captivating that it is impossible for me to notice ways to overtly sin. I don't know if during those times I was sinning by accident in one way or another, but as far as impulses and temptations, I just didn't have time to entertain them. HE was too present. And my love for HIM was true, "first love!" I do not believe this was anything I did nor do I believe there is anything I can do to get it back, but I can seek HIM with all my heart and I can ask and I can be available. And my desire is that before I die, my every waking moment and sleeping moment is this way of life. Now, that is up to HIM, but as for me, HE will find me stirring myself up attempting to take hold of HIM.

And let me ask you a question, even if I were wrong, do you think HE is upset about that kind of passion? No. I was so thankful to find my Lori, my precious wife had waited for me not wasting herself on every guy that had come by just as I had saved myself for her till our wedding night. That was intimate and precious and if that was the response I had, how do you think our Groom (Jesus) will feel? The desire even if unfounded and immature, (which it is not, it is a sign of deep maturity), had got to be something that even makes Jesus say right now, "Dad, I want to go get that bride!!!!" Is HE saying that right now about the Body of Christ? Not so much. However, maybe that's part of what this book is for. Getting a Bride to set itself apart and wait for their mate. We should do this in spirit and flesh.

Can you stop and make that agreement? If you have already gone away for other lovers, can you stop right now and repent and say you are sorry to the Holy Spirit and recommit to wait now?

So, let's go on into the harmony concept.

Why I use the word, "harmony…" Harmony is a better description than balance. Balance describes something that holds another thing in check. The Bible and the Spirit do not hold each other back or in check. Actually, the perfect mix and life in the middle of the both of them is where there is more release of power and harmony. They work together not against each other. I want to live in between the lines of Spirit and Bible and I want to see what they do in my life when they work together. The Spirit brings the WORD to life inside of me. And the Spirit cannot utilize the WORD inside me without my ingesting it. And Jesus is the WORD and the kicker is that HE said we had to eat HIS flesh (as well as we had to eat every word from HIM) and we had to ingest HIS blood. We are consumers of only one thing in the world. We consume all of Jesus (John 1 says that HE is the WORD made flesh).

This sounds strange, but it is true. Ingesting everything about the WORD that was made flesh allows the Spirit to utilize it in us and HE strikes the chords with the very nearness of HIS being. HE can take the WORD of GOD, which gives us a framework for what is possible in the Kingdom, and then teach us to play to the edge of the boundaries. This reminds me of that study in kids playing in a playground that never left the monkey bars until the playground had a fence added around it and then the kids played to the very edge of the fence. Everything inside us desires the safety of that defined boundary. The Spirit gives us the ability to play to the edge. I learned in soccer that I did not give up till the ball crossed the full line. I became a good player at the edge of the field and I would use other's fear of the edge to my advantage. So, the Spirit can take the fear out of the RISK which we so value in faith life. And HE makes things alive and fun. And when the Spirit is in it, fruit of the Spirit are as well. So, if someone knows a lot of WORD but they do not have fruit of the Spirit, which are love, joy, peace, patience, kindness, goodness, gentleness, faithfulness, and self-control, and even if they are lacking in one, then you can be assured they are not in harmony with the Spirit. The Spirit gives authority to the WORD and brings power behind our words as HE makes it resonate from us into other believers as well as through the WORD HIS power often follows with demonstration.

At any rate, there is harmony between the Spirit and the WORD that is earthquaking.

In this era, we must bring two sides of Christianity into harmony of Spirit and Truth.

We have the Truth guys which are all into intellect and we have the Spirit guys which are all into feeling and emotion and we need to be in the middle of the harmony of the two.

THE DANGERS OF ONE WITHOUT THE OTHER

Without intellect and WORD to anchor us, we are out in a ship in a storm batted around with no stability. Without Spirit and simply intellect, we are arrogant and deceived by our own minds, which the Bible says man cannot even know and that the Spirit is the only one that can know it. The Bible also says that this kind of faith is calloused and dry.

SAFETY IN THEIR HARMONY IN EVERYDAY LIFE

Our safety in the harmony of the Spirit and the WORD is that the Spirit creates hunger for the WORD, the WORD brings foundation to the believer and then the Spirit comes back and sparks that Truth to bring the believer into harmony with GOD's will daily as HE reveals the Father at work daily in alignment with Scripture.

Harmony between the Spirit and Word creates a kind of dissonance that is like wave theory and can literally move things, break things and like an earthquake the harmonics in the working of the Spirit hand in hand with the truth moves things and people. We need to be the kind of worshipers that are in harmony with the Spirit and Word having a Kingdom dissonance that resonates in the deepest parts of them and they are MOVED into action. Activity and social change becomes an outflow from relationship. It is overflow. We are not DOING IT for GOD. We are doing it "with" GOD. WORD cannot resonate with the Spirit if it is not inside you.

GROWING IN INTIMACY

The description of a vine being attached into a branch is an intimate connection. There is oneness there. John 15:5 says that Jesus is the vine and we are the branches. There is more HE says in that passage so read it later, but what I want to say here is that this branch being in the vine is like the umbilicaling of a baby into a mother. The branch receives nutrition and draws all source and resource from being connected into the vine. We have to ask ourselves the questions; "are we like a baby in a mother drawing all our nutrition from the mother? Are we able to live detached?"

I would say that the answer in the majority of our lives is, "NO!!!!!!"

Therefore, the Intimacy of the Kingdom IS the key to everything in the Kingdom.

All of our ability in HIM starts in knowing we can do NOTHING WITHOUT HIM!!!!!!!!

So, let's look at ways we can grow in intimacy even though we may not be deeply in the WORD. Where is a good place to start? A great place to start is by praying to the Father in Jesus' name and worshiping HIM. Also, we can talk to Holy Spirit and when we do this, we often do not know how to pray. I suggest using Scripture to pray and then you are ingesting the WORD as well as communing with the Spirit. And let me tell you, HE so desires to lift Jesus up and so knows that Jesus is the WORD that HE absolutely loves this stuff. And don't worry. This is not the end of it. This is just a beginning model to get you jumpstarted!

<u>Watch Dustin's video now on having a growing, dynamic relationship that is intimate with Holy Spirit.</u>

GROWING IN HAVING A POWERFUL PRAYER LIFE

Using GOD' WORD to frame prayer as well as to use in prayer is key. I suggest using some of the following as you learn to pray. In the next parts of this chapter, you will find my writings on the Apostolic Prayers and The LORD's Prayer. I include these because there is no part of the church that questions the authority of these prayers and since they are Scripture straight out of the Bible, we can use them literally and know that they are a good model as well as simply good prayers to use anytime. We can pray them with authority and we should use them in all situations.

THE POWER PRAYERS

The Power Prayers were prayers prayed by the Apostles and the early church, written into the letters the apostles wrote as prayers and petitions for the believers they were written to or by Jesus. You can easily know that these are good to literally pray right now, so, pray them if you cannot think of other things to pray. As a matter of fact, I have learned that the more I memorize and use Scripture in my daily life, the more I am changed into its likeness. In other words, you can use these to pray until your prayers become like them. It is not a rule. This is a learning tool and the prayers are good and true. So, use them. Here they are.

1. Ephesians 1:17-19
"..the Father of glory, may give to you the SPIRIT OF WISDOM AND REVELATION IN THE KNOWLEDGE OF HIM, the eyes of your understanding being enlightened; that you may know what is the HOPE OF HIS CALLING, what are the riches of the GLORY OF HIS

INHERITANCE IN THE SAINTS, and what is the exceeding GREATNESS OF HIS POWER TOWARD US."

2. Ephesians 3:16-19
"..that He would grant you, according to the riches of His glory, TO BE STRENGTHENED WITH MIGHT THROUGH HIS SPIRIT IN THE INNER MAN, that Christ may dwell in your hearts through faith; that you, being rooted and grounded in love, MAY BE ABLE TO COMPREHEND with all the saints what is the width and length and depth and height-- to know the love of Christ which passes knowledge; that you may be filled with all the fullness of God."

3. Philippians 1:9-11
"And this I pray, that YOUR LOVE MAY ABOUND still more and more in knowledge and all discernment, that you may APPROVE THE THINGS THAT ARE EXCELLENT, that you may be sincere and without offense till the day of Christ, being FILLED WITH THE FRUITS OF RIGHTEOUSNESS which are by Jesus Christ, to the glory and praise of God." (Phil. 1:9-11)

4. Colossians 1:9-12
"We do not cease to pray for you, and to ask that you may be filled with the KNOWLEDGE OF HIS WILL in all wisdom and spiritual understanding; that you may have a WALK WORTHY OF THE LORD, fully pleasing Him, BEING FRUITFUL in every good work and increasing in the knowledge of God; STRENGTHENED WITH ALL MIGHT, according to His glorious power, for all patience and longsuffering with joy; giving thanks to the Father who has qualified us to be partakers of the inheritance of the saints in the light."

5. Romans 15:5-7
"Now may the God of patience and comfort GRANT YOU TO BE LIKE-MINDED toward one another, according to Christ Jesus, THAT YOU MAY WITH ONE MIND AND ONE MOUTH glorify the God and Father of our Lord Jesus."

6. Romans 15:13
"Now may the God of hope FILL YOU WITH ALL JOY AND PEACE IN BELIEVING, THAT YOU MAY ABOUND IN HOPE by the power of the Holy Spirit."

7. Romans 10:1
"My heart's desire and prayer to God for ISRAEL is that they may be

saved."

8. 1 Corinthians 1:4-8
"I thank my God always concerning you for the grace of God which was given to you by Christ Jesus, THAT YOU WERE ENRICHED IN EVERYTHING by Him in all utterance and all knowledge, even as the testimony of Christ was confirmed in you, so THAT YOU COME SHORT IN NO GIFT, eagerly waiting for the revelation of our Lord Jesus Christ, who will also confirm you to the end, THAT YOU MAY BE BLAMELESS in the day of our Lord Jesus Christ."

9. 1 Thessalonians 3:9-13
"..we rejoice for your sake before our God, night and day praying exceedingly THAT WE MAY SEE YOUR FACE and PERFECT WHAT IS LACKING in your faith Now may our God and Father Himself, and our Lord Jesus Christ, DIRECT OUR WAY TO YOU. And may the Lord make you increase and ABOUND IN LOVE to one another and to all so that He may ESTABLISH YOUR HEARTS BLAMELESS IN HOLINESS before our God and Father at the coming of our Lord Jesus Christ with all His saints."

10. 2 Thessalonians 1:11-12
"Therefore we also pray always for you THAT OUR GOD WOULD COUNT YOU WORTHY OF THIS CALLING, AND FULFILL ALL THE GOOD PLEASURE OF HIS GOODNESS AND THE WORK OF FAITH WITH POWER, that the name of our Lord Jesus Christ may be glorified in you, and you in Him, according to the grace of our God and the Lord Jesus Christ."

11. 2 Thessalonians 3:1-5
"Finally, brethren, pray for us, THAT THE WORD OF THE LORD MAY RUN SWIFTLY AND BE GLORIFIED, just as it is with you, and that we may be delivered from unreasonable and wicked men; for not all have faith. But the Lord is faithful, who will establish you and guard you from the evil one. And we have confidence in the Lord concerning you, both that you do and will do the things we command you. NOW MAY THE LORD DIRECT YOUR HEARTS INTO THE LOVE OF GOD AND INTO THE PATIENCE OF CHRIST."

12. Acts 4:29-31
"Now, Lord, look on their threats, and GRANT TO YOUR SERVANTS THAT WITH ALL BOLDNESS THEY MAY SPEAK YOUR WORD, BY STRETCHING OUT YOUR HAND TO HEAL,

AND THAT SIGNS AND WONDERS MAY BE DONE through the name of Your holy Servant Jesus. And when they had prayed, the place where they were assembled together was shaken; and they were all filled with the Holy Spirit, and they spoke the word of God with boldness."

13. John 17:24-26
"Father, I desire that they also whom You gave Me may be with Me where I am, THAT THEY MAY BEHOLD MY GLORY which You have given Me; for You loved Me before the foundation of the world. "O righteous Father! The world has not known You, but I have known You; and these have known that You sent Me. "And I have declared to them Your name, and WILL DECLARE IT, THAT THE LOVE WITH WHICH YOU LOVED ME MAY BE IN THEM, and I in them."

THE LORD'S PRAYER BROKEN DOWN

Over time, I had been reading Jesus' demonstration of prayer and Holy Spirit taught me in my own personal prayer time to pray the way the LORD's Prayer is framed. I could see that the different parts of this prayer that Jesus prayed with the disciples in order to teach them to pray was much deeper than the simple text we quote often in our church meetings.

I call these the "Phases of Prayer" or the "types of prayer." After the worksheet part you see here, there is more explanation to the use and what it all means.

(I have made the LORD's Prayer here into a Practice Worksheet. Copy it and use it in your prayer time or rewrite it and put it in the back of your Bible or journal and use it so you learn the actual phases and types of prayer Jesus used in HIS Prayer to the Father).

These DO NOT need to be done in any specific order, however, I find that the beginning and end are best to stay the same at least. Just make sure you touch on each phase for a balanced love relationship. It's a conversation and it is a give and take conversation.

Matthew 6:
"This, then, is how you should pray:
"'Our Father in heaven,
hallowed be your name,
[10] your kingdom come,
your will be done,

   on earth as it is in heaven.
[11] Give us today our daily bread.
[12] And forgive us our debts,
   as we also have forgiven our debtors.
[13] And lead us not into temptation,
   but deliver us from the evil one.
   for yours is the kingdom
   and the power and the glory forever.
   Amen."

PHASES OF PRAYER BASED ON MATTHEW 6

(Try this as a series of steps into intimate fuller prayer).

FIRST: Identification and praise. A recognition of who God is and his Glory. "Our Father in heaven, Your name be honored as holy." This is when we recognize how incredibly awesome and praiseworthy our God is and we fall to our knees because of it.

SECOND: Agreement and alignment. Recognizing that God's plans are sovereign and submitting ourselves to His vision. "Your Kingdom come, Your will be done, on Earth as it is in Heaven." Or in the words of a Christ Tomlin song "You're the God of this City...Greater things are yet to come."

THIRD: Petition/supplication. A request to take care of us, not just physically but spiritually, materially, and inter-personally. "Give us this day our daily bread." (Also, ambiguity of language means that just as the divine name suggests past, present and future tenses, so too does this passage suggest a remembering of yesterday's promise to live in tomorrow's provision today)

FOURTH: Forgiveness. The Next line in the Lord's prayer "Forgive us our debts as we also have forgiven our debtors" assumes that we don't hold any unforgiveness. It assumes that we have let go of any grudges or hurts we have received and reminds us that even though we are forgiven our sins by His grace, that we still must pass it forward and forgive others as well.

FIFTH: Confession, repentance. "And forgive us our debts as we also have forgiven our debtors." This one takes me ages. I mean if I actually sat down and named out every single sin I was guilty of I'd probably never get off my knees but there are days when that's exactly what I do. I confess my sins to my lord and repent of them so that I can more fully walk in His presence.

SIXTH: Future protection and deliverance from current circumstances. "And do not lead us into temptation but delivers us from evil."

SEVENTH: Worship (in closing). "For Yours is the Kingdom, and the power, and the glory forever." (This kind of) Worship is different from praise and might be better referred to as "adoration." In this final place of prayer, I adore God. I love God and demonstrate my love for him in any way I can manage.

And from this point, we are better led into the phases of worship with GOD as I stated before.

We start here in prayer and worship and THEN AND ONLY THEN at the end of phases of worship can we find the OVERFLOW to act in Ministry and Giving. Ministry and giving come from outflow of encounter with GOD as we become intimate in prayer and worship. GRRRRRRR!

PHASES OF PRAYER WORKSHEET

1 – Call to Worship | Praise & Thanksgiving | Identification

Verse | "Our father in heaven… hollowed is your name…" Example | "Good morning LORD, its' me again. I just want to lift you this morning…"

2 – Agreement | Aligning with GOD's Plans

Verse | "Your Kingdom Come… Your Will be done…" Example | "Today, can you come and bring my heart into alignment with what you want to do today? Will you do exactly what you want today? I want to lay down my plans for this day and I want to pick up yours…"

3 – Petition | for both Spiritual & Physical Personal Needs

Verse | "Give us this day our daily bread…" Example | "Jesus, will you take care of everything I need to today? I need _____, _____ & _____."

4 – Forgiveness | Prerequisite to Confession & Repentance

Verse | "…As we have forgiven our debtors…" Example | "Please forgive me for holding hurt, pain and bad memories…" "I forgive _____ for hurting me…" "I allow you to wash over my mind forgiveness toward this bad memory. I will hold it no longer…" "Help me forgive _____ for hurting me and help me find a way to contact them and convey my forgiveness."

Intercession | Praying for Others

Since Jesus here includes other people in the personal prayer here, I also add intercession here. An intercessor is someone that stands in between someone and another. In other words, in a courtroom, there is a judge, a prosecuting attorney who is sharing the accusations with the judge and then defending attorney and the defendant.

If we are the defendant, Jesus would be our defending attorney to the Father who would be the judge against the Devil who would be our accuser and prosecuting attorney.

Jesus in that picture is the intercessor.

On the Earth in this current overlap of Kingdoms, we are the intercessors for our friends, family and others who are believers or not and others can be our intercessors. We stand between heaven and that person and petition for that person to have GOD answer them in their situation.

So, here are some tips about intercession:

A - When someone asks for prayer, stop right where you are and pray with them and intercede for them. Just pray, "GOD, I agree with _____, please answer this prayer about their _____ issue. In Jesus Name." (It really is that easy. I do this all the time).
B - Keep a list of people you pray for and their needs.
C - Journal when GOD answers prayers. It is encouraging.
D - Have a top 5 people you pray for every day to know Jesus. Ask GOD for opportunities to share with them.
E - Pray daily for your lists.

5 – Confession & Repentance | Which leads to receipt of Forgiveness from GOD

Verse | "Forgive us our sins." Example | "GOD, I have sinned in these ways _____." "Please forgive me!" "I repent, which means, I am NEVER GOING BACK!"

Sidenote: Some sins to think about here are:

1 – Any unforgiveness we have held against a brother or sister.
2 – Any doubtful thing that we hide in the back of our heart whether we know if it is really sin or not… If it makes us carry guilt, it IS SIN!

3 – Any time we have offended or not listened to the Holy Spirit.

4 – Anything we know that we have done against our brother or sister that is not loving them above ourselves and any time we have not loved GOD above all.

5 – And of course, the BIG TEN!

We must STOP immediately and ask for forgiveness for each area here mentioned.

6 – Future Direction & Protection | Knowing He allows temptation and trial for our maturing, we embrace HIS will above, yet always ask for HIS hand in guiding us through it.

Verse | "Lead us not into temptation… And deliver us from evil…" Example | "Guide my every step." "Direct me away from anything evil and from temptation." "Please keep me strong and able to run back to the WORD when trials and temptation comes."

7 – Adoration & Worship
Verse | "…For yours is the Kingdom and the Power and the glory forever…" Example | "You own it all!!!!" "I lift you up!!!" "I bless your name with all my soul!!!" "This is me dancing for you Poppa!"

THE PHASES OF WORSHIP START HERE…. (Go to that chapter and try them after doing this worksheet and just see what happens. This is so awesome to grow in). And then continue in listening...

Listening (Communion) | Communion of spirit with GOD alone and/or with others while together with GOD

Thus, we enter the phases of worship, which really culminate in our ability to LISTEN TO GOD. (I have a separate list based on the phases of the Heart in the Habits Chapter of the Warriors Manual).

Again, here, I have further attempted to take the LORD's prayer and as simply as possible, look at the different phases that Jesus is illustrating with this amazing model prayer.

Now, the key is to remember that this is NOT a defined structure that MUST be taken in exact step as noted below. You can go through these phases in any order you would like. The key is to remember that each phase is important and though they may be mixed, in order to have a more mature prayer life, we DO NOT encourage you to leave any out.

Also, if you notice, it both starts and ends with a mode of worship. It starts with a real "Call to Worship," or Praise and thanksgiving, honoring talk and ends with more Adoration kind of worship.
Matthew 6:9-14

Prayer is…

Intimate and personal. "Go into your private room, shut the door, and pray to your Father who is in secret." I shut out the world and create space for God to come and meet with me one on one. NO distractions, no mess, just him and me. Better than date night.

Direct. "Don't babble like the idolaters, since they imagine they'll be heard for their many words…your Father knows what you need before you ask Him." No need to beat around the bush, there's no need to play games or hit the formula just right or just so, God is there and already knows our needs and desires so anything extra comes out of our love for Him not out of a need to placate Him.

Gaining Strategy
The Warrior's Ear
Being Watchful
1. Do I listen to GOD?
2. Am I running at too fast of a pace to hear GOD daily?
3. How do I know what HE is saying?
4. Is it possible HE is talking all the time and I am unable to hear?
5. Pray with me, "Father, are YOU trying to get my attention? Have I been missing YOUR subtle hints? I desire to know and do YOUR will and join YOU in YOUR activity. Help me know better when YOU are speaking, recognize YOUR invitation, respond with obedience immediately and join YOU in adventure. Help me shrug off fear and walk in love. Amen."

7 THE WARRIOR'S EAR

Hearing & Doing GOD's Will

Before you run out and decide that you are going to hear and obey the voice of GOD, please understand that there has to be a relationship FIRST! If you are from the Psychic, Spiritist, Occult or New Age Background, I caution you in trying to come at this the same way you would with your background and history. Again, this first relies on the fact that you agree with John 14:6 and second that you have a personal relationship with Jesus.

It is NOT formulaic, you cannot do traditions. These are only guidelines that have been helpful to my personal relationship with HIM and cannot be simply used as a legalistic checklist. GOD will change up how HE speaks. The items you see below are guides in the process of learning the person, character, will, ways and purposes of GOD. And you MUST REPENT OF THAT SIN before being able to fully hear GOD. He is not interested in your getting your kicks from this, you being able to promote yourself and/or your being more powerful. YUCK!

I encourage you to read the book by Henry Blackaby, "Experiencing GOD" for more information on the daily experience of GOD.

This relationship with GOD I am talking about must be real and relevant and you must first be available for that relationship approaching it the same way you would with a significant other such as spouse or boyfriend/girlfriend. You cannot think that GOD is some Genie or some means of getting what you want. He is NOT YOUR DOG. He will not roll over, play dead and do tricks.

Also, as you approach this relationship, you may find like me that it is to your advantage to make a space and a time for continued talks. I always have a prayer closet wherever I live and have designated times when the kids are in bed, no one is up and I have already kept all my commitments or lived my values for the day. So, both early in the morning and late at the evening, I seek HIM for relationship that is deep. The rest of the day, we just talk as we go. Sometimes, HIS talk gets heavier or stronger and drives me to hiding away with HIM or to my knees immediately. This is all subject to the way you and Poppa GOD converse and the way the Holy Spirit is able to teach you. It is different for every person.

For more on building a prayer closet, watch this video now!

<u>For more info on having a relationship with GOD through worship and time with HIM, watch this video by Dustin, here, now.</u>

George Mueller's Points on Learning to Hear the Voice of GOD:
Here is how Muller summed up the way he entered a heart relationship with God and learned to discern His voice:

1. I seek at the beginning to get my heart into such a state that it has no will of its own in regard to a given matter. Nine-tenths of the trouble with people generally is just here. Nine-tenths of the difficulties are overcome when our hearts are ready to do the Lord's will, whatever it may be. When one is truly in this state, it is usually but a little way to the knowledge of what His will is.

2. Having done this, I do not leave the result to feeling or simple impression. If so, I make myself liable to great delusions.

3. I seek the Will of the Spirit of God through, or in connection with, the Word of God. The Spirit and the Word must be combined. If I look to the Spirit alone without the Word. I lay myself open to great delusions also. If the Holy Ghost guides us at all, He will do it according to the Scriptures and never contrary to them.

4. Next I take into account providential circumstances. These often plainly indicate God's Will in connection with His Word and Spirit.

5. I ask God in prayer to reveal His Will to me aright.

6. Thus, through prayer to God, the study of the Word, and reflection, I come to a deliberate judgment according to the best of my ability and knowledge, and if my mind is thus at peace, and continues so after two or three more petitions, I proceed accordingly.

To read more on George Mueller, click through right here and go to our page on HIM in the Revival Life website.

DUSTIN'S TIPS FOR DISCERNING THE VOICE OF GOD:
When you hear something that you feel might be GOD's speaking to you, run through the following quick checklist:

1 – The voice sounds like your own voice, but it is a good thing you could never think of.

The Bible states that we are not able to even desire to do good. So, apart from GOD, we cannot think up purely altruistic behavior. This at the very beginning becomes a sign to me when I have a good idea to help someone and I truly get nothing from it.

When these ideas come, I usually immediately think to myself, "Oh, that's not GOD, that's just me…"

However, seriously, how often do you ever think about whether or not something is GOD when it is a mundane task? Satan's greatest trick for the

empowered child of GOD is to trick them into thinking that the wonderful drawing of the Holy Spirit is just their imagination or idea!
If it is good according to the BIBLE, it is "not just you!"

2 – It will ALWAYS go in accordance with Scripture.

The Bible is my root, my anchor and my authority. Now, the key is that I cannot function fully in being able to quickly react to the WORD of GOD if I do not have it INSIDE ME ALREADY! We have to become the greatest students of the WORD so that when we are in the middle of something or when GOD directs, we don't have to say, "Hey wait a minute GOD or wait a minute so and so…" "I have to go read the Bible and see what to do!"

Get it inside you BEFORE you need it. The same is true of temptation. On a side note. Be ready to take the devil on before he takes you on! Get the WORD of GOD inside you!!!!!!

Think about it. I have said this hundreds of times and I am saying it again here. Do you tune a guitar before or after a concert? Do you practice before or after the concert????? Think about it!!!!

3 – If it is in accordance with Scripture and it is a good thing you could never think of under normal conditions, then, it will come in alignment with Godly Counsel in your life.

I run to people I trust that hear GOD more than me or at least as much as me. Once I have gone to Scripture and I am still not sure, the multitude of counsel the Bible says is your safety net.
And how do you know who to run to for counsel? Find some GODly person with grey hair. And not just that, look at the chapter on the Maturing Warrior and read what a mature believer looks like. Those are the people that are able to give counsel. They are mature when you see fruit, purity and stewardship.

4 – It does NOT feel like you are wearing wet shoes although it will likely make you uncomfortable in a different way.

This last point is ALWAYS LAST!!!!! Never make this first!!!!!! First go through the other steps and then trust your gut. Have you ever had wet shoes? Have you ever heard someone say something in church or do something in church and attribute it to GOD and it just feels like you stepped in something yucky? That is most likely discernment. And when you discern between a good and bad spirit, you are hearing GOD. The same is true here. If you go through the steps and you may still feel uncomfortable, but you definitely KNOW IT'S GOD or you feel the fire of GOD burning in your gut, then you KNOW here at this point it is HIM. However, if you get through the other points and you still are not sure and you get here and it feels iffy. Not that you are scared, but that something just ain't right as my grandma used to say… Stop and wait. It may be GOD's protection. The Bible talks about this when it says to NOT lay on hands hastily. We must always be in step with GOD. See John 5:19.

At any rate, I feel like the waiting thing is the least of our worries. We have had so few people on fire and sharing and doing the work of GOD that we need to GO GO GO!!!!! Right?!

<u>Watch Dustin's video now on hearing GOD and obeying HIS voice.</u>

Now, when I say "hear," let me make this perfectly clear as to what I am meaning. I have learned both through experience, the Bible and from others' experiences with me that there are a number of ways we can "hear."

GOD MAY SPEAK TO US BY:
1 – Another believer
2 – The church
3 – His WORD
4 – Circumstances
5 – His Holy Spirit

However, he also may sovereignly speak or He may speak through the Holy Spirit. And if we are available, literally saying, "GOD, speak to me. Show me your will. Show me where to join you as you are working. Help me have the courage to join you." He will speak to you and lead you step by step through your day. Now, when HE speaks through HIS Spirit or Sovereignly, which means the following:

1 – He can speak sovereignly through simply talking out loud where everyone hears it.

2 – He can speak sovereignly through simply talking out loud and we are the only ones that understand HIM where others may hear nothing or hear thunders.

3 – He may move us and we not know how or why we are moving and doing what we are doing. (This is not scary and IS NOT possession. GOD is a gentleman and is careful with us. This often feels precious like a Father leading a child).

4 – He may give us a feeling, impression and even a lurch in our stomach that reminds us of butterflies mixed with aching or a pulling from within one's core. (This of course IS NOT the same as stomach cramps that may be physical although, sometimes these feel almost the same at the height of intercession).

5 – Someone may see something visibly that they know is not there or an image inside their head while praying. (It could be a word, a sentence or an image).

6 – An impression. (This is the hard one. It's just a feeling or sense about something. Usually discernment).

7 – A strong desire

8 – A voice inside you that sounds just like your voice and thoughts, but is too good to explain away.

Please hear me in this. THESE THINGS MUST BE BROUGHT under the above steps to discerning whether the experiences match up with GOD and HIS known character. YOU NEVER SHOULD SIMPLY MOVE OFF OF THE ABOVE 8 ITEMS!

And the catch is that the younger we are in this, the more scary this can be. Gifting is never an indicator of maturity. We need maturity BEFORE we have HUGE ability in anything such as hearing GOD. Therefore, cultivate the relationship through worship first.

This list is NOT exhaustive. And I am only trying to get you to see that there is more to this walk than you can imagine. Have fun!

Listen to a sermon here by Dustin as he walks a church through the steps of hearing GOD.

In closing, here is one more video we wanted to share where Dustin goes through some next steps as well as some resources for you as you continue in Growing in the Spirit.

Getting Dressed
The Warrior's Gifts
Being Watchful
1. Does GOD give everyone spiritual gifts?
2. Who gives them and where do they come from?
3. What are they? What are the specific 9 main spiritual gifts mentioned in the Bible?
4. Why do we need them? Can't we do without them?
5. Isn't the church fine as it is?
6. What is their purpose?

Pray with me, "Father, help me not be afraid. And help me to desire all that YOU want for me and for YOUR Son's bride. In Jesus' name, Amen."

8 THE WARRIOR'S GIFTS

PREFACE: PLEASE DO NOT BE AFRAID.

Before we jump into this chapter, I want to take a moment and ask that we do ourselves a favor and we first, let go of what others have defined these to be. There are people on Television, in churches and who have mega-churches in America who talk about what they believe these things to be and there are many that either do not know what they really are or they have hyper-spiritualized them. So, we need to normalize the gifts. The gifts are supposed to be normative for believers. Some people who act weird as they say they are manifesting spiritual activity or working in a gift, I believe are attempting to get attention or platform the gift. I have tried to not only do my prayer, worship and giving in secret, but as well to also function in gifts in secret and below to the radar while going through the day at work or anywhere else. The fact that gifts have been made "weird" is a sad thing. I have learned to function in them with no one largely knowing any different. They however, DO KNOW when GOD encounters them through the activity of the gift.

So, let's detach a bit from what extremist denominations and TV evangelist type people say gifts are. I feel like people have stolen these terms. They have stolen "gifts" and "Baptism of Fire" by using the terms the wrong ways. I do not believe most people who use these terms currently even know the fullness of what they are.

So, right here and now, rather than allowing people who abuse the Bible, manipulate people's reactions or act weird in order to attract attention to tell us what the gifts are, let's ask Holy Spirit, the great teacher that Jesus said would bring us into all truth to teach us what they are. We need to take these terms back. Just because someone says they know what it is doesn't mean they do. We cannot be afraid to go back to the New Testament and the original design and learn what they are. We cannot allow someone else's "weird" activity and strange reactions to emotion stop us from living fully in the Kingdom. Let's take the terms back and let's re-teach even these people what they really are. Many people manipulate others with what they call gifts that really are not.

DIGGING DEEPER

The sad thing about this chapter is that I grew for the first half of my life not knowing that these actually existed and the last while in life I have had to deal with people that didn't deserve them. The catch about the grace gifts is that they really are like little "grace-lets" that GOD has given people not for their own pleasure or to abuse and manipulate others nor are they for people to use to gain a platform, pedestal or power. And yet, immature believers have used them this way so many times.

Deep and powerful gifting is dangerous. Since the stronger we are in something, it often becomes our weakness in the Kingdom, the gifts have a real ability to corrupt. Big gifting in a person is not a sign of maturity. Too many times in the past, the church has called someone a prophet who neither was mature and demonstrating fruit, stewardship and purity over the long haul, but they were not even able to prophesy.

I have actually met people the church called prophets who were unable to call forth things nor were they able to speak what Holy Spirit was saying about the future. Of course they were gifted, but it was in the ability to do words of knowledge and words of wisdom.

And these people had been elevated to the office of "prophet" in the Western church. This is a sad thing. It sets the person up for a "fail" when they are tested over true prophecy that was incorrect and sets the church up for a fail when secular media gets ahold of them, or someone's expectations were not met or when they just plain break under the stress of trying to be someone they are not with a co-dependence between them trying to find their identity in what the church said about them and the church trying to find their fix in what they could divvy out.

Not a good thing. So, one way to fix this issue with those offices is to more clearly define what the gifts look like. I never was able to find a book on the gifts when I was a young person and I grew up in a church that did not believe the gifts were still in existence, but over time I have functioned in every one of them. (To read more, get my book, "A Warriors Tale").

And in the little church I grew up in, there were very real gifts that showed up. They just often were not understood, noticed or sanctioned. Now I have learned how to demystify them as well as how to function in them while no one really noticing in the working world in which I exist. Being a high level IT Development Company Owner now and having spent over a decade in the public sector doing finance, support, corporate sales, management, development and IT as well as much more in the jobs in which I flourished, I found ways to do the gifts as a part of my daily life and flow. As a matter of fact, I even shared my faith life openly and my love of Jesus and most of my co-workers knew I was a believer and I ministered to them and saw many of them grow into the church or grow more in love with Jesus through this faith walk together and the largest percentage were shocked in the end when they found out I have been an undercover pastor. They were shocked when they realized they had been prayed for and shepherded for years. (Get the other book for more of that story).

So, when I write this, I come from the standpoint that this is natural stuff for the believer and it works best when people don't walk away thinking, "That guy should be somebody important on TV…" And instead they walk away thinking, "Man, I love Jesus more… I need to get in church this weekend…"

The gifts do NOT exist for the edification of the single believer but the larger body of Christ and for people to come to know Jesus. IT IS NOT TO MAKE YOU RICH!!!! STOP WASTING THE GIFTING! YOU ARE IRRELEVANT TO THE WORLD IF YOU ABUSE GIFTS! Treat them with respect and use them wisely as a good steward like anything else GOD has given you. Eagerly desire them, but seek HIS face more than HIS hand.

There are two passages that speak a lot about gifts but before I add them here, I just want to mention that 1 Corinthians 13 says that all gifts will pass away, but love will continue on in the age to come. Keep that in mind. If gifts are not functioning inside the framework of GOD's passionate, furious love for everyone, especially the Bride and the lost, then they are of NO USE!!!!!!! They are noisy commotions. You must first be a person that is abiding in the Vine with an outflow of love before you can join GOD in what HE is doing for gifts to be effective. But notice I did not say, "for them to work." I said for them to be truly effective.

Here are the two passages on the Gifts I want to share:

Romans 12
3 For by the grace given me I say to every one of you: Do not think of yourself more highly than you ought, but rather think of yourself with sober judgment, in accordance with the faith God has distributed to each of you. 4 For just as each of us has one body with many members, and these members do not all have the same function, 5 so in Christ we, though many, form one body, and each member belongs to all the others. 6 We have different gifts, according to the grace given to each of us. If your gift is prophesying, then prophesy in accordance with your faith; 7 if it is serving, then serve; if it is teaching, then teach; 8 if it is to encourage, then give encouragement; if it is giving, then give generously; if it is to lead, do it diligently; if it is to show mercy, do it cheerfully.
9 Love must be sincere. Hate what is evil; cling to what is good. 10 Be

devoted to one another in love. Honor one another above yourselves. 11 Never be lacking in zeal, but keep your spiritual fervor, serving the Lord. 12 Be joyful in hope, patient in affliction, faithful in prayer. 13 Share with the Lord's people who are in need. Practice hospitality.

1 Corinthians 12

Now about the gifts of the Spirit, brothers and sisters, I do not want you to be uninformed. 2 You know that when you were pagans, somehow or other you were influenced and led astray to mute idols. 3 Therefore I want you to know that no one who is speaking by the Spirit of God says, "Jesus be cursed," and no one can say, "Jesus is Lord," except by the Holy Spirit.

4 There are different kinds of gifts, but the same Spirit distributes them. 5 There are different kinds of service, but the same Lord. 6 There are different kinds of working, but in all of them and in everyone it is the same God at work.

7 Now to each one the manifestation of the Spirit is given for the common good. 8 To one there is given through the Spirit a message of wisdom, to another a message of knowledge by means of the same Spirit, 9 to another faith by the same Spirit, to another gifts of healing by that one Spirit, 10 to another miraculous powers, to another prophecy, to another distinguishing between spirits, to another speaking in different kinds of tongues, and to still another the interpretation of tongues. 11 All these are the work of one and the same Spirit, and he distributes them to each one, just as he determines.

THE GIFTS EXPLAINED

Paul is clear enough on what is expected of the gifts and how they work. He is also clear on our attitudes about them as well as the fact that he desired for everyone to know about them. So, let me take a little time and share what I have learned personally about these gifts. This again, is what I have learned through functioning in them around the world.

Something before we jump in.

A - Gifts can be for someone to have for life but also may be for the moment.

B - The Holy Spirit may have someone who is not gifted in a certain gift function in any and all gifts when needed and yet that person not "keep" that gift. John Wimber called this the "Dancing Hand of GOD.'

C - Gifts are for the entire Body's growth and encouragement. THEY

ARE NOT TO BE USED TO LORD OVER OTHERS. They are for serving others.

D - Those that are gifted in any gift should be aware that it is a great responsibility and should work out their salvation and life in intimacy with the Holy Spirit, exhibiting fruit of the Spirit and maturing in the faith. I have seen many ruined by gifts that they did not have the maturity to handle.

E - We eagerly desire spiritual gifts. We more eagerly desire the gift giver. Do not put gifts above the giver. And yet, DO DESIRE GIFTS! Ask for them. And realize you are asking for an entire life of service to the giver of the gifts by serving the Body.

F - Just because you have a powerful gift does not make you mature.

G - Everyone has gifts. We need to recognize them, pray for impartation of them by the Holy Spirit and laying on hands and pray for them to be stirred up. (This is the Biblical model).

H - Gifts should be natural, not pedestaled. I feel like you can know when you are functioning the best in them when no one at your job or work knows what just happened after you function in one, all they know is GOD is real when you are done.

I - So, watch your language!!!!!!! We do not need to say, "THUS SAITH THE LORD…" We can say, "Have you ever thought this; _____," (fill in the blank with the word). If the person says, "How did you know that?" We then respond with, "GOD is revealing HIMSELF to you right now and HE wants you to know HE is real. HE spoke that through me. I couldn't know that…" or we can say on the start, "I feel GOD wants you to know, _____," (fill in the blank with the word." We need to dumb it down for the regular world so they can hear what we are saying. I learned from my uncle that is a scientist that if I do not dumb down my words when I am talking about something that is higher level learning, a kid will never understand it. The need to sound smart or to be viewed as gifted or intelligent will thwart our ability to be natural about the gifts.

J - Gifts are the natural state of the church. A healthy church has love, is safely intimate, is growing, has fruit of the Spirit, is being discipled and is discipling and is natural in worship and the gifts.

THE 9 GIFTS

The Apostle Paul enlists in 1 Corinthians 12:4-11 nine supernatural grace-let gifts of the Spirit. We can divide them into three groups as follows:

MANIFESTATIONS OF WISDOM AND KNOWLEDGE BY THE HOLY SPIRIT

1. The gift of words of wisdom, verse 8

Words of Wisdom are guidance in Wisdom and understanding for Scripture and application as well as sometimes wise counsel that goes along with it for a person's life. For example, someone is dealing with a specific issue that you are praying for and as you are praying, and then Holy Spirit speaks into the back of your mind a Scripture that really directly deals with they are dealing with and how it applies. And the person says, "That's exactly what I was sensing… Thank you…"

It's the ability to know something "Wise" in application to Scripture or in relation to Scripture that the Father is speaking into the person or situation at that moment.

THE GREEK:
The spiritual **gift** of wisdom, like the **gift** of **knowledge**, is also referred to as the "**word** of wisdom" or "utterance of wisdom." The Greek **word** for wisdom is sophia and it refers to the intimate understanding of God's **Word** and His commandments which results in holy and upright living.

2. The gift of words of knowledge, verse 8

Words of Knowledge are sentences, words or phrases that GOD speaks divinely by the Holy Spirit in leading someone in speaking into another person's life. You are NOT receiving a "Word of Knowledge" if it is something you knew already about the person, or if there are things you are picking up in their mannerisms. It is NOT profiling.

We must be careful in how we do this because it can be mistaken for psychic work and we have to be careful not to "read" people in order to manipulate or get a certain response. These little words from GOD for another are precious and should be treated with respect. If we do not have a specific word for someone then we need to keep it to ourselves.

This works best when we don't know the person we receive the word for. When you get something you cannot know for someone you do not know, it is the greatest sign to both you and that person that GOD is encountering them and interacting with them.

The goal of these words often is for salvation and/or healing. When someone hears the words that are spoken, they usually have an "aha" moment as the Spirit reveals exactly what is in their hearts that only they and GOD could know. And at that very moment, that person even if an unbeliever often will immediately believe that GOD is real. (See the chapter on King and Country. I discuss Power Encounters and Kingdom Collisions happen. This gift is great for a Kingdom Collision).

When you receive what you believe to be a word for someone that is divine knowledge that only GOD could know and you are working through whether or not it is correct or if the timing is correct to share, get counsel. (You can also refer to the chapter on "Hearing GOD" in this book).

THE GREEK:
The spiritual gift of knowledge is also known as the "word of knowledge" or "utterance of knowledge." The Greek word for this gift is Gnosis and it simply means knowledge. The Scriptural emphasis in 1 Corinthians 12:8 is on the ability to speak this knowledge to others in a given situation or knowing things about a person's life we cannot know without the Holy Spirit of GOD revealing it to us. (Revelatory Understanding).

SOME TIPS FOR SHARING A WORD OF KNOWLEDGE:

A - Be sure to only say what you hear. If it is only one word, don't add to it. Just say exactly what you heard. Do not try to figure it out or even give people explanation. GOD does not need a lawyer. He needs a messenger. One time I got the word, "Macaroni & Cheese" for someone. I didn't get anything else. I shared that word and they broke down in tears since it was a trigger word that only GOD could know for them. (That is another story you can find in my book, A Warriors Tale).

B - You must cultivate relationship and intimacy in order to be able to walk in a way where GOD can trust you as HIS servant and secret keeper. So, check out the chapter on The Warriors Center. Tune your guitar before the concert.

C - Just because you get a word doesn't mean you need to share it immediately. We have to ask GOD about timing. A lot of times for people in my family or people I know well, I do not share immediately because GOD is not directing. I pray over the specific thing and sometimes HE leads me to share and sometimes HE has them come to me another time. Most of the time in public if I get a word and directive from GOD for someone, the time to share is often right then. I have learned that most of the time I get a gut dropping sensation and feel overwhelmed with having to do it. I am not an extrovert so it is hard for me to step out in faith like this. This may be hard for some to believe because I have stepped out hundreds or possibly thousands of times in my daily life over the years. (See my other book for these stories). Be sure to ask Holy Spirit what HE is doing and where you can join the Father in HIS work.

D - Practice, practice, practice. We have a high regard for failure in my community. We love failure as long as it is mixed with humility, honesty and we all learn from it. My definition of success is; "Success is getting up one more time than you fall down."

E - Learn to practice in a safe environment as with all gifts. I love doing ministry in small groups meetings in homes. This is a great place to learn. See my chapter on the Warriors Comrades for more information on having people in your life that will keep you accountable and help you grow.

F - DO NOT BE AFRAID! These words are not your problem, plan or directive. We are just obedient servants that are joining GOD in what HE is doing, so keep asking, "What are YOU doing, LORD…" And listen. It gets easier the more you try and it is a ton of fun!!!!

3. The gift of discernment, verse 10

Discerning spirits is the ability to sense what spirits are in the room. A discerning person picks up on what is going on with the spiritual world, the angelic, the demonic as well as the Holy Spirit in a space. Are they always discerning? Maybe not, however, the more mature that have this gift are a real asset since they are more able to sense if the group is in one accord or not and what is happening in the room as well as sometimes when there is a need of repentance in the group.

Discerning of spirits is a needed gift in the church. These folks are more sensitive in a "sixth sense" kind of way. They have "intuition" that is from the gift at work in them by the Holy Spirit. As with all gifts, this gift is not just for the person that has it but for the whole Body of Christ. I feel that this gift is like a "firewall" or a safety mechanism in the church.

A Discerner is the handmaiden of Holy Spirit. Sensitivity to what the Spirit is saying should never be ignored and is not overrated. We have too often offended the Holy Spirit in our churches and we need to become more and more sensitive. We need discernment back.

THE GREEK:
The spiritual gift of discernment is also known as the gift of "discernment of spirits" or "distinguishing between spirits." The Greek word for the gift of discernment is *Diakrisis*. The word describes being able to distinguish, discern, judge or appraise a person, statement, situation, or environment. In the New Testament it describes the ability to distinguish between spirits as in 1 Corinthians 12:10, and to discern good and evil as in Hebrews 5:14.

The Holy Spirit gives the gift of discernment to enable Christians to clearly recognize and distinguish between the influence of God, Satan, the world, and the flesh in a given situation. The church needs to function in this gift to warn believers in times of danger or keep them from being led astray by false teaching. See also I Corinthians 12:10, Acts 5:3-6; 16:16-18; 1 John 4:1.

MANIFESTATIONS OF THE POWER OF THE HOLY SPIRIT

4. The gift of faith, verse 9

Faith is both something we have in Jesus and a supernatural gift. The gift of faith I have found is an extra measure of faith in the face of insurmountable odds. There are times we face certain realities in our world and we have to ask for more faith. The gift of faith shows up when there are insurmountable odds and the person or persons faced with these issues have no fear. They instead have peace and a deep down indescribable awareness of GOD's plan and desire in the situation and they have no way of doubting.

Gifts of Faith happen a lot in pioneering works. People that are doing church planting in foreign countries with no church presence or in the underground church as well as church planters here in the states function in this.

It can go hand in hand with the other two gifts listed below and sometimes this gift is imparted into a person by a Word of Knowledge, a Word of Wisdom or a Prophetic Word. All of these give people an "Aha" moment and that revelation in a very real, personal and current way can spark this gift of Faith that just stays with someone.

We should really ask for this gift. It is so necessary. The Father in the story of Jesus healing his demon possessed son said, "I believe, help my unbelief..." Jesus said that belief made it so nothing is impossible.

If we need miracles and/or healing, we should start with the foundation of faith.

Hope is the building blocks faith is built out of. So, be sure to put your hope in no person but Jesus. "Hope deferred makes the heart sick..." - Solomon. Be careful to keep your hope safe. Do not let anyone steal your hope or cause you to hope in them. Faith is the substance of things hoped for. And do not forget, the core of love from 1 Corinthians. "Love always believes..." If we are intimate and in loving relationship with Holy Spirit, we will have faith. And I believe that this intimacy is the anchor point for the Gift of Faith. Nothing like a love-struck girl when she reads a love note from her new fiancé. She can read it over and over and she can "wait forever" if necessary for her love to come! The Bible is that love note. Jesus is that fiancé. We are awaiting with great hope (Faith) which is birthed out of love and intimacy! Faith keeps oil in the lamp and the light burning. As Jesus said, "When the Son of Man comes will HE be able to find faith on the earth?"

Let's answer HIM with a resounding yes from our hearts of love!

THE GREEK:
The word for faith in the New Testament is *Pistis*. It carries the notion of confidence, certainty, trust, and assurance in the object of faith. The gift of faith is rooted in one's saving faith in Christ and the trust that comes through a close relationship with the Savior. Those with this gift have a trust and confidence in God that allows them to live boldly for Him and manifest that faith in mighty ways.

In the Bible the gift of faith is often accompanied by great works of faith. In Acts 3:1-10 we see this gift in action when Peter sees a lame man at the Beautiful Gate and calls on him to stand up and walk in the Name of Jesus. Jesus said even a small amount of this faith could move mountains (Matthew 17:20; 21:21). Paul echoed this truth in 1 Corinthians 13:2.

The Holy Spirit distributes this gift to some in the church to encourage and build up the church in her confidence in God. Those with the gift of faith trust that God is sovereign and He is good. They take Him at His Word and put the full weight of their lives in His hands. They expect God to move and are not surprised when He answers a prayer or performs a miracle.

5. The Gift of Healing, verse 9

Gifts of healing are just what they say they are. Having been healed by GOD miraculously, I can tell you that GOD still heals of anything. We need to go to HIM first and pray for healing before the doctors. And when the doctors give us the news that they can do nothing else, that is when we have to see GOD move. GOD can! HE IS ABLE! Everything HE did in the past, HE can do today.

If there isn't anyone you know that functions in this gift already, do what the Bible says in James and get the elders of the church community together and have them lay hands on you and pray. Confess anything that is unforgiveness or sin in your life and have them pray for the Father to heal you in Jesus' name. Don't let people pray cheesy prayers like, "…if it be your will, oh Lord…" Those prayers disgust me. It is proof someone does not know their standing with GOD nor do they know how the Kingdom works.

See the chapter on King and Country. What is GOD's will? It is the coming of everything that is in the Kingdom to come. Is there perfect health in the Kingdom to come? YES! Then we can know that right now it is available and as Jesus prayed, "YOUR Kingdom come, YOUR will be done on earth as it is in heaven," we must agree. Healing come and break through now.

Lastly, do not be afraid to pray wrong. If someone prays for someone to be healed and they are not, what do we do? Schedule another time to pray. Jesus prayed for a blind man twice. If HE had to twice then we may have to 20! DO NOT BE AFRAID to look dumb. As I have said many times to my teams, "If my daughter is sick and in the hospital dying, somebody better come and pray some dumb prayers like, 'little girl get up in Jesus' name.'" If it doesn't work, what happens? NOTHING! But what if it does????

I have prayed for MANY people in deathbed situations and seen them get up when the doctors said they could not and they were done. One man had a shotgun blast through his brain that disfigured his face, was brain dead on life support and was given hours to live, another had a double colostomy in ICU with hours to live, another with a brain tumor at 70 years old and hours to live and so many more. All of those were healed. (If you want to read more, get the book A Warriors Tale). And for a reference when praying for the sick to be healed, go to the chapter on "The Warriors Prayer."

THE GREEK:
Charismata iamaton is literally translated "gifts of healings." This spiritual gift is closely related to the gifts of faith and miracles. All spiritual gifts are to be exercised in faith, but gifts of healings involve a special measure of it. This gift is interesting in that there is no guarantee that a person will always be able to heal anyone he or she desires. It is subject to the sovereign will of God, as all spiritual gifts are.

6. The gift of working of miracles, 9

This includes anything ever done in the Bible that is considered a miracle.
A - Parting of the Red Sea
B - Plagues
C - Teleportation
D - Multiplication of Food
E - Divine Guidance
F - Water from a rock
G - Axe head floating
H - Cleansing of Water
I - Calming the Sea
J - Killing a tree
K - Aged or Barren having children
L - Armies defeated by themselves
M - Fire falling from heaven
N - Virgin Birth

There are so many more. The Bible is full of stories where GOD did miracles. Are these miracles relevant? They are relevant to the people that needed them to happen or needed GOD's answer. Are they relevant today? Absolutely. We have seen many miracles happen some of which I have questions in my mind about even though GOD did them right in front of me. My mind does not have to comprehend for GOD to be able to do HIS work. I just have to believe. "Trust in the LORD with all your heart, lean not on your own understanding, but in all your ways acknowledge HIM and

HE will direct your paths." -Proverbs 3:5-6 (My life verse).

See in that verse, it says, "…lean not on your own understanding…" Miracles are not an intellectual feat and sometimes intellectualism can be a hindrance. It is not always a hindrance, but it can be. "…lean not on my deep intellectual ability…"

Jesus took fishermen and made men marvel at what they knew by simply being with HIM for 3 years. There is something kinesthetic in the learning model that comes with the demonstration of GOD through a miracle that takes theology and makes it practical and we know from learning models for kids that this makes the truth STICK!

No better way to teach the kids than to experience GOD working together and to put a landmark in our lives to go back to in years to come.
Jesus said, "If you believe, you can tell this mountain to be displaced and go into the sea and it will do it…"

Was HE being literal about this physical phenomenon in the natural world. Surely Jesus doesn't care about that kind of thing and it wasn't literal. Well, if you do not think it was literal, HE said it after withering a tree that did not give HIM food when HE wanted it. Was that literal and natural?

When Jesus says the mountain will move, HE means that literal land mass will be displaced not by plate tectonics but by the hand of the Creator that literally created it. Booyah! GRRRRRR!

Take it from someone that has seen miracles. Don't listen to anyone trying to teach you about these gifts and miracles in specific if they have never had any experience with them. Humans are idiots if they believe that their human world view and limited life experiences totally define GOD's reality when approaching us on the Earth.

THE GREEK:
The spiritual gift of miracles is described in Scripture much like the gift of healing. It is found in 1Corinthians 12:10 and the Greek phrase *energemata dynameon* literally translates "workings of powers." The double plural most likely means that these gifts were diverse and were not permanently available at the will of the gifted believer, but instead were bestowed at various times and circumstances. This means that they are all subject to GOD's plan, HIS hand.

SPECIAL INSTRUCTIONAL UTTERANCES BY THE HOLY SPIRIT

7. The gift of prophecy, verse 10

This is very simply put, foretelling or forth-calling by the Holy Spirit. There are soothsayers and fortune tellers out there that have a form of Catholicism or some kind of Christian cult or who are simply witches or into divination. This gift needs no props and calls on no spirits. It gives all glory to GOD. All other kinds of fortunetellers are in witchcraft and are evil.

Foretelling means to be able to speak what is about to happen in the future. Forth-calling is the ability to speak something that GOD is speaking through us to the person and when it is stated, certain steps begin to align or the words themselves cause awakening in the soul of the person to which we are speaking.

The gifts ALWAYS LIFT JESUS UP!!!!!! NOT HUMANS!!!!!

We must have discernment when approaching this gift.

The person that speaks something in prophecy tells something that will come to pass in the future and it happens.

Also, the gift can call things out in a group of people such as in Jonah's story where he said what would happen should Nineveh not change and they responded the way GOD intended with repentance and then the country was moved by the prophet's words into alignment and thus were forth-called into the Kingdom alignment they were to be. They entered their calling again with GOD.

This gift is not to be confused with the office. The office of a Prophet is given to someone that is 100% on with the forth-calling and foretelling over many years, demonstrates maturity as we discussed in the chapter on the Maturing Warrior and is above reproach with love for the Bride and Body and is already bringing the Bride and Body into alignment with GOD's design. See the chapter on the Warrior Bride for more on the office of the prophet. Too often someone functions in the gift one or two times and we elevate them to an office. I have watched these men over and over succumb to arrogance, pride and hubris and I have watched as many have fallen into sin and taken many weak believers with them. Call them what they are… "Gifted. Normal Christians." I do not blame these men for their hurting the church and destroying understanding about the offices. I blame all of us that put their gift on a pedestal and did not put maturity (fruit, stewardship, and purity and creating disciples) on the pedestal first.

I also believe that part of the reason the Body of Christ has cast off restraint and is dying is because of what we see in Proverbs 29:18, "Where there is no Prophetic Revelation, the people cast of restraint…"

We need it back. Our churches need it back, our families need it back, our culture needs it back. We must start praying especially for this gift to return and we must repent for ever holding it back in the church we have offended the Holy Spirit by killing or hurting HIS prophets and forbidding the prophetic words HE wants to share.

We need this back. We need revelation. In a personal sense, not a corporate or cultural sense:

Revelation leads to awakening
Awakening leads to repentance.
Repentance leads to revival
Revival leads to cultural revolution or shift.
WE MUST HAVE PROPHETIC REVELATION BACK IN THE CHURCH!

Our world, culture and churches does not have a sin problem. They have a PROPHETIC REVELATION problem. They would stop casting off restraint if they all had "aha" moments! BRING BACK THE AHA TO THE CHURCH, OH GOD! Pray that with me. Let's keep praying that!

THE GREEK:
The Greek word for the gift of prophecy is *propheteia* which is the ability to receive a divinely inspired message and deliver it to others in the church. These messages can take the form of exhortation, correction, disclosure of secret sins, prediction of future events, comfort, inspiration, or other revelations given to equip and edify the body of Christ (1 Corinthians 14:3-4, 24-25)

Paul says in 1 Corinthians 14:1 to "Pursue love, and earnestly desire the spiritual gifts, especially that you may prophesy." This gift is a blessing to the church and should not be quenched or despised (1 Thessalonians 5:20). Those who have the gift of prophecy differ from the Old Testament Prophets who spoke the authoritative Word of God directly. Their words were recorded as Scripture as they proclaimed, "Thus says The Lord," whereas the messages from those with the spiritual gift of prophecy must be tested (1 Corinthians 14:29-33; 1 Thessalonians 5:20-21; 1 John 4:1-3). In the New Testament the Apostles, not the prophets, took over the role of Scriptural proclamation from the Old Testament Prophets.

8. The gift of tongues, verse 10

- Tongues is like encryption for our messaging service with GOD. Since only the Holy Spirit can know the heart of man and man cannot even know his own heart like the Bible says and since only the Holy Spirit knows the heart of GOD, this medium or gift is an amazing advantage for all of us since when the gift is in function, we commune with the Father in a way that is very intimate. It is a purposeful thing.

- It is not required for people to have been Baptized in the Spirit however in the Bible, it most often is a demonstration of when the Spirit fell.

- It's like putting up a spiritual antennae and your "hearing" gets better for Words of Knowledge and Words of Wisdom as well as the prophetic.

- This gift is largely personal in nature. Therefore, I tell people to largely do it in secret. Jesus already said that we should do our praying in secret and even more so this intimate kind of prayer. Just like I do not go running around in public in my skivvies, I do not go around parading my prayer language. I do it in secret and unless I sense that GOD has someone nearby that will interpret with a prophetic utterance, I do not even do it loud when in ministry times. I pray with intelligible words when praying for others.

- This gift is to only be used in the Body if it goes hand in hand with interpretation.

- The literal translation of the gift "tongues" in the New Testament Greek is really "unknown tongues." For those out there that think this is translatable languages that are known to man, you are wrong. Read the Bible. I guarantee you do not want to say it is in error. The Bible is not in error, so our theology must be if it is incorrectly leaving out the word, "unknown."

- 1 Corinthians 13 says that they will pass away when the fullness of GOD comes and that love is more important than all of these gifts.

- 1 Corinthians speaks of tongues of men and of angels. I have seen times where evil people function in a type of tongue that is not a human language. In history, we see the use of glossolalia outside of the church in pagan practice. We need to be careful not to assume that everyone speaking in another tongue is speaking in the unknown tongue which is the gift of the Spirit described here. Remember, we test folks with the gift and we test the spirit. This is where the gift of discernment is needed.

THE GREEK:
The Greek word for tongues is *glossa*, which literally means "tongue." When it is used in the New Testament addressing the subject of spiritual gifts it carries the contextual meaning of "languages." Speaking in tongues is the utterance of prayer or of a message glorifying God, typically spoken to God (1 Corinthians 14:2), in a language that is unknown to the one speaking it.

9. The gift of the interpretation of tongues, verse 10

Plain and simple, this is the ability to understand and interpret the special prayer language that GOD gives called, "The Gift of Tongues."

I have as well had GOD translate someone else's language into my ears and I heard them in English. This happened 3 times in Kenya and not only were the people shocked that experienced it, I was shocked and did not know what had happened even though I was convinced that the person that was speaking in Kisii tribal language was speaking to me in English. Even my American cohort with me saw it all and we were both blown away.

Sometimes you just know what is in the unknown language people pray in tongues and something comes out usually that is revelatory and prophetic.

This is a gift that I believe is required for someone to function in tongues in the open in the larger Body of Christ. Tongues were not meant to be used in the larger Body unless this gift of interpretation goes hand in hand with it, then the personal gift of tongues becomes something for the edification of the whole Body.

THE GREEK:
The Greek word for interpretation is *hermeneia* and simply means to

interpret, explain, or expound some message that is not able to be understood in a natural way. Thus, this spiritual gift is the supernatural ability to understand and explain messages uttered in an unknown language.

My Encouragement…

Go and play kids. As John Wimber used to say, "GOD keeps HIS best toys on the bottom shelf." And "Everyone gets to play." We need to lighten up in the church and allow space for people to learn. Fear is faith in the opposite direction and as long as we are fearful or confused on the gifts, the better Satan can hold grasp on the world around us and the church.

So, know that the gifts are for today. They have not passed. They have been around through every era in different forms and they are important. We must desire them and they will be a part of what brings the Body into health. We cannot go any further without them. We must stop trading the Presence and Power of GOD for performance and programs in the church. It will not be much longer that the church is simply deemed irrelevant as an artifact of a passing dark era. This is not the case. This is not the truth. The church cannot die. The Gospel and the Kingdom is ALWAYS RELEVANT. Those that receive the benefit of these gifts will see the Kingdom demonstrated in front of them. They will see Luke 4 alive and the Bible as well as the GOD of the Bible will be relevant immediately.

I preach only one message and that is the message of the Cross. –Paul

If we do not preach, no one will hear. And we do not preach with wise and persuasive words but with a powerful demonstration of the Spirit. –Paul

Preparing the Way
The Warrior Bride
Being Watchful
1. Is the church more than a building?
2. What defines the church?
3. Is everyone important?
4. How should it function? And how can it grow better?
5. Who are the group of people that are for bringing the church into maturity? And why does it matter if they are mature?

Pray with me, "Father, in Jesus' name, bring the Body of Christ together in maturity and unity and let them be edified and grow. Please bring back all the five different offices in the church again. Please forgive us for giving the wrong people titles. In Jesus' name, Amen."

9 THE WARRIOR BRIDE

PREFACE: DO NOT BE AFRAID

Let me preface this chapter here. This is more for the current church to understand and the future "elect" to decipher what is happening in the Body of Christ around them. Before you read this chapter, please understand that the Body of Christ is more than any one denomination. It is the whole Christian Body of believers around the world. Even if there are groups and denominations that you do not agree with, wholly, they are on the same team and in the same Body as long as they believe what we discussed in the Apostle's Creed at the beginning of this book. This is important!!!! If any group does NOT agree with that Creed and the core theology that is behind it, they are NOT a part of the Body of Christ, they are a cult or sect of Christianity.

Also, just saying that you agree to that Creed is not enough. We have to further have made a commitment to Jesus Christ, have repented of sin and asked Holy Spirit to live inside of us as well as submitted to Jesus' LORDSHIP and confessed HIM as well as believe that HE died and rose again and lives now. If we are this kind of believer, then we are in the Body of Christ.

So, with that said, you may want to skip this chapter if you are not comfortable with discussing the leadership of the church, however, I believe that it is of the utmost importance for every person to see what is going on inside the church organization today that is NOT truly led of the Spirit as well as not functioning in the Body. I believe that in a future time where the "very elect would be deceived," it will be important to know what is "not" the true church of Jesus Christ. So, please hear me. Right now, the church does not work and function in wholeness. We are well outside the Biblical model. This is not my design. It is HIS. And that being the case, I share this chapter to give us a foundation in which we feel safe building the Body if we have to in a day that is largely secularized all the way into the church offices as well as a culture that may be post-Christian. So, with that said, please read on with skepticism and check everything you can against the Bible.

HOW THE BODY WORKS:

ORGANISM VERSUS ORGANIZATION

The church is not an "organization" in the business sense, even though it is very much an organization. Every living thing is organized in its working.

There are "systems" in place inside of a living being and entity that are each one very organized such as the nervous system, limbic system and cardiovascular systems. All of these systems are organized to do exact and specific functions. However, this organization that is in each living entity is for the actual organism to not just "survive" but to "thrive."

This being the case, we need to realize that Jesus never discussed the Bride of Christ, the Church and its members in a business, organization since. Believe me, his disciples could have easily done this with a number of them running fishing businesses, a tax collector who could do business accounting and one that was over the accounting for the group. Jesus HIMSELF was most likely schooled in business having grown up in a household where his father likely had a carpentry shop and even though Mary and Joseph knew this child was different, it is highly likely Jesus was schooled in carpentry and the business around it.

This being the case, it's interesting that Jesus focused on teaching HIS followers on being one with HIM in a vine, being one as HE and HIS father were "one" and even saying that they had to be one in ingesting HIS body and blood as well as Paul being led by Jesus' Spirit being led to describe the church as a living "Body" like a human's is interesting.

They did not address the "Body" of believers as an institution nor as an organization as we see it today with club like status and membership. Things didn't come up for a vote. It wasn't a democracy. It was a theocracy with GOD as head. The whole idea of Israel having a King was a bad idea to GOD. Before Saul, GOD attempted to have this model, but Israel begged for a King. GOD said they would regret it and they did.

Instead of a business or a democracy, they said it was like hands, feet, arms, legs, torso, hidden unmentionable parts and Jesus as the head.

Why is it we treat the members of this "Body" with disrespect? Why do we personally treat one person as more important than another? It's because we do not realize just how important each person is to another and we are immature in our thinking. We believe that we do not have to have this person or that person and that we would be better off if that person is not a part of our Body.

Not to mention, in America, we see the Body of Christ as the church or denomination we are a part of. Jesus never saw this nor did the early Apostles. There was ONE BODY. THERE WAS ONE HEAD. The Body of Christ spans the globe and has every tribe, tongue and culture involved.

It has all denominations involved and it is bigger and more unified than we can imagine. We, together are ONE.

And in Western culture, we are so big on rugged individualism, however, this is not the way of the cross. Jesus says that there is no greater thing that someone can do than lay their own life down for another. What if laying down your life is not a one time thing? What if Jesus meant we are to be in a constant life laying down culture? And Jesus described the best leaders as being the ones that could wash feet. Now, some people desire to wash feet in a religious sense because it makes them look bigger because Jesus said it. But, what if washing someone's feet was not just literal as Jesus demonstrated but was even more. What if it was a constant lowering of self and building others up. Not in mock humility and piety, but in a true partnership with the Holy Spirit's leading.

And this rugged individualism has led us to the belief that it is better to be a self-made person and a person that steps on others to get to the top and all that really matters in life is getting to that greater goal. People live this way in life, family, business and even ministries. We teach our kids inadvertently that we have to do everything we can even at the cost of our own very morals to get what we want. We teach our kids that it doesn't matter if your wife of 30 years makes it with you as you get to the top, who cares as long as you get there and you make yourself bigger doing it and write a book about it when you are done that sells millions teaching people to do the same things you did. And on top of that, dump that old wife when you "make it" and get a brand new younger one!

We teach that character traits are not as important as personality changes and outward appearance changes. None of which are true. This country was founded by people who woke early in the morning, worked hard every day and took care of their community. They wrote more and spoke more about right and wrong, more about motives and character in their first 50 to 100 years of America than our last 100 years combined.

So, let's say this; a baby is "dependent." A teenager becomes "independent." (This is seen as the height of maturity in America). A dysfunctional adult is "Co-dependent." And a truly mature person (of which there are few in American culture compared to the larger population) is "inter-dependent."

A person that is interdependent sees that it is too childish to be dependent and knows that a dependent adult has problems as does a co-dependent adult. They know that these people are truly unable to have healthy relationships as an adult. This person realizes that it is better to be independent where you are self-sustaining, but also has matured enough and has enough personal identity settled in themselves to know that things just go better in "teams." They realize that the concept of synergy really works and that they can get more than double the return when they work together with another in a mutually beneficial way. They understand that there is give and take and that they do not always get their way, but they are always looking for ways where both sides can "win" and come to consensus. They know it is not good enough for them to just get their way in things and it is not good enough for another person to only get their way, but for both to work through every single issue in a Biblical way, seeking GOD's central will in all things and looking for the answer that gives both parties and sides an answer where the both move forward together. To do this, the individuals involved have to truly want the best for their brother or sister and they have to truly be unselfish and yet not totally selfless.

It is a give and take. There is shared interest, shared vision, shared gains, shared losses and shared growth. This is community at its best. And Jesus, the Holy Spirit and the Father best demonstrate this unity and community of anything in all creation. They are unified as one and yet they are 3 separate personalities and occupy 3 separate spaces in reality and yet they are unified in one Spirit. The Trinity has been unexplainable from the beginning, however, the affect of the fullness of the Manifest Presence of GOD in the Body of Christ as the head comes into place in the organism is unmistakable. It is "One Accord." This term in Acts is the keynote affect of the incarnation of GOD's Presence in the church. It is GOD in the center and lead. And GOD is LOVE. LOVE works.

And in the concept of the Body itself, it would be an organism that knows it cannot function the way it should without every part. It has hands, feet and all the other parts. All the parts know their roles and own those roles. They are not trying to be any other part. This is a sign of maturity. The simplicity of that obedience is powerful, And the Body knows that when one part of the Body is hurting, you do not lop it off, you tend to it and carry its load as best you can till it heals.

If churches thought this way, how different would everything be? And as we look at this organism it becomes very apparent that this thing cannot get arranged as it should unless someone is a part of bringing it together.

Thus, enters the offices...

THE OFFICES OF THE CHURCH

Before we really even dig into the office, I want to say again that Gifts are not a sign of maturity. So, we are wrong when we place people into offices based solely on gifts and not on maturity. Maturity is measured by the fruit in a person's life. And missing fruit is missing relationship.

The office should only come after a long fruit-filled life is demonstrated in someone that has a tested gifting. And beyond that, making sure we know exactly what gift is what is key. We called a lot of people prophets in the church that missed the mark in prophecy over and over literally. Yet, they did function well in words of knowledge or words of wisdom. This is key. We need to make sure we are calling the person the right thing. We accidentally give men and women platforms they should not have either due to their having the wrong gifting and being mislabeled or their inability to demonstrate fruit, which is a sign of immaturity. Neither should be elevated to an office. And no one should be placed into an office unless they are truly showing the fruit of humility, are subject to accountability and submissive to GOD not being swayed by men. And who surround themselves with GODly counsel.

THE OFFICES AS WE FIND THEM IN THE BIBLE:
Pastor
Teacher
Evangelist
Prophet
Apostle

Let's frame this as well with the understanding that we do not give offices to people like interviewing and hiring people for a job. We are not "taking resumes." And we do not "choose" them. The anointing of GOD for the office is either on them or it is not. There is no grooming process for gaining that anointing. There can be training in maturing those that are showing signs of anointing for the specific office at a young age. Samuel was a child when he first heard GOD's voice and received his first prophetic word and word of knowledge. However, it was not until Eli's passing and many years of maturing in fruit and life before GOD until he was the judge and prophet of Israel.

WE RECOGNIZE THE OFFICES ARE:
1 - Holy Spirit revealed.
2 - The person demonstrates the results and fruit of maturity and the fruit of the office possibly years before they are known to be in it.

We agree with what GOD is already doing in and through a person who is beginning to function in an office and the office is confirmed and then blessed by the laying on of hands.

(Laying on hands is simply when we place our hands on someone as we pray for them like they did in the Bible before "setting someone apart for the work of the LORD." And it is believed as well as sometimes you even can tangibly feel that the Holy Spirit anointing is conferred more, released and/or demonstrated during these moments as people are there together doing it in Jesus' name).

These people have not "worked up" the gifts and offices or manipulated to get there. As a matter of fact, I have found that often the people called into an office do not even want to be known that way nor do they want a title.

True story, this is a side note and not directly related, but if you find someone who is good with finance, faithful in all they do and does NOT want to look after the books of the church because they fear GOD and they do not like touching money, they usually make the BEST person to be bookkeeper. Beware the person that HAS TO HANDLE MONEY or they are not happy. Just saying.

Back to what I was saying. But, these people do not work it up. They are it. You already see the fruit of it in their lives. For instance:

A pastor is someone that people are seeking out for counsel, leadership and life development, nurture in Spiritual life, discipleship and who has a following of people he or she is developing in the faith. If there is no one following them, they are not a pastor. You don't "teach" or "hire" this kind of stuff. It either is or isn't. A pastor cannot help but shepherd those that are around them no matter the setting and those that are around them are becoming more mature in the life of Christ. (Reread my chapter on signs of maturity).

A teacher has people around them following them who are learning. These people have found that this person "the teacher" is just easy to learn from. They have such a way of wording things that just makes sense and they cannot help themselves but to teach in all ways at all times using all methods. You can see people getting "aha" moments around them and they unveil the Kingdom easily.

An evangelist cannot help but draw people to Christ. And its a side effect of their daily lives. It's awesome to watch these people. They don't work anything up, they simply have a gift and an office and people sometimes literally seek them out begging for them to lead them to Jesus. "What must I do to be saved…" I have actually seen this happen. You cannot make this stuff up.

A prophet says things that come to pass over and over without being "off" and is able to call things into being in people, countries, communities and creation. This is different than having moved or been used in the "gift of prophecy." One can be used in the gift and never have the office. It takes a long term fruitfulness in the gift and a maturity in forcing out their "soulish" interpretations, a purity of hearing the simplicity of the voice of GOD and a long term life of fruit of the Spirit, Stewardship and Purity. These folks must be deep in 1 Corinthains 13 love. The office requires maturity. If they are not, there words are sounding gongs and clanging cymbals. And they can function in the gift of prophecy without being mature in gift or fruit and they are NOT A PROPHET.

An Apostle functions in all gifts and offices as needed and brings things into agreement, has a regional and sometimes national or international authority as well as vision of what the church looks like. They have planted the Kingdom work in communities missionally. They shepherd shepherds and offices of the church, all of which are not planned or performed but are a result of day-to-day natural living.

These are GOD-ordained parts of the Body of Christ and these offices are not to LORD their role over others or gain prestige. They exist to see the Body served, equipped, functioning, healthy and blessed. Theirs' is the role of chief foot washer.

The maturity in fruit, stewardship and purity is prerequisite and more important than gifting.

We have run into problems today by putting immature, highly gifted people into offices. GOD did not ordain this. It's our failure.

METRICS FOR DISCERNING THE OFFICES:
1 - Fruit, stewardship, purity and discipleship as discussed in 1 Timothy, 2 Timothy, Matthew 28 and Galatians 5.
2 - Demonstration of the aforementioned fruit of the Spirit.
3 - THEN AND ONLY THEN, NUMBER 3 is the "Gifting" and "Ability" or "Anointing."

Then, before any hasty hands laying on event; fasting prayer and meditation should be observed in seeking GOD's will above our "ability to recognize" the office. The local community should be unified in this and they should be together as the Spirit leads all "mature" believers to one accord. This was the model in Acts for replacing Judas and was the first design in how they released leadership. This also was the model in selecting the first deacons.

Now, the key to remember about the offices is that they ALL WORK TOGETHER FOR ONE GOAL! THEY MUST HAVE EACH OTHER AND ALL OF THEM ARE NEEDED FOR THIS GOAL. HOWEVER, THIS GOAL IS TO GET THE BRIDE INTO HER GLORY. Therefore, these guys and gals are not just great additions to the church, but they are NECESSARY for the final work. I believe in the season of Malachi 4:5-6, they will be the "fathers" that turn the children back to relationship. So, even though there is very little room for them in the schematics of our denominations and even though there are some others that have been hired into their offices without being truly anointed, when they do show up whether inside the church as it exists or beside it, we MUST recognize the gifting, anointing and maturity and agree with the Holy Spirit's directive to give them authority in our lives and churches. We NEED THEM for this Bride to grow up. I am convinced there is no other design that will work for the church to come into true readiness for Jesus' return without them. Let's begin to watch and develop this generation till they show up on the scene again. GRRRRRR!

DEACONS & ELDERS

I want to add one more section here as I have learned much about it and that is the deacons and elders.

The leadership model in the Body of Christ is an upside down model. This is due to the belief as Jesus stated to the disciples that if one of them wanted to be the greatest among them, they must be the greatest servant. This means that the pastor is a servant and demonstrates Servanthood above all others. Then the elders and the deacons, with the needs of the lost, immature believer, aged, poor, widow, orphan, broken, foreigner and young placed above all; being the ones we serve.

-As Jesus said that we would serve washing feet as he did.
-We are called to have the mind of Christ that considers others above ourselves.
-The second greatest command where we love others as ourselves.
-Consider the poor, the widow, the needy, the broken and the foreigner

since he is their protector. -we should realize that the greatest in the Kingdom is the one who can serve.

-the first is last and the last is first.

-so, all of our leadership functions in a heart of serving and love.

MATURITY IN DEACONS AND ELDERSHIP

Maturity again is required for people to walk in the various levels of the church. Servant leadership (the deacons) is the best training ground for the leadership. I think that someone needs to be at the church and demonstrate a life of serving for 6 months before serving in any capacity as a servant leader. I would further require another 6 months before they can serve as an elder. This is on top of the Biblical qualifications listed here.

MATURITY REVIEWED:

We believe maturity includes:

1- fruit of the Spirit (at the elder level, this would require someone to demonstrate a more consistent life of fruit)

2- purity

3- stewardship

4- creating disciples

At the servant leader level, we often have invited people that demonstrated some level of these above traits in maturity and we have invited them to grow into maturity as the grow in ministry. At the elder level there must be a deepening of this life that demonstrates a long term life of fruit, stewardship, purity and a life style of creating disciples. There should be life lived that prove the maturity. As well as much mentoring younger believers.

SERVANT LEADERS (DEACONS)

The Original Purpose of Deacons: (Servant Leadership)

-Acts 6:1-6 Now at this time while the disciples were increasing in number, a complaint arose on the part of the Hellenistic Jews against the native Hebrews, because their widows were being overlooked in the daily serving of food. So the twelve summoned the congregation of the disciples and said, "It is not desirable for us to neglect the word of God in order to serve tables. "Therefore, brethren, select from among you seven men of good reputation, full of the Spirit and of wisdom, whom we may put in charge of this task. read more.

-1 Timothy 3:8 In the same way, deacons are to be worthy of respect, sincere, not indulging in much wine, and not pursuing dishonest gain.

The purpose of the servant leadership is to create a team of people that each oversee a specific ministry. They meet regularly to report what is happening in their ministry area and offer support to each other. They support each other for developing ministry, maturing as well as creating movement in the larger body for larger joint events.

They meet, report, pray and encourage as well as look for opportunities to grow the body of Christ as well as each other's ministries and communicate upcoming events.

MENTORS, COUNSEL & COACHES (ELDERSHIP)

Elders or overseers are akin to pastors in the church in that they care for the shepherding of people. They are duties and tasked with the oversight and development of the church as well as the leading of it. They have been servants and walk in maturity in the faith. They have the fruit of the Spirit, they are servants of the Body and therefore, they are trustworthy in not just the direction of the church, but the spiritual direction and development of the Body of Christ. They are the chief servants under the pastoral team. The elders feel great humility and are deep in honor for those around them, esteeming others higher than themselves as they realize their position requires great grace and is an honor. They are wise and they are deep in the Bible as well as the Spirit, worshiping in Spirit and Truth. They abide in the vine and demonstrate the definition of maturity. They meet regularly in order to pray, seek GOD's face, worship, fellowship and then out of overflow of Holy Spirit's leading, make decisions and prayerfully direct the church. All questionable things in the body as well as the directives of the administration of the body come here to this group for prayer and leading out of one accord. This position is a great honor and demands great humility. Again, these must be deep in Scripture, founded and anchored in the Bible, "holding to the WORD as taught." There is no way to lead the church without having love, walking in the Spirit, which is demonstrated by the fruit and being invested in the Bible as well as well studied in it, hiding the WORD in their hearts (Psalm 119:11).

-1Timothy 3:1-7 Here is a trustworthy saying: Whoever aspires to be an overseer desires a noble task. 2 Now the overseer is to be above reproach, faithful to his wife, temperate, self-controlled, respectable, hospitable, able to teach, 3 not given to drunkenness, not violent but gentle, not quarrelsome, not a lover of money. 4 He must manage his own family well and see that his children obey him, and he must do so in a manner worthy of full[a] respect. 5 (If anyone does not know how to manage his own family, how can he take care of God's church?) 6 He must not be a recent convert, or he may become conceited and fall under the same judgment as the devil. 7 He must also have a good reputation with outsiders, so that he will not fall into disgrace and into the devil's trap.

-1 Peter 5:1-4 So I exhort the elders among you, as a fellow elder and a witness of the sufferings of Christ, as well as a partaker in the glory that is going to be revealed: shepherd the flock of God that is among you, exercising oversight, not under compulsion, but willingly, as God would have you; not for shameful gain, but eagerly; not domineering over those in your charge, but being examples to the flock. And when the chief Shepherd appears, you will receive the unfading crown of glory.

-Titus 1:6-7 5 This is why I left you in Crete, so that you might put what remained into order, and appoint elders in every town as I directed you— 6 if anyone is above reproach, the husband of one wife, and his children are believers and not open to the charge of debauchery or insubordination. 7 For an overseer, as God's steward, must be above reproach. He must not be arrogant or quick-tempered or a drunkard or violent or greedy for gain, 8 but hospitable, a lover of good, self-controlled, upright, holy, and disciplined. 9 He must hold firm to the trustworthy WORD as taught, so that he may be able to give instruction in sound[f] doctrine and also to rebuke those who contradict it.

-Acts 14:23 And when they had appointed elders for them in every church, with prayer and fasting they committed them to the Lord in whom they had believed.

-James 5:14 Is anyone among you sick? Let him call for the elders of the church, and let them pray over him, anointing him with oil in the name of the Lord.

I believe that the elders, deacons, pastors, evangelists, teachers, prophets and apostles are all required in the most Biblical definition in the Body of Christ for the Body of Christ to become the revealed Bride of Christ GOD desires for HIS SON'S betrothed.

PREPARATION AND REVELATION OF THE BRIDE

Revelation 21 and 22 talks about the Bride of Christ, (the Church in its fullness and unity) being ready for Jesus' return as well as what it is going to look like when Jesus is being presented her. So, bridal language is the norm when thinking about the final revelation of the Church or Body of Christ.

Jesus even talks about our waiting for the return of the Son of Man being like brides awaiting their groom. There is a description here of anticipation and preparation.

There is intimacy conveyed here. There would be wooing and courting of a bride and groom and there would be gifts, a build up and a day where the groom would come and take his bride away from the bride's fathers house and she would become a part of the groom's father's house. So, when we look at the future of the Body of Christ, we should realize that there should be a current build up to a crescendo. Just because our reality may present us a picture of a dirty, unprepared, slothly bride, that does not mean we have to buy in to that. That is not the truth of what is to come. This Bride is going to be ready for her groom and her groom is going to be excited to find her anticipating, chaste and radiant. HE IS COMING AGAIN!

So, if our present reality is not presenting this "Church/Bride" in our era, we begin to realign with our first love and take heed to the call of the Angel in Revelation and come back to our first love. We begin to beg heaven on our knees with tears again for the gift of repentance to come upon the church and for the Spirit of Revelation to come with the Prophets of GOD and call us back into revelation of the coming day. We can ask GOD for revelation to come. As HE reveals truth to us, repentance is always the response. Don't buy into the lie that just because it has not happened for many years that it cannot happen now. IT CAN HAPPEN! Pray for the Bride to be revived and awakened to love again.

The Revelation passage shares a picture of what this Bride will look like and how amazing in the last chapter is her revealing to the world. She is so beautiful as a "Holy City" and a "Holy People," that John the disciple who is writing down the revelation falls down in worship overcome by the revelation. He does this out of turn and is told by the Angel to not do that. The Angel even says that John is going to get them both in trouble for worshiping the wrong person. Was John so immature that he wouldn't know that already? No! If anyone was mature in the faith, it was John the disciple. By the time he was on the Isle of Patmos in jail, he would have likely been in his 80's. He would have walked with Jesus for over 70 years. He would have discipled some of the greatest lineage of disciples of the church's history who became fathers to the early church fathers and gave credence and credibility to the historicity of the origins of the canon of Scripture we have today.

John knew better.

What happened here?

Let's just say that the text must not capture fully just how amazing this picture was. This revelation was so great that it would cause a mature believer/leader of the church to fall down and worship the wrong person. WOW!

We should be praying today that GOD reveal this to us today! I believe if we had just a slight understanding of how amazing this Bride is and how amazing the Coming LORD is we would be ruined for life for anything else.

We can read this passage over and over and pray for revelation. That is a good place to start and then we can begin to develop the 5 offices of the church. These guys and gals are supposed to bring us into the communion of the Saints that will bring this Bride into a readied state. We need the 5 offices back. And we do not need to sell short. Don't fill the roles with just anyone. Look for the fruit of maturity, the fruit of the anointing of the office and then look at the long life with Jesus and stayed-ness through trials.

And remember, Christ in us is the hope of Glory as well as the whole earth groans and waits for the revelation of the Sons and Daughters of GOD. This again is a Bridal revelation. It must be pretty awesome, this, "hope of glory." And the revelation of the Sons and Daughters of GOD must be amazing if the whole world is not just holding its breath, but aching and groaning for them to show up and bring the whole world back into alignment with GOD's plan when they walk in!!!!!!!

I believe through the Holy Spirit, there will be a realigning of this Body and she is going to grow from tottering child to beautiful young lady under the direction of the Holy Spirit and the guidance of the 5 Offices until she goes from a tripping baby to a dancing Bride. The gifts, the fruit, the humility, the love will all be seen. The unity will be unmistakable. The fact that she is focused and waiting will be unquestionable.

Do we see this Bride right now? I would have to say no. However, I have to say that I so believe in this revelation and the purposes of GOD I know she will come. Maybe you will help her mature. I pray that you use every gift GOD gives you in order to benefit this goal. I believe in you. You've read this book this far. You have to have something different inside you to keep reading since much of this stuff makes no sense without the Holy Spirit revealing. So, if that's the case, I believe you are already in the middle of a season of the revelation of this Bride and you are called to grow her up.

You cannot do it.

However, you know the ONE who can do it through you. Never forget that in your weakness HE is strong. And dance Bride, dance. HIS heart leaps inside thinking about how much you want HIM. HE WANTS YOU MORE! HE IS COMING! All of the Kingdom and purposes of who we are are focused on this. The whole thing, the Kingdom and everything else is a love story written and planned by a Father who wants a Bride for HIS Son. He bet the entire world on it. And if HE is so interested in a wedding feast and a big marriage, SO AM I! GRRRRR!

Even so LORD, come!

Watch this video here about keeping the fire while we wait on the LORD…

DUSTIN HEDRICK

Learning the Battle
The War & Weapons
Being Watchful
1. Should I be afraid of the enemy?
2. How can I defend myself and prepare to battle?
3. Is he even real?
4. Why should we not focus on him and only allow Jesus to be the center of attention?
5. How do we overcome him?
6. Pray with me, "Father, please keep me safe from the evil one, please help me worship Jesus more, please teach me the ways of growing mature and deep and help me put on the armor YOU have given so that I can stand against the devil. In Jesus' name, Amen."

10 THE WAR & THE WEAPONS

FIGHTING THE ENEMY
We war not against flesh and blood…
(Do we or do we not?)

Satan is a brilliant tactician. You have to realize that he has been studying humans and the way they think, act and fight for thousands of years. And if the scientists are right, then millions of years. How arrogant must we be to think that we understand anything about what he does or how he works! How arrogant we must be to think that we innately in our human ability or after being simply "born" can figure out his activity, schemes or strategies.

Since he has been around for thousands of years, he has come up with amazing ways to subdue anything human and earthbound. However, he is not more powerful than the Sons and Daughters of GOD who are in Christ Jesus.

I have long noticed that he has an ability to show up in third world countries and the demonic seems to be working out in the open there and yet he is not seemingly noticeable in the United States or more developed nations. I wondered for a couple years in the first of my ministry career if it were that demons were not just more evident but also more in number in 3rd world countries or undeveloped nations than in developed countries.

After 20 years of ministry, I have scrapped that theory and now firmly believe that the demonic is actually more populous in developed countries especially in the United States and is actually becoming more evident in areas that are populated by more people or that are more important to the demonic strategy.

Before we dig into this, know the following:
1- Fear is faith in the wrong direction.
2- GOD is LOVE and perfect love casts off all fear. So, LOVE come, fear go!
3- We cannot speak fear, we must speak faith.

I do not believe that I understand all of what they are doing, but after years of interaction and having been involved with over a hundred deliverances of people truly demonized, I have drawn the following conclusions.

1 - Demons best defense is allowing humans to believe they do not exist.

2 - When humans do recognize that demons exist, they use fear tactics to attack humans, both spiritual and physical.

3 - Different areas, regions, states and nations face different demonic controllers. They are not all the same and their characteristics show up in the people that are controlled by them, thus culture wide characteristics that I say are sociological events or what I call a sociological happening where multiple things ironically happen the same way. Or theories of probability don't apply and chance seems too lame an explanation.

4 - They like us to either ignore their control or to become overly preoccupied with them.

5 - They come as "good" messengers. They never overtly reveal their real motives to humans, especially the ones they control.

6 - There are two camps out there. One that doesn't believe in demons and one that believes too much in them. I simply come from the perspective that I have to deal with them and when I enter the normal world, we are against each other. I walk in Jesus' calling, "...I have come to destroy the works of Satan..." And since that is the case, every single day of my life in the real world is a conflict of good and evil and it is a clash between the Kingdom of Heaven inside me and around me and the kingdom of Hell that is in control of fallen man. My walking in allows the Father to have access to fallen man and when they are freed from Hell's grasp, they become a child of the Kingdom and the world that is around them is also brought into alignment with the will of the King of the Kingdom that is now and not yet.

I have seen that oftentimes the moment a demonic entity reveals itself, believers either become overly fearful or they dig into the faith with their eyes opened. After the first encounter my wife had with the demonic, as you read in my other book about my life story, she so woke up that she wanted to go back to before she "knew that the other side existed." However, the reaction to it was we both became even more focused on Jesus after we saw a little more of how nasty the demonic is. Thus, it is better for them to own unwitting, clueless normal humans and leave them believing they are in control of their own lives than to show their real identity and scare the crud out of them.

In undeveloped nations, the fear tactic dominates. I like this better, because once people are believers in Jesus Christ, it becomes easy to equip them with the tools necessary to fight back and once believers just see how powerful Holy Spirit is, they overwhelmingly defeat the enemy in their areas and are even more empowered when it comes to dealing with supernatural issues.

The most important thing to remember is that Satan's main problem is that he wanted to be the center of attention. He was thrown out of heaven for desiring to be worshiped. He wanted what could only be given to GOD. So, that goes along with my belief that my main purpose is to worship GOD and bring HIM glory, to be known by GOD and to be loved by HIM! If that is the case, then always remember as we go further into this, the attack that best slaps the devil in the face is not an outright conflict with HIM, but is a life of pure love relationship and worship to GOD. In the face of this, Satan must always flee. This is the KEYYYYYYY!!!!!!! SO REMEMBER IT!!!!!

REMEMBER FIRST LOVE BEFORE YOU MOVE ON! FIRST LOVE OF JESUS IS THE FIRST WEAPON AGAINST SATAN!!!!!!

If you are not in love with Jesus, stop reading and ask Holy Spirit to bring you into more love relationship with Jesus and go back and read the chapter of this book on intimacy and washing Jesus' feet.

Now, as I head into the Scriptures, let's look at tools and weapons you need to fight this battle.

If you are having a hard time believing in this part, stop and walk away and do not read any more. OR… Stop right now and ask GOD to reveal or open your eyes to what is really going on around you. HE WILL. Do NOT FEAR! AND DO NOT DOUBT! Simply pray and ask for revelation.

THE WAR
Ephesians 6:10-20
10 Finally, be strong in the Lord and in his mighty power. 11 Put on the full armor of God, so that you can take your stand against the devil's schemes. 12 For our struggle is not against flesh and blood, but against the rulers, against the authorities, against the powers of this dark world and against the spiritual forces of evil in the heavenly realms. 13 Therefore put on the full armor of God, so that when the day of evil comes, you may be able to stand your ground, and after you have done everything, to stand.14 Stand firm then, with the belt of truth buckled around your waist, with the

breastplate of righteousness in place, 15 and with your feet fitted with the readiness that comes from the gospel of peace. 16 In addition to all this, take up the shield of faith, with which you can extinguish all the flaming arrows of the evil one. 17 Take the helmet of salvation and the sword of the Spirit, which is the word of God.

18 And pray in the Spirit on all occasions with all kinds of prayers and requests. With this in mind, be alert and always keep on praying for all the Lord's people. 19 Pray also for me, that whenever I speak, words may be given me so that I will fearlessly make known the mystery of the gospel, 20 for which I am an ambassador in chains. Pray that I may declare it fearlessly, as I should.

We have to stop looking at the human side of everything and start asking what is behind what we are seeing. We aren't finding humans.

WARRIORS' WEAPONS

We do not understand what we already have within our grasp. Some of these things like the name of Jesus "of whom Paul preached," is so powerful that even an unbeliever can use it and it will work against the enemy. Seriously, think about Acts where the 7 sons of Sceva used "the name of Jesus whom Paul preaches" to cast out demons and it worked!!!! At least it worked until a demon that was more powerful than their unbelief could handle.

So, these are weapons. Use them. Meditate on them and remember them when you are in the middle of the battle. Also, frame the battle this way. The primary battle Satan and the demonic is focused on the mind of man. Satan wants to keep us "double-minded." He wants to keep us focused on himself more than GOD. We must battle back and learn to discern between our thoughts, GOD's thoughts and the enemy's thoughts he places inside our heads.

We have to recognize.
Then, we have to fight back. We have to fight to bring our minds under the control of the Holy Spirit. We know that our minds can be renewed by the Bible, so, memorizing, reading, meditating on and journaling on Scripture will renew our minds. We must wash our minds with Scripture. I literally not only read Scripture, I listen to it on recordings and allow it to wash over me.

Filtering our thoughts from the enemy's becomes easier when we have Scripture in there to literally filter them. The sword of the Spirit is able to do this.

1 - Saying the name of Jesus, WORD of GOD, Blood of Jesus & worshiping out loud or internally is powerful. As a matter of fact, we do it outwardly and loud to battle Satan. He cannot hear inside our heads. So, saying out loud what is powerful and what we are claiming is a push back against HIM. (Focus on Jesus and meditate on HIS name so that you can call on HIM when the attacks happen).

Think about this:

- Jesus fought the Devil in the wilderness and used the Scripture against him. The Devil tempted Jesus and Jesus didn't sin. Jesus quoted Scripture, so it must be important for us too.
- Worship needs to be on and done all week long. I encourage you to keep it running in the house. Keep a life of worship going.
- WORD needs to be everywhere around you if you are fighting so you have a weapon to grab at any time. WORD is the Sword of the Spirit. Have swords everywhere as well as daggers and knives of the Spirit. Surround yourself with WORD. Literally take verses and write them on your walls or on cards and tape them to the walls. Put them everywhere.

2 - Filter the voices. The Bible says that Christ cannot say evil and that we cannot even do anything that is good apart from GOD. Romans and Psalms state this. So, if we are the righteousness of Christ once Jesus is LORD and we can assume all bad thoughts are demonic temptations and should be externalized as well as dealt with overtly and externally in voice and deed since they really cannot know your thoughts since the only one that can know a man's heart is the Holy Spirit, not even man himself.

3 - Think about this, in the story that Jesus tells, who changed the prodigals' clothes? We don't change our own clothes and we don't fix ourselves. So, we can relax and stop trying to "fix" ourselves. Instead, we can allow Holy Spirit to have access to us and HE fixes us. ISN'T THAT GREAT NEWS!!!!! HE CHANGES MY CLOTHES! HE MAKES ME CLEAN!!!! When Satan says in my head that I am not clean, I can say back that it's not my problem! AWESOME!

- Success is simply getting up one more time than you fall down.
- stop judging yourself and start allowing GOD to clean you up, put your clothes on and simply receive grace.

4 - The armor of GOD is required. We cannot fight this battle unless we

understand the armor of GOD and unless we actually put it on.

What is the armor?

THE ARMOR OF GOD:

A - The belt of truth

Seriously, TRUTH is a person and when you keep yourself in the center of "TRUTH" as a value and a characteristic, you will never be caught with your pants down and you will have something to tuck your skirts in when you need to run. So, you will not be tripped up.

The literal belt of a soldiers attire would have kept their clothes out of their way whether it kept something held up or it kept something from being around their legs to trip them.

So, we need to be people that don't live in any way inside of lies or deceit. As a matter of fact, let me say here that if you are telling white lies, or half-truths, they are total sin. Don't be deceived. Let your "yes" be "yes" and your "no" be "no." There is not such thing as a half-truth or a white lie. It is all a lie and sin.

And truthfully, if you are hiding something in untruth, then trust me, demons when encountered will bring that up to fight you. I have had demons tell my greatest fears to me out loud and even things said to my wife in secret through another person who could not know it. Now, this does not scare me but it can make it a problem if I am having to repent for my sins in the middle of a demonic battle before I have a leg to stand on with them. It can trip you up.

And if you are battling demons that are attacking you, if you are walking in lies, then you are not going to have a legal right to tell them to get out of your life and house. They have a right into our lives through the very sin we allow in. So, become a person of truth first.

B - The breastplate of righteousness

Purity is built into this, which you can read about in my chapter on Maturity. However, righteousness is not just about purity. There is so much more to it. First, you need to understand that our righteousness comes from who Christ is and what HE did. It is not of ourselves. It is something received not worked for. However, you HAVE TO receive it. We need to know who we are inside of Jesus Christ.

And beyond that, I would suggest a word study throughout the Bible on what the Bible defines as a "righteous" man or woman. I actually, personally have read through Proverbs every month for many years because I believe that internalizing the truths of Wisdom can have the affect of bringing out characteristics of Wisdom. The Bible says in Psalm 119:11, which I quote again here that hiding HIS Word in our hearts makes it where we have an outflow of right living before HIM.

C - Feet fitted with the readiness that comes from the gospel of peace

We should NOT hit the streets to any kind of social work or justice work unless we already are surrounding ourselves with the Gospel. The Cross and Resurrection are the keystones to our faith. Paul said that he did not preach anything except the cross and it was in its foolishness that men were saved. He said over and over that was all he intended to know, preach and do. If Paul was this centered on that message, why are we not the same?

It's possible that many of us have never encountered Christ and the Cross. There has been no actual forgiveness or true change of ownership of our lives from ourselves to Christ's LORDSHIP.

If this has taken place, then the story we share is not simply the story of how Jesus died and rose again 2000 years ago but as well what that has done inside of us.

Being fitted with this Gospel means we are aware of and able to give an answer at all times for the hope we have in Christ by sharing what happened 2000 years ago in that act as well as what has happened inside of us directly. This makes the story of the Gospel relevant for today. It is relevant because we are able to tell the person we are sharing with how it is relevant to us and what it did in us and if we are being honest, there should be a life that is proof that we are living so that people see our lives, hear our stories, hear Jesus' story and then say, "aha!"

The light goes off inside of them and we have just engaged the enemy in the battle of the ages and the Holy Spirit through our story convicts someone and they encounter HIM, repent, pray and repent from the story and confess Christ coming under HIS LORDSHIP, believing HIS cross story true because of the demonstration they've seen right in front of them.

We need to practice sharing daily as witnesses to the world about what

GOD is currently doing in our lives. We need to show our thankfulness for every single thing HE does and share with the world the hope we have.

Doing this also situates us in battle ever ready to see the Kingdom of GOD expand into the hearts of others and keeping the enemy at bay, forcing him away and keeping him from being the center of attention in our lives and homes. We ought to every day as families confess Christ and share what we are thankful about HIS activities in the past and present and speak hope into the future.

D - The shield of faith, with which you can extinguish all the flaming arrows of the evil one

Faith is both a fruit and a gift. Staying in contact with the WORD and Spirit in harmony in our lives can largely keep the faith inside of us. However, there is a gift of faith that is beyond the actual faith we have as believers. We should ask Holy Spirit for more faith every single day. As a matter of fact, I encourage you to ask HIM to reveal HIMSELF, HIS PURPOSES and HIS WAYS every day and through daily interaction for HIM to grow your faith. Every time we see GOD do something that is unexplainable, it increases our faith and we learn HIM by a new name. If GOD has healed you, you learn that "GOD IS YOUR HEALER."

Learn to see where GOD has done things in the past and in your present and begin to write down the stories. Going back to these stories and giving GOD credit for what HE has done can truly develop your faith and make you stronger in the Kingdom.

E - The helmet of salvation

Knowing who we are in Christ is powerful. It trains our brain. Meditating and living inside of the reality that we are Sons and Daughters of GOD is like wearing a helmet on our heads. Anyone knows that if our head is hit under attack we can be killed. By wearing a helmet, we are protecting ourselves from concussion and death.

We put on this understanding every single day. We wake in the morning with the belief that we are believers and are Sons and Daughters of GOD. We do this by walking into HIS Presence and engaging HIM in conversation. We need a constant abiding awareness of who HE is and who we are.

This will keep our minds trained and focused and will make it so that the enemy is unable to divide our minds. I discuss our minds being divided in other chapters and areas. Read more later.

F - The sword of the Spirit, which is the word of God.

The WORD of GOD is powerful in itself. Jesus like I said used the WORD of GOD to fight Satan in the wilderness. It must be powerful if HE used it to push Satan back. However, recognize that in that same story, Satan used the WORD of GOD against Jesus. What made the WORD right when Jesus said it and wrong when Satan did? Satan twisted the WORD out of context to get what he wanted. That is manipulation. And did you know the Bible says that manipulation is the same thing as doing the sin of witchcraft?!

Jesus used the WORD of GOD in alignment with the WILL OF GOD. And the only way we can know the will of GOD, the Bible says is through interaction with the Spirit of GOD. And Jesus went into the wilderness "led by the Spirit of GOD," so HIS communing with Holy Spirit and using the WORD had a kick tail affect!

So, asking Holy Spirit daily to speak to us about the WORD of GOD is powerful for fighting the enemy. We need to practice this daily. You cannot expect to know Scripture and use it in the middle of an attack if you have not hidden it in your heart before said battle.

That's like tuning your guitar after the big concert. That makes no sense. You can't do the concert if you are not tuned. And you cannot fight this battle if you are not already steeped in memorized Scripture. Then you can say back to the enemy out loud, "The Bible says…. _____(fill in the blank with the verse), So, back off devil, in Jesus' name. Father, rebuke this enemy in accordance with YOUR WORD by the name of Jesus! GRRRRR"

Sounds funny, but it works. You won't be laughing when there is an attack and Satan won't be laughing when you are done with his demon should you understand and practice this truth.

The WORD OF GOD IS POWERFUL!!!!!!!! The Bible says so, so, I believe it! When I used to live in the inner-city and I slept in an old warehouse, homeless with the homeless we were getting off the streets and there were no doors or windows in their holes and anyone could come in and attack us, I slept with it on my chest. I believe in the power of the WORD!

5 - The demoniac and the sinful woman at the well became 2 of Jesus' first missionaries... Why?

Because they new the demons in an intimate way and due to those years of attack they had been inadvertently equipped the best way possible to aggress against those very attackers.

I have often asked myself why it is that Jesus did not send the demons out of the area. Why did HE send them into the pigs and why did HE allow them to stay in the very area they had come from?

Jesus knew that HE had the exact person perfectly equipped for the job to head right back into that city and take on those exact demons. He knew that sending them away without filling that place with the Holy Spirit would mean they would bring back 70x the attack next time.

He knew that with only an afternoon and no deep theological or seminary training, he had the exact person he needed to kick their tails. He knew that person would know the way they thought, the way they attacked and even the means by which they did it. He knew that missionary, the once demoniac had the right tools and had encountered HIM and knew HIM and knew the HE (Jesus) was LORD and HE knew that is all it took. So, when that guy just wanted to keep following HIM around, while HE still kept the disciples with HIM and did not send them out to change the world, this guy, HE sent immediately. And the secret to this empowerment I believe was wrapped up inside of the very thing that he mentioned about the sinful woman. He had been forgiven much and he had gotten ahold of the fact that he had. That once demoniac was someone to be reckoned with.

This is good news if you are in that situation. Maybe Satan is on you so much because you are his greatest fear.

6 - Does Satan waste resources? NO!

So, then if you are under attack and it is more visible than with other people, don't look down on yourself and think you are the worst, recognize that Satan sees something that you don't and it is likely the fact that you are an important piece to the Kingdom. Remember, the first two missionaries Jesus sent out were the woman at the well and the demoniac in the cemetery.

7 - How long has Satan been doing what he does? Think about it. He has been at this for eons. He isn't stupid!!!!! Stop trying to fight the devil, tell him that, "Father, rebuke this demon in the name of Jesus Christ!" We are not scared of HIM but we also aren't ignorant and arrogant. Don't poke the sleeping dragon. And don't fight demons you don't have to. However, when led into an engagement by Holy Spirit, DO NOT BACK DOWN! We know the end of the story. We win. And we know that Jesus already has the keys to Hell and the grave. He is already the winner and we already rule with Jesus in the era of overlap that I discuss more in the chapter on Kingdoms.

8 - Remember like I already said that in the book of Acts - Jesus' name is so powerful unbelievers used it to fight demons. "Seven Sons of Sceva."

9 - Engaging Demoniacs

You need to know before anything is done that not everything is a demon. Don't just assume it is. I encourage someone to pray for another person through the 5 Step Prayer Model first which I mention in the chapter on the Warriors Prayer and then if while going through it either it becomes revealed that the issue is demonic or if the demon manifests itself and not simply psychological (which requires a licensed and trained psychologist or psychiatrist) and it is not physical (which we defer to a medical professional first), then we go ahead and plan a time to deal with the demonic issue in a more stable and safe environment. Do not hastily lay on hands like the Bible says. You've got time. Pray, prepare and move wisely.

(Also note, there have been rare occasions where I have had people try and make me believe that something was demonic that was not. This is really hard. I have had to learn to listen to the Spirit with the Gift of discernment and to pay attention to whether something demonstrated supernatural ability before moving forward. It is rare, but there have been a couple people that just wanted attention and had truly real, different psychological disorders. I default to sending people to psychologists first in those cases).

However, if someone comes and they demonstrate true demonic supernatural issues and the medical profession and psychological profession cannot find a solution and medicine does not work or if I am in an undeveloped country and there is not another solution, I move forward. Again, I live in an enlightened era and I am not interested in calling things something they are not. If it is a headache, I am calling it a headache and allowing a doctor to prescribe Tylenol as I pray for healing of it. I live in a very balanced naturally supernatural place. Let's be honest and not over mystify things. Call it what it is and then deal with it. I see many people twisting things today to both extremes. Some call everything a demon. Others call nothing demonic. I don't have any interest nor do I make any gain in what I do, so there is a really great amount of honesty right here where I live. It is what it is. So, deal with it.

And since for so many years people have come for deliverance and they have been delivered, I think that it is time to call that what it is as well. There was no book to buy and read when I was a kid like this. This book is coming from life experience. It isn't cute and cuddly. It is real and precise.

Now, before we can ever fight Satan, we must know Jesus. I mean, you actually don't have to since we see the 7 sons of Sceva did not, but I believe it essential for your safety that you do since you don't want to be beat up and sent off naked.

And on top of Jesus being our LORD, we must be continually filled with Holy Spirit. The Bible says that we should not be drunk with wine, but continually filled with the Spirit. (Think Acts 2) And do not allow the people you are casting demons out of to be refilled by demons due to emptiness. This requires a long walk and accountability.

Before you engage someone who is under the control of a demonic entity, be sure to have spent time in prayer and fasting. We do not pray and fast in order to get what we want or to make GOD do something, we pray and fast with an attitude of a servant just desiring to be obedient to our LORD's direction. As you are in the prayer and fasting stage which could last hours or days, allow the Spirit to lead you and ask GOD to bring you into alignment with HIS will, not your own.

So, if you are battling to cast out a demon, you don't have to use long prayers or even some special formula. However, you know that worship music, Scripture, the name of Jesus and the Blood of Jesus are powerful.

When you are able to get the person to shut up and the demon is made quiet, you need to ask the affected person if they know what is happening to them and if they want to be delivered. If they say "yes," go on. If they say "no," get out of there. There is no good you can do. If they are in your house, make them leave. That thing can only stay where it is welcomed.

Again, if someone does have a demon finally cast out of them, you need to make sure that they come to know Jesus as LORD immediately. Take them through the path I mention in chapters one and two. Have them accept Jesus' LORDSHIP and then pray that they are Baptized in the Holy Spirit with gifts and fruit immediately and that HE refill every empty place in them. This also may be a good point to take them through the 5 Step Healing Model I mention in the chapter on the Warriors Prayer as well as the Cross prayer if they have unforgiveness and pain which usually they do. (There is usually a legal right that allowed the demon in in the first place).

10 - When dealing with people who face real demonic, day in and day out battles and even after you see them healed, don't leave them without some tools.

Help people externalize the battle. Get it out of them by them framing it out of them and their bodies. They have to fight. People that have demons will need to be warriors for life. Once you've dealt with a demon for real and up close and personal, you won't ever want to be on that team and you are awake to reality and cannot go back to believing they don't exist.

They need to refill their time and replace their old habits. This book is filled with ways to do that. So, hand them the book.

11 - Demons' greatest attacks are: 1 - pretending they don't exist (for those who don't believe). 2 - fear (for those who know they do). So, tell them to fight back. Recognize when the enemy attacks, don't be afraid and then move on to worship GOD.

12 - Remember that "fear is faith in the wrong direction."

13 - Safety is in the multitude of counsel. two are better than one since they pick each other up. And there is safety in taking on the battle with another. DO NOT BATTLE ALONE and DO NOT DO DELIVERANCE ALONE! Get backup. At least if someone else is with you, they can pray for you and cover your back if something is happening. And they can agree with you. The Bible says that where two or more are gathered in HIS Name, HE will be in the middle of them. So, get together and say, "We are here together in Jesus' Name…" And then you have the Spirit of GOD as backup. Believe!!!!!!!!

14 - Eyes can be closed by GOD or others AND Jesus' power of revelation is powerful enough to change men's lives forever. (Proverbs 28:19 "Without prophetic revelation, the people perish *or cast off restraint*).

So, pray for GOD to reveal things to people. Pray for HIM to open their eyes. HE can and will do this. Sometimes it happens in a moment and like the chapter on gifts discusses, words of Wisdom and words of Knowledge can give people an "aha" moment as the Holy Spirit uses them to reveal that HE is in the place and that HE is real. This can shift the room in a power encounter in a moment. I will discuss "Power Encounters" in the chapter on the King & Country.

15 - If Satan hates something, I love it. I surround myself with everything he hates. I literally write Scriptures on my walls. If they are on the walls and I get called into a battle in the middle of the night, I can walk around the house and I have something to remind the devil of. If you cannot write on your walls, use note cards or post it notes. Stick them on the walls. Stick them on your mirror. Some verses that are great for the battle are:

AT THE END OF THIS CHAPTER, THERE IS A LIST OF BATTLE VERSES TO MEMORIZE AND USE. USE THEM!

16 - There are two lists. 1 - the list of the Lamb's Book of Life. 2 - the list of people the Devil knows. I want to be on both.

You get on the first one by Knowing Jesus and HIS knowing you. You get on the other as the enemy has had enough encounters with you. I want him worried about me. The way I do this? Focus on my first love and be ready in all things.

17 - Bitter Roots and judgments. (See the passage on the Warriors Prayer)

18 - The Cross Prayer (See the passage on the Warriors Prayer)

19 - Meditate on the name of Jesus and believe in HIM and pray, "help my unbelief if you don't." And use HIS name even in dreams. (I mentioned this before).

20 - Worship and pray at all times and pray in all kinds of ways. The Bible even says that we need to pray all the time in all kinds of ways. Stay in a constant contact with Holy Spirit. (See the chapter on intimacy for more).

21 - When things begin to go wrong in your life, don't immediately run to a doctor or another for input. Stop, slow down and listen. Sometimes it

is attack from the enemy. Realign with GOD's will and HIS heart and repent for any unconfessed thing. If there is nothing to do in this area, wait still and ask GOD to reveal why HE is allowing it? HE may be using the trial to direct you another way in life. Whatever you do, do not be downhearted. Be prepared, aware and excited. We are framing our reality around the fact that "all things work to the good of those who love the LORD." This is a hard thing to believe but it is true. And always give HIM glory as well as right to rule your steps.

22 - Remember the story of Joseph. Even the prison times are for aligning you in the will of GOD for the next step. GOD does strange things in HIS steps toward revealing HIMSELF. Think about it. So, don't give the devil too much credit. Satan likes being the center and getting credit. GOD is the kind of GOD that waited to give Abraham a child till he was 100 years old. He left Joseph in a prison for possibly 3 years. He allowed Paul to be shipwrecked and bit by a snake. He allowed Paul and Silas to be imprisoned and beaten. And in that story, HE allowed it so they could bring salvation to the prison guard's house. SEE THE PURPOSE OF GOD. CHOOSE TO BELIEVE THE BEST!

23 - GOD is less interested in our happiness than our nearness. And joy has an expression that is happy, however, our emotions do not dictate our reality. What dictates our reality? THE WORD OF GOD! So, when your emotions are off, wake fully up and remind your reality of what GOD SAYS IN HIS WORD and watch that reality come into continuity and sync with Heaven's Kingdom!

DEALING WITH THE DEMONIZED
A STEP BY STEP WORKSHEET (This is a model and not the rule. It works for me).

First, you need to understand that 20 years ago when I was facing this stuff for the first times, there was no book I could read and there wasn't anyone I could talk to. One man who was the father of a friend of mine in college that I knew had actually done some kind of exorcism. I said back then to myself as these people began to show up in my life and in the church where I served as youth minister that if I ever learn how to effectively deal with this stuff, I am going to make sure the next generation after me doesn't have to struggle so much with it. So, that's what I am doing. I haven't found something that takes all the mystery or fear out of it so that's why I am writing this. This just has to dumb it down and make it nothing. We need to take it in stride and this just needs to be a side affect of doing the Kingdom not a focus. I am tired of the Devil getting so much attention when it comes to the demon possessed!!!!!!!

When dealing with anyone that is truly demonized or possessed, please do NOT rush into ministry time unprepared. Take time to listen to the LORD. The Bible says we should not hastily lay on hands. I believe that if at all possible, take time to pray, fast and hear GOD and then engage in the process as GOD leads. DO NOT RUSH ANYTHING. Satan loves to rush us and get us ahead of GOD's timings. As a matter of fact, remember, you really do not want to engage the enemy on his territory and if HE engages you, it is possible HE wants visibility or center of attention.

However, there were times that Jesus cast demons out of people after they ran up and said, "What have you to do with us Son of GOD?" HE did it usually with a word. Possibly a single word. HE did not allow them to take center stage and HE dealt with them decisively. Only once did HE seemingly allow them to bargain with HIM but it was for HIS advantage for them to stay because HE had a plan for the person HE would send to deal with them as a missionary and it was the man freed from them who was schooled in their ways.

Jesus did not allow them to be the focus and neither did the disciples in Acts. When a demonized girl followed them around yelling truthful information about them, they did not allow her to take credit or look like an authority. They cast the fortune telling demon out of her. Remember, Satan loves to be the center of attention. It is the original thing that got HIM into trouble.

So, often when someone needs this kind of ministry we want to jump in or they want us to hurry and lay hands on them and begin to work the deal out. I have found that often I need to use some time to speak to the person and get some details through an interview process if I can before I engage.

Before I even begin, I do the following if I have the chance. (On a side note, since when I am in 3rd world countries, people run up and engage me or they come to a meeting where I am speaking and they manifest before I have a chance to prepare, I have already done these first items BEFORE I EVER PREACH OR GO ON MISSION. I anticipate these encounters so I prepare in advance).

1 - I pray and fast. I do this to come into agreement and alignment with the LORD.

2 - I confess hidden sin, and confront anything in my life that is

questionable and if I have aught against a brother or sister or they against me, I deal with that and try to come to an agreement.

3 - I ask GOD to reveal anything else that is an issue with my life.

4 - I take time to eat well and rest well. This can be really important if you have to deal with something that is time consuming. I prepare for longer issues and if they take less time that is great.

5 - Schedule a time after praying and fasting. Put it on your timeframe and choose a location that you have control over. Maybe not your own home or near your spouse and kids unless they are also believers and are ready to engage.

6 - Get resources together. Anointing oil, Scripture you can pray and quote. Using the Apostolic prayers that are listed in the chapter on Prayer is very helpful. Get Bibles and have them marked to passages you need. Get worship music and have it ready to praise as you battle. Good lighting is important and do it during the day if you can. Take all of the devil's weapons away.

7 - Get backup and support. The Bible talks about bringing those that need healing to the elders and for them to confess so they will be healed.

8 - Again, choose a place where the Devil will not be able to be the center of attention and bring shame to you or the church.

After I have prepared, then I engage:
1 - have interview time with the person and find out the story behind their demonization.

2 - find out if they want to become a believer and have Jesus as LORD. If they do not, then end this meeting.

3 - find out if they want the demon issue to stop and if they want to be free of its control. If they do not, end the meeting.

4 - As you feel led, begin to pray and praise. Ask GOD for guidance on what and how to pray as you pray and invite the Holy Spirit into the place you are at.

5 - Invite the affected person to confess sin and involvement with witchcraft, occult or "sorcery" (which includes using chemicals to enhance

their perception of reality which if you think about it does include drugs).

6 - Begin from the beginning to lift Jesus' name on high, speak the Blood of Jesus over the person, command the enemy to leave and be quiet since the person does not want them any longer.

7 - As the person is cogent (or if they are not, command them to come forward and speak to you in Jesus' name. Call the affected person by name and say, "Speak to me _____, in Jesus' name). Ask them to tell the demon to leave them and that they no longer want it. Then as they are able or if you need, command them again and ask them to accept Jesus Christ as LORD walking them through confession, repentance, belief in the cross and resurrection and profession of faith in Jesus being their LORD.

8 - Command the demon in Jesus' name to leave the person alone and pray sealing over the person's profession of faith. And have the person repeat the commands for it to leave as well as pray after you as you feel led.

9 - Command it to go and pray the prayers, praise and worship Jesus and continue to repeat as needed until they are free.

10 - This may take some time. You can lay hands on the person as needed and use anointing oil as needed. I mostly simply put a little on my hands and pray over the person directly. I do not pour it on them.

11 - once the demon leaves, pray that the Holy Spirit seal them up and that nothing comes back since they are filled with the Holy Spirit.

12 - Lead the person to ask GOD for the Baptism of fire of the Holy Spirit and for gifts they can use in walking as a warrior. They will never be the same and they are now a warrior for life.

13 - Don't forget that using the 5 Step Prayer Model from the chapter The Warriors Prayer and walk the person through forgiveness and healing as well as the Cross Prayer as needed for anything that comes out during the whole thing.

14 - Disengage at any time it does not feel safe and be free to have them get psychological help if they are not truly demonized.

15 - Pray over all of those involved and make sure to pray covering and that there be no backlash in the name of Jesus on them or their families and that all fear would go in Jesus name.

After this has past, I give direction for afterwards:
1 - Go and sin no more…
2 - Get in church.
3 - Read the WORD
4 - Worship regularly.
5 - take command of your thoughts.
6 - put Scripture up around you to cling to
7 - get accountability.
8 - get discipled somewhere. Get in a Bible Study and/or New Members' class.
9 - Turn Worship on all the time.

DEMONIZED

If someone you know or you are attacked by demons and you need to fight back, you can personally take much of this and use it for yourself. You can fight by using the same methods Jesus did as well as surrounding yourself with Scripture, memorizing it and meditating on it. You can take every thought captive and you can detach from all evil thoughts as well as rebuke the demonic spirit overtly out loud.

BATTLE VERSES

The following are scriptures to use in fighting an enemy, be it the Devil, a demon, or anything else.

THE ATTITUDE OF BATTLE (Humility and Obedience to God)

"Do not rejoice when your enemy falls, and do not let your heart be glad when he stumbles; lest the Lord see it, and it displeases Him, and He turn away His wrath from him." Proverbs 24:17

"If your enemy is hungry, give him bread to eat; and if he is thirsty, give him water to drink; for so you will heap coals of fire on his head, and the Lord will reward you." Proverbs 25:21

"Therefore submit to God. Resist the devil and he will flee from you." James 4:7

"If you walk in My statutes and keep My commandments, and perform them … you shall eat your bread to the full, and dwell in your land safely. I will give you peace in the land, and you shall lie down, and none will make you afraid; I will rid the land of evil beasts, and the sword will not go through your land. You will chase your enemies, and they shall fall by the sword before you. Five of you shall chase a hundred, and a hundred of you shall put ten thousand to flight; your enemies shall fall by the sword before you." Leviticus 26:3

"For the Lord your God walks in the midst of your camp, to deliver you and give your enemies over to you; therefore your camp shall be holy, that He may see no unclean thing among you, and turn away from you." Deuteronomy 23:14

ANOINTING TO APPROACH BATTLE

"Behold, I give you the authority to trample on serpents and scorpions, and over all the power of the enemy, and nothing shall by any means hurt you." Luke 10:19

"Then He called His twelve disciples together and gave them power and authority over all demons, and to cure diseases." Luke 9:1

"And He called the twelve to Him, and began to send them out two by two, and gave them power over unclean spirits … and they cast out many demons, and anointed with oil many who were sick, and healed them." Mark 6: 7.13

"And when He had called His twelve disciples to Him, He gave them power over unclean spirits, to cast them out, and to heal all kinds of sickness and all kinds of disease." Matthew 10:1

"But go rather to the lost sheep of the house of Israel. And as you go, preach, saying, 'The kingdom of heaven is at hand.' Heal the sick, cleanse the lepers, raise the dead, cast out demons. Freely you have received, freely give." Matthew 10:6

"No weapon formed against you shall prosper, and every tongue which rises against you in judgment you shall condemn. This is the heritage of the servants of the Lord, and their righteousness is from me," says the Lord. Isaiah 54:17

"Through You we will push down our enemies; through Your name we will trample those who rise up against us. For I will not trust in my bow, nor shall my sword save me. But You have saved us from our enemies, and have put to shame those who hated us. In God we boast all day long, and praise Your name forever." Psalm 44:5

"For the eyes of the Lord run to and fro throughout the whole earth, to show Himself strong on behalf of those whose heart is loyal to Him." 2 Chronicles 16:9

"… but the people who know their God shall be strong, and carry out great exploits." Daniel 11:32

"This is the word of the Lord to Zerubbabel: 'Not by might, nor by power, but by My Spirit,' says the Lord of Hosts. Zechariah 4:6

"But you shall receive power when the Holy Spirit has come upon you; and you shall be witnesses to Me in Jerusalem, and in all Judea and Samaria, and to the end of the earth." Acts 1:8

"For our gospel did not come to you in word only, but also in power, and in the Holy Spirit …" 1 Thessalonians 1:5

"For the kingdom of God is not in word but in power." 1 Corinthians 4:20

"… in mighty signs and wonders, by the power of the Spirit of God …" Romans 15:19

"Truly the signs of an apostle were accomplished among you with all perseverance, in signs and wonders and mighty deeds." 2 Corinthians 12:12

"God also bearing witness both with signs and wonders, with various miracles, and gifts of the Holy Spirit …" Hebrews 2:4

"And they went out and preached everywhere, the Lord working with them and confirming the Word through the accompanying signs. Amen." Mark 16:20

"And with great power the apostles gave witness to the resurrection of the Lord Jesus. And great grace was upon them all." Acts 4:33

"But the anointing which you have received from Him abides in you …" 1 John 2:27

"But you have an anointing from the Holy One, and you know all things." 1 John 2:20

"Then fear came upon every soul, and many wonders and signs were done through the apostles." Acts 2:43

"No man shall be able to stand before you all the days of your life; as I was with Moses, so I will be with you. I will not leave you nor forsake you. Be strong and of good courage …" Joshua 1:5

"Blessed be the Lord my Rock, who trains my hands for war, and my fingers for battle – my loving kindness and my fortress, my high tower and my deliverer, my shield and the One in whom I take refuge, who subdues my people under me." Psalm 144:1

"For You are my lamp, O Lord; the Lord shall enlighten my darkness. For by You I can run against a troop; by my God I can leap over a wall. As for God, His way is perfect; the word of the Lord is proven; He is a shield to all who trust in Him." 2 Samuel 22:29

"It is God who arms me with strength, and makes my way perfect. He makes my feet like the feet of deer, and sets me on high places. He teaches my hands to make war, so that my arms can bend a bow of bronze … I have pursued my enemies and overtaken them; neither did I turn back again till they were destroyed, I have wounded them, so that they were not able to rise; they have fallen under my feet. For You have armed me with strength for the battle; you have subdued under me those who rose up against me." Psalm 18:32

GOD'S STRENGTH AND BOLDNESS

"I can do all things through Christ who strengthens me." Philippians 4:13

"The Lord is my strength and my shield …" Psalm 28:7

"In the day when I called out, You answered me, and made me bold with strength in my soul." Psalm 138:3

"O God, You are more awesome than Your holy places. The God of Israel is He who gives strength and power to His people." Psalm 68:35

"He gives power to the weak, and to those who have no might He increases strength." Isaiah 40:29

"For the Lord will be your confidence, and will keep your foot from being caught." Proverbs 3:26

"Yet the righteous will hold to his way, and he who has clean hands will be stronger and stronger." Job 17:9

"They shall walk after the Lord. He will roar like a lion. When He roars, then His sons shall come trembling from the west …" Hosea 11:10

"If you faint in the day of adversity, your strength is small." Proverbs 24:10

GOD'S PROTECTION
"Have you not made a hedge around him, around his household, and around all that he has on every side?" Job 1:10

"The Lord is my rock, my fortress and my deliverer; the God of my strength, in Him I will trust, my shield and the horn of my salvation, my stronghold and my refuge, my Savior, You save me from violence." 2 Samuel 22:2

"Truly my soul silently waits for God; from Him comes my salvation. He only is my rock and my salvation; He is my defense; I shall not be greatly moved." Psalm 62:1

"But the Lord is faithful, who will establish you and guard you from the evil one." 2 Thessalonians 3:3

"Many are the afflictions of the righteous, but the Lord delivers him out of them all. He guards all of his bones; not one of them is broken." Psalm 34:19

"And the Lord will deliver me from every evil work and preserve me for His heavenly kingdom." 2 Timothy 4:18

"The Lord is my rock and my fortress and my deliverer; my God, my strength, in whom I will trust; my shield and the horn of my salvation, my stronghold. I will call upon the Lord, who is worthy to be praised; so shall I be saved from my enemies." Psalm 18:2

"But the salvation of the righteous is from the Lord; He is their strength in time of trouble. And the Lord shall help them and deliver them; He shall deliver them from the wicked, and save them, because they trust in Him." Psalm 37:39

"I will lift up my eyes to the hills – from whence comes my help? My help come from the Lord, who made heaven and earth. He will not allow your foot to be moved; He who keeps you will not slumber. Behold, He who keeps Israel shall neither slumber nor sleep. The Lord is your keeper; the Lord is your shade at your right hand. The sun shall not strike you by day, nor the moon by night. The Lord shall preserve you from all evil; He shall preserve your soul. The Lord shall preserve your going out and your coming in from this time forth, and even forevermore." Psalm 121:1

"… Deliver me speedily; be my rock of refuge, a fortress of defense to save me. For You are my rock and my fortress; therefore, for Your name's sake, lead me and guide me. Pull me out of the net which they have secretly laid for me, for You are my strength. Into Your hand I commit my spirit; You have redeemed me, O Lord God of truth." Psalm 31:2

"Oh, how great is Your goodness, which You have laid up for those who fear You, which you have prepared for those who trust in You in the presence of the sons of men! You shall hide them in the secret place of Your presence from the plots of man; You shall keep them secretly in a pavilion from the strife of tongues." Psalm 31:19

"The Lord is my light and my salvation; whom shall I fear? The Lord is the strength of my life; of whom shall I be afraid? When the wicked came against me to eat up my flesh, my enemies and foes, they stumbled and fell. Though an army should encamp against me, my heart shall not fear; though war should rise against me, in this I will be confident." Psalm 27:1

"The Lord is on my side; I will not fear. What can man do to me? The Lord is for me among those who help me; therefore I shall see my desire on those who hate me. It is better to trust in the Lord than to put confidence in man. It is better to trust in the Lord than to put confidence in princes. All nations surrounded me, but in the name of the Lord I will destroy them." Psalm 118:6

"If God is for us, who can be against us?" Romans 8:31

"God is our refuge and strength, a very present help in trouble. Therefore we will not fear, though the earth be removed, and though the mountains be carried into the midst of the sea … God is in the midst of her, she shall not be moved; God shall help her, just at the break of dawn." Psalm 46:1

"Whenever I am afraid, I will trust in You. In God I will praise His word, in God I have put my trust; I will not fear. What can flesh do to me? … In God I have put my trust; I will not be afraid. What can man do to me?" Psalm 56: 3,11

"When they went from one nation to another, from one kingdom to another people, He permitted no one to do them wrong; Yes, He reproved kings for their sakes, saying "Do not touch my anointed ones, and do My prophets no harm." Psalm 105:13

"Give us help from trouble, for vain is the help of man. Through God we will do valiantly, for it is He who shall tread down our enemies." Psalm 60:11

"For the Lord God will help me; therefore I will not be disgraced; therefore I have set my face like a flint, and I know that I will not be ashamed. He is near who justifies me; who will contend with me? Let us stand together. Who is my adversary? Let him come near me. Surely the Lord God will help me; who is he who will condemn me? Indeed they will all grow old like a garment; the moth will eat them up." Isaiah 50:7

"Those who trust in the Lord are like Mount Zion, which cannot be moved, but abides forever. As the mountains surround Jerusalem, so the Lord surrounds His people from this time forth and forever." Psalm 125:1

"Oh, bless our God, you peoples! And make the voice of His praise to be heard, who keeps your soul among the living, and does not allow our feet to be moved." Psalm 66:8

"Even to your old age, I am He, and even to gray hairs I will carry you! I have made, and I will bear; even I will carry, and will deliver you." Isaiah 46:4

"He who dwells in the secret place of the Most High shall abide under the shadow of the Almighty. I will say of the Lord, "He is my refuge and my fortress; my God, in Him I will trust. Surely He shall deliver you from the snare of the fowler and from the perilous pestilence. He shall cover you with His feather, and under His wings you shall take refugee; His truth shall be your shield and buckler. You shall not be afraid of the terror by night, nor of the arrow that flies by day, nor of the pestilence that walks in darkness, nor of the destruction that lays waste at noonday.

A thousand may fall at your side, and ten thousand at your right hand; but it shall not come near you. Only with your eyes shall you look, and see the reward of the wicked. Because you have made the Lord, who is my refuge, even the Most High, your habitation, no evil shall befall you, nor shall any plague come near your dwelling; for He shall give His angels charge over you, to keep you in all your ways.

They shall bear you up in their hands, lest you dash your foot against a stone. You shall tread upon the lion and the cobra, the young lion and the serpent you shall trample. Because he has set his love upon Me, therefore I will deliver him; I will set him on high, because he has known My name. He shall call upon Me, and I will answer him; I will be with him in trouble; I will deliver him and honor him. With long life I will satisfy him, and show him My salvation." Psalm 91:1-16

GOD, WHO FIGHTS OUR BATTLE
"The Lord is a Man of War; the Lord is His name ... Your Right Hand, O Lord, has become glorious in power; Your right hand. O Lord, has dashed the enemy in pieces. And in the greatness of Your excellence you have overthrown those who rose against You; You sent forth Your wrath which consumed them like stubble." Exodus 15:3,6

"The Lord shall go forth like a mighty Man; He shall stir up His zeal like a Man of War. He shall cry out, yes, shout aloud; He shall prevail against His enemies." Isaiah 42:13

"I will go before you and make the crooked paths straight; I will break in pieces the gates of bronze and cut the bars of iron." Isaiah 45:2

"For you shall not go out with haste, nor go by flight; for the Lord will go before you, and the God of Israel will be your rear guard." Isaiah 52:12

"Therefore understand today the Lord your God is He who goes before you as a consuming fire. He will destroy them and bring them down before you; so you shall drive them out and destroy them quickly, as the Lord has said to you." Deuteronomy 9:3

"The Lord will fight for you, and you shall hold your peace." Exodus 14:14

"Be strong and courageous; do not be afraid nor dismayed before the king of Assyria, nor before all the multitude that is with him; for there are more with us than with him. With him is an arm of flesh; but with us is the Lord our God, to help us and to fight our battles." 2 Chronicles 32:7

"... For I will contend with him who contends with you." Isaiah 49:25

"... since it is a righteous thing with God to repay with tribulation those who trouble you." 2 Thessalonians 1:6

"The eternal God is your refuge, and underneath are the everlasting arms; He will thrust out the enemy from before you, and will say, 'destroy!' Deuteronomy 33:27

Do not say, "I will recompense evil," wait for the Lord, and He will save you." Proverbs 20:22

"I will bless those who bless you, and I will curse those who curse you." Genesis 12:3

"Many a time they have afflicted me from my youth; yet they have not prevailed against me … The Lord is righteous; He has cut in pieces the cords of the wicked." Psalm 129:2

"It is God who avenges me, and subdues the peoples under me; He delivers me from my enemies. You also lift me up above those who rise against me; You have delivered me from the violent man." Psalm 18:47

"Plead my cause, O Lord, with those who strive with me; fight against those who fight against me. Take hold of shield and buckler, and stand up for my help. Also draw out the spear, and stop those who pursue me. Say to my soul, "I am your salvation." Psalm 35:1

"When my enemies turn back, they shall fall and perish at your presence. For You have maintained my right hand and my cause; You sat on the throne judging in righteousness." Psalm 9:3

"Do not be afraid of their faces, for I am with you to deliver you," says the Lord. Jeremiah 1:8

"God is a just judge, and God is angry with the wicked every day. If He does not turn back, He will sharpen His sword; He bends His bow and makes it ready. He prepares for Himself instruments of death; He makes His arrows into fiery shafts." Psalm 7:11

"He will guard the feet of His saints, but the wicked shall be silent in darkness. For by strength no man shall prevail. The adversaries of the Lord shall be broken in pieces; from heaven He will thunder against them. The Lord will judge the ends of the earth. He will give strength to His king, and exalt the horn of His anointed. 1 Samuel 2:9

"… For we have no power against this great multitude that is coming against us; nor do we know what to do, but our eyes are upon You … Then the Spirit of the Lord came upon Jahaziel … thus says the Lord to you: 'Do not be afraid nor dismayed because of this great multitude, for the battle is not yours, but God's … You will not need to fight in this battle. Position yourselves, stand still and see the salvation of the Lord, who is with you, O Judah and Jerusalem!" Do not fear or be dismayed; tomorrow go out against them, for the Lord is with you." 2 Chronicles 20:12-17

"Behold, all those who were incensed against you shall be ashamed and disgraced; they shall be as nothing, and those who strive with you shall perish. You shall seek them and not find them – those who contend with you. Those who war against you shall be as nothing, as a nonexistent thing. For I, the Lord your God, will hold your right hand, saying to you, 'Fear not, I will help you.' " Isaiah 41:11

"When the enemy comes in like a flood, the Spirit of the Lord will lift up a standard against him." Isaiah 59:19

"Now I know that the Lord saves His anointed; He will answer him from His holy heaven with the saving strength of His right hand." Psalm 20:6

"Though I walk in the midst of trouble, You will revive me; You will stretch out Your hand against the wrath of my enemies, and You right hand will save me. The Lord will perfect that which concerns me ..." Psalm 138:7

"When you pass through the waters, I will be with you; and through the rivers, they shall not overflow you. When you walk through the fire, you shall not be burned, nor shall the flame scorch you." Isaiah 43:2

"For they did not gain possession of the land by their own sword, nor did their arm save them; but it was Your right hand, Your arm, and the light of Your countenance, because You favored them." Psalm 44:3

"You marched through the land in indignation; You trampled the nations in anger. You went forth for the salvation of Your people, for salvation with Your anointed. You struck the head from the house of the wicked." Habakkuk 3:12

"The righteous cry out, and the Lord hears, and delivers them out of all their troubles." Psalm 34:17

"And I commanded Joshua at that time, saying, 'Your eyes have seen all that the Lord Your God has done to these two kings; so will the Lord do to all the kingdoms through which you pass. You must not fear them, for the Lord Your God Himself fights for you.' " Deuteronomy 3:21

HIS ANGELS BATTLE FOR YOU

"The angel of the Lord encamps all around those who fear Him, and delivers them." Psalm 34:7

"For He shall give His angels charge over you, to keep you in all your ways." Psalm 91:11

"And let the angel of the Lord chase him … And let the angel of the Lord pursue him … Let the destruction come upon him unexpectedly." Psalm 35:5-8

"Behold, I send an angel before you to keep you in the way and to bring you into the place which I have prepared." Exodus 23:20

"Are they not all ministering spirits sent forth to minister for those who will inherit salvation?" Hebrews 1:14

"Then the Lord commanded the angel, and he returned his sword to its sheath … but David could not go before it to inquire of God, for he was afraid of the sword of the angel of the Lord." 1 Chronicles 21:27, 29

"And it came to pass on a certain night that the angel of the Lord went out, and killed in the camp of the Assyrians one hundred and eighty-five thousand; and when the people arose early in the morning, there were the corpses – all dead." 2 Kings 19:35

"Then immediately an angel of the Lord struck him, because he did not give glory to God. And he was eaten by worms and died." Acts 12:23

"Do not forget to entertain strangers, for by doing so some have unwittingly entertained angels." Hebrews 13:2

Learning to Run
The Warrior's Bounty
Being Watchful
1. What is the endgame and the goal?
2. Why is it important to dream?
3. What is revival and awakening?
4. Does GOD really still do that stuff today?
5. What is the historical record?
6. Pray with me, "LORD, help me to dream big and ask big for YOU. Help me to believe that YOU can still move today and then help me to ask and keep on asking, seek and keep on seeking and to knock and keep on knocking and help me draw others to ask with me. We need revival. In our day and in our time, make YOURSELF KNOWN AGAIN! Lift YOUR Son high. In Jesus' name, Amen!"

11 THE WARRIOR'S BOUNTY

Habakkuk 3:2
LORD, I have heard of your fame; I stand in awe of your deeds, LORD. Repeat them in our day, in our time make them known; in wrath remember mercy.

2 Chronicles 7:14
...if my people, who are called by my name, will humble themselves and pray and seek my face and turn from their wicked ways, then I will hear from heaven, and I will forgive their sin and will heal their land.

The Warrior is after something. He is after the same thing Jesus was, "...Your Kingdom come, Your will be done on earth just as it is in Heaven?"

And Jesus said that "The Kingdom of Heaven suffers at the hand of the violent and the violent takes it by force..."

Did Jesus mean it? Will the Kingdom be taken hold of by those who are passionately seeking it? Is the violence HE is talking about bad or did HE believe that seeking should have some unction or some drive behind it?

The Bible also says that whoever seeks GOD must believe that GOD hears those prayers and is a rewarder of those who diligently seek HIM.

Do we have the passion to seek GOD with unction and a drastic kind of no holds barred desperation?

I believe the higher the desperation in a person, the more likely they are to get answers.

Remember the lady that grabbed Jesus' cloak and was healed of the issue of blood? (I saw a lady healed like this once of this exact thing, read my other book for the story). She had such desperation, that she knew she would face certain ridicule if not stoning to death for touching Jesus and making HIM unclean. In the Bible, she was commanded to walk around town yelling, "unclean, unclean" and was to stay afar from others not touching them because the moment she did touch them, they were made unclean and they could not go into the Temple and they could not take part in religious ceremony.

However, did she force Jesus to become unclean by grabbing HIM?

NO! As a matter of fact, Jesus says something very interesting; HE said that HE felt power go out of HIM and into her. What happened here? Did her sickness make HIM unclean? No, her violent, desperate, grab for healing and for Jesus' touch had a power encounter. And WHO WAS MORE POWERFUL? Was her sickness, flesh or enemy that was attacking her more powerful than Jesus' power of the Holy Spirit from the Father? NO! As a matter of fact, this violent, desperate act was not rewarded with stoning for making Jesus unclean. It was rewarded with a return of the power of GOD that surged from Jesus' being and took hold of her flesh, making it clean.

The uncleanness in her did not overtake the cleanness of Jesus. It swallowed it up and made her well.

She was violent. She was desperate. And yet, what did it get her? Healed.

In Isaiah, GOD says that HE looked the entire world for a person to "Rise up and take hold of HIM." He found no one in that day. Will HE find someone in this day? Will we rise up aggressive with love and passion for GOD to in break into our reality?

John Wesley said that men would come for miles around to watch him burn as he stirred himself up and set himself on fire for GOD.

Henry Blackaby asked me personally to be a man that would rise up and stir myself up for GOD. He said the world has still yet to see what one man totally sold out to the cause of Christ can do. He said, "Be that man!" And that's just what I have been doing for 20 years.

I have seen what happens when young people are stirred up for GOD and begin to cry out for mercy and pray for days, weeks, months and even years for GOD to move in their community and to save their family members. I have seen with my eyes what Holy Spirit fire baptism on a community looks like. I have seen revivals and awakenings and have moved in them. I have had the Holy Spirit power and Presence fall on meetings and the unexplainable happen. I know what happens. I have seen a youth ministry spread revival over communities, churches, schools and more. I have seen outbreaks of unexplainable responses for Gospel altar calls in church as well as in schools both public and private and from elementary schools to junior high, high school and colleges and universities. I have seen the unexplainable work of GOD where even people come up and cry out, "What must I do to be saved?" in public unprompted. I have seen the Presence of GOD hit people I have not even talked to as they walked by me.

I have seen it. I have also spent years praying people would be stirred up and that GOD would do this kind of thing. I have spent hours a day in a prayer closet as well as planted churches, youth ministries, campus ministries and prayer ministries focusing them in on the fact that GOD can do the impossible and that if we pray and seek HIS face, HE WILL ANSWER! AND I AM PROOF HE DOES. (Read about all of those stories in my other book).

So, as I write this, let me say that I believe a little bit different than most folks and I am a little more serious about this. Also, I am desperate in a way that others may not understand because I have seen these movements and I ache inside for it to happen again. I believe that even if it does not happen in my time that I have lived the life I have lived to help guide another generation into the Presence of GOD and not to screw it up. I want to say with all my heart that this book may well be a way I do that. And if you are in the middle of a movement of GOD right now that is starting up and people are excited about what you are doing and they are crediting you for the Kingdom activity and you are getting a lot of attention, without being falsely humble, keep on your knees in prayer and keep a right attitude with GOD and stay humble. GIVE GOD ALL THE GLORY and don't even feel people's back pats and applause. Have a heart that is seeking the applause of the ONE. When others notice you, stay concerned about being in the closet for HIM to stay in close nearness and relation with you. Go back and read the chapters on intimacy and on maturity. And get some GODly counsel. You will need it.

So, with that said, let me say a few things here about what I believe about revival and awakening.

I believe our desperation has to exceed our fear and inaction.

I believe our passion and unction has to exceed our inability and complacency.

I believe our revelation has to exceed our laziness.

However, there will be another day when there are a young people aching for the power of GOD again. They will likely be made desperate by something whether it is a sickness or cultural issues, poverty, loss, grief or something. And when they realize that they can see change only by the hand of GOD and not from any social justice that they can do, they will stop trying to "save the Earth" and begin to try to save their souls. They will stop rising up to change things by their own power and will begin to bow the knee to GOD and beg for HIS power to intervene.

At some point, we have to come to a place where we have exhausted all the options that the world affords us such as doctors, money, people and stuff we can own or recreation and once the emptiness leads us to a place where nothing else will satisfy this insatiable desire for something more than the normal life we are handed and we ache like the slaves in Egypt and begin to cry out for GOD to send a deliverer, HE will. HIS Kingdom is already always available and ready to break into our current reality.

So, what does the fullness of that Kingdom inbreaking look like? I believe we have seen it is seasons of revival and awakening. When these seasons happen, it's times where the veil between the world that is and the world to come is very thin.

MANIFEST PRESENCE

In our time we need something more than a simple flash in the pan excitement in our churches for something that is cool. We do not simply need our churches to grow through creating the best performance and best marketed experience in the area. I do not want to be the "best show in town."

I want to see the day again where GOD shows up and shows off and it's not the worship band, cute preacher or even soft spoken message or any number of other cool effects we have in our services that get people in the door. I want to seek the GOD who seeks men until HE comes in the door. What if some Sunday you came into a service and before you noticed anything else, your spirit inside you leapt and you felt the Holy, Heavy Presence of GOD in the room. What if all of a sudden the whole reality that GOD was real was more real than the birds chirping outside. What if you had an encounter so real that you swore you heard HIS voice out loud and you felt as if you had entered the Holiest place.

Manifest Presence is simply the fullness of all the Kingdom of GOD which means that the Father on the throne, the Son beside HIM and the Spirit as well as all of the fullness of the throne room and Heaven that is to come, came into the room with us. What if we saw it right there in front of us and around us, right now?

Jesus said, "I will 'show myself' to them..."

And the Father fully demonstrated this many times throughout the Bible. We see it best described in Solomon's dedication of the Temple. The priests were knocked down under the heaviness of GOD's Presence and everyone was pressed to the ground and no one could get up to even minister to GOD.

It could be said that the fire and cloud that led the Israelites in the desert was GOD's Presence and Kingdom manifested. There are manifestations of GOD's Presence when human beings come into contact with the greatness of GOD and then respond to HIS power.

All of this is not the goal. They are indicators. The goal is to be in HIS Presence and to worship HIM alone. However, we need to know that the Manifest Presence of GOD is missing from the church largely right now. We are not walking into an awakened awareness wall when we come in the doors and for the most part people are not celebrating coming into HIS house. The expectancy that GOD will heal, save, deliver, free, cleanse and manifest in our services is largely gone. If this expectation were there and the desperation were there, then the manifestation would be there.

Let's pray and ask GOD right here to stir up our expectancy and desperation for HIS Presence to manifest and for Jesus to be lifted HIGH!!!!!!!! Stop and pray now before we go on...

Pray with me. "LORD, stir up my hunger and expectancy. Help me believe that YOU are able to do more reviving work just as YOU have done in the past. Help me to believe that YOU can use me and that YOU are working right now. I pray YOU will lift Jesus high and use me at all costs. Amen."

REVIVAL & AWAKENING

I have seen these take place. My definitions are below. However, let's look at what the world defines these things to be to start to get an understanding.

Taken from Wikipedia:

Christian revival is a term that generally refers to a specific period of increased spiritual interest or renewal in the life of a church congregation or many churches, either regionally or globally. This should be distinguished from the use of the term "revival" to refer to an evangelistic meeting or series of meetings (see Revival meeting).

Revivals are seen as the restoration of the church itself to a vital and fervent relationship with God after a period of decline. Mass conversions of non-believers are viewed by church leaders as having positive moral effects.

Historians have different numbering and dating systems. There were "Awakenings" around the years 1727, 1792, 1830, 1857, 1882 and 1904. More recent revivals include those of 1906 (Azusa Street Revival), 1930s (Balokole), 1970s (Jesus people) and 1909 Chile Revival which spread in the Americas, Africa, and Asia among Protestants and Catholics.

Evan Roberts felt there were steps that would lead into revival. If you do not know who he is, his story is one of the most amazing and tragic.

Evan and friends were touched in a revival meeting where young people were stirred by the Manifest Presence of GOD. So, Evan began to go to various towns to speak of his changed life. "Oh, Syd," he said to his best friend, Sydney Evans, in late 1904, "We are going to see the mightiest revival that Wales has ever known - the Holy Spirit is coming just now." In great anticipation, he added, "We must get ready. We must get a little band and go all over the country preaching." Then Roberts stopped, looked at Sydney, and said, "Do you believe that God can give us 100,000 now?"

Within six months, 100,000 souls were converted in Wales.

One writer of the time said that the social impact was similarly reported. Judges were presented with white gloves signifying no cases to be tried. Alcoholism was halved. At times hundreds of people would stand to declare their surrender to Christ as Lord. Restitution was made, gamblers and others normally untouched by the ministry of the church came to Christ. In fact, esteemed G. Campbell Morgan recalled a conversation with a mine manager about profanity. The manager told him, "The haulers are some of the very lowest. They have driven their horses by obscenity and kicks. Now they can hardly persuade their horses to start working, because they have no obscenity and kicks."

Do you long to see God move like that in our day? What if, one hundred years later, God so moved in our nation that hundreds of thousands of people, even millions, flooded the churches? If so, remember there is never great, widespread revival without personal revival. Do you seek a personal, deep, Spirit-led movement of God in your life?

Then consider these aspects of personal revival taught by Evan Roberts, known as the Four Points:

You must put away any unconfessed sin.
You must put away any doubtful habit.
You must obey the Holy Spirit promptly.
You must confess Christ publicly.
May God raise up a generation of people with this passion.

Charles Finney said there are specific signs of revival when it comes.

Taken from: Charles G. Finney, "What a Revival of Religion Is" (1835)

Charles G. Finney (1792-1875) was perhaps the most successful revivalist of the Second Great Awakening. The awakening began on the frontier of Kentucky in 1801. Finney, working in the North, gained his fame during a series of revivals in Rochester, New York.

Finney Says:

"It is presupposed that the church is sunk down in a backslidden state, and a revival consists in the return of the church from her backsliding, and in the conversion of sinners."

1. A revival always includes conviction of sin on the part of the church. Backslidden professors cannot wake up and begin right away in the service of God, without deep searching of heart. The fountains of sin need to be broken up. In a true revival, Christians are always brought under such convictions; they see their sins in such a light, that often they find it impossible to maintain a hope of their acceptance with God. It does not always go to that extent; but there are always, in a genuine revival, deep convictions of sin, and often cases of abandoning all hope.

2. Backslidden Christians will be brought to repentance. A revival is nothing else than a new beginning of obedience to God. Just as the case of a converted sinner, the first step is a deep repentance, a breaking down of heart, a getting down into the dust before God, with deep humility, and forsaking of sin.

3. Christians will have their fair renewed. While they are in their backslidden state they are blind to the state of sinners. Their hearts are as hard as marble. The truths of the Bible only appear like a dream. They admit it to be all true; their conscience and their judgment assent to it; but their faith does not see it standing out in bold relief, in all the burning realities of eternity. But when they enter into a revival, they no longer see men as trees walking, but they see things in that strong light which will renew the love of God in their hearts. This will lead them to labor zealously to bring others to him. They will feel grieved that others do not love God, when they love him so much. And they will set themselves feelingly to persuade their neighbors to give him their heart. So their love to men will be renewed. They will be filled with a tender and burning love for souls. They will have a longing desire for the salvation of the whole world. They will be in agony for individuals whom they want to have saves; their friends, relations, enemies. They will not only be urging them to give their hearts to God, but they will carry them to God in the arms of faith, and with strong crying and tears beseech God to have mercy on them, and save their souls from endless burning.

4. A revival breaks the power of the world and sin over Christians. It bring them to such awakened sense that they get a fresh perspective towards heaven. They have a new foretaste of heaven, and new desires after union to God; and the charm of the world is broken, and the power of sin overcome.

5. When the churches are thus awakened and reformed, the reformation and salvation of sinners will follow, going through the same stages of conviction, repentance, and reformation. Their hearts will be broken down and changed. Very often the most abandoned profligates are among the subjects. Harlots, and drunkards, infidels, and all sorts of abandoned characters, are awakened and converted. The worst part of human society are softened, and reclaimed, and made to appear as lovely specimens of the beauty of holiness. . . .

You can see from what Charles Finney is saying that we in the church at this present moment are not in a state of revival and you can see that it would take a miracle for the whole Body of Christ to be moved into what we read above.

However, as Finney also says in another part of this same writing, it is impossible for us to go any further without asking GOD to stir up an excitement in our hearts and without religious fervor to come back. We need to beg GOD for Heaven come down. As a matter of fact, some of my favorite worship songs today have this theme in them.

Also, let's not stop here in looking at what the greats say about revival. Jonathan Edwards talks about the signs that the work of GOD through revival and manifested Presence in a human being is authentic. We do need to be able to test authenticity of what may seem weird or inappropriate. Remember, with GOD, things that seem inappropriate such as Abraham sacrificing his child or David dancing naked may not be inappropriate at all. GOD showed HIS hand in saving Isaac and Michal was struck barren for judging David's dance attire. Sometimes we have to say with David, "I will be even more undignified than this…" And we may have to dance some more. Since this is the case, we cannot assume that everything people do is a good response to the Presence of GOD and it may not even be the Presence of GOD they are responding to. (Read the chapter on the Gifts of the Spirit. We need discernment here with people's responses to GOD's Presence). And as well, read on what Edwards says. I believe this is a good basic tool for making sure something is GOD's activity in a person or not.

Jonathan Edwards' way to discern the Spirit's working:

In 1741 Jonathan Edwards wrote The Distinguishing Marks of a Work of the Spirit of God. He called his readers to evaluate the awakening by looking past the enthusiastic behavior to see the fruit. He wrote of five distinguishing marks of the Spirit's work. He stated that Satan would not counterfeit activities that led to these responses. If we can answer yes to these then we should regard the manifestation as genuine even if it is unfamiliar to us.

Does it bring honor to the person of Jesus Christ?
Does it produce a greater hatred of sin and a greater love for righteousness?
Does it produce a greater regard for Scripture?
Does it lead people into truth?
Does it produce a greater love for God and man?

These are good tools to use along with the gift of discernment to keep things safe as we see revival. And we need to be very careful not to hurt the Holy Spirit who can be truly deeply offended. HE is offended when people attribute HIS true work with the enemy. So, be slow to call something "evil or Satanic." Look at it deeply and watch not just the person's immediate reaction, but watch for the change in their lives. We all need to have maturity enough to have capacity that this does not scare us and we will not throw the baby out with the bathwater. We need to take our time and deal with immaturity wherever it shows up however as well to teach and help the people who do not understand; to understand what the Spirit is doing and instead of judging and closing off, we need to open up and ask for MORE! MORE LORD!

People say to me all the time that revival and awakening do not matter anymore or that it will never happen again. However, I cannot give up the hope I have that they will take place again. As a matter of fact since I experienced awakening, revival and since I have at times been a carrier of the Presence of GOD, for the rest of my life I am ruined for the normal, mundane way people do church and religion. This has hurt and grieved me so often. Sometimes, you wish you could just go back to not knowing, however, being lost in purposelessness is much worse than being ruined for the world.

Once you truly encounter the greatness and power of GOD in the fullness of HIS Presence, you cannot go back. The memory is etched in your mind and being forever. As a matter of fact, I always say that the proof of a true encounter with GOD no matter how weird it is, is tested by the way a person walks afterwards. Does it change their lives? Is there a demonstration of fruit? Is there new maturity? Are they different than they were before the encounter?

The depth of the encounter should at the very least be equal to the level of change afterwards. Every time in the Bible where you find someone coming face to face with GOD's glory, you find them changed.

And people all the time say to me, "Isn't the Holy Spirit" the same as the "Presence of GOD" you are talking about? And I say, "no." Actually, when people say this to me, I know they have not encountered the Presence of GOD in a revival or awakening sense and they probably have not walked in the power of the Holy Spirit as well.

In Ezekiel, the prophet says that he was taken up "by the Spirit" to the Temple as they were together watching the "Glory of GOD" depart from the temple. Where was the Spirit? …With Ezekiel. What is this "Glory of GOD?"

Well, I believe it is related to the same thing going on in the early church when Ananias and Sapphira were killed for a simple lie. Here two actual believers were killed for lying to the Holy Spirit. Does the Holy Spirit kill every person in the church for every single lie they say? Well, judging by the sheer amount of lying and deceit that is actually in the church today and the way believers are so slothly in their approach to GOD and HIS holiness, I would say we would have a lot more dead believers and a lot scarier churches in the world if it were simply A+B=C. I do not think that is how it works. In those days there was a Presence on the church that was a bit different and the Bible talks about it. There was a heaviness on the church so that every time they assembled to pray, the place they prayed in was shaken and/or someone had a demonstrable encounter such as Peter's release from prison. (See Acts).

The Bible talks about the sheer thousands added to their number in a moment as well as the way that they enjoyed all grace and peace among even the non-believers of that time. What was happening here? It had to be something different. It could not be "church as usual" that we enjoy today (or actually, endure today).

There is historic precedent from that time till now in the church of more times where there was some kind of real, tangible, heavy, different Manifest Presence of GOD on the church, communities and whole cities where GOD was moving. Stories are told over and over of whole cities being overwhelmed with the heaviness of GOD's Presence when Father Nash came to town and began to intercede and by the time Charles Finney rode in, people who did not know the man nor cared for anything to do with Christianity would be bowed over on the sides of the road outside the town overcome by the Presence of GOD and they would be crying out for mercy.

Stories are told of how even the places where he would stay whether hotels or boarding houses would have people along the corridors on bended knee crying out for GOD's mercy.
Was this normal in that day? No. Was it due to Charles Finney's fame? No. Many did not even know of the man. What was it?

Something unseen, something tangible and real. GOD was coming NEAR.

There are stories of the First Great Awakening as speakers such as Jonathan Edwards or George Whitefield would be preaching, people would fall and swoon under some unseen power overcome by an overwhelming need to repent. In Edward's meetings people at one point in a group had an open revelation that Hell had opened before them in the floor. Many people saw this phenomenon at the same time.

During the Welsh Revival, the Presence would come so heavily on a place that the people of GOD with no preacher, no worship leader nor any guide and often led by a young person as young as 5 years old would come to church every night of the week and sing songs that had never been written. Let's get this straight. This is a group of people singing the same exact lyrics at the same time for a new song that had never been written and heaviness of GOD would come so strongly that people would be overwhelmed and leave the church singing down the streets.

Or what about the group of young people in the 14th or 15th century in France that would come together and pray in a street and yell, "MERCY!" And everyone for blocks around would fall to their knees and beg for GOD's mercy.

There are so many more stories to tell from history and I have seen it myself. So, now, it is time to add some definition, so we can take some steps to become reacquainted with the Presence and power of GOD in our time. You may be reading this long after my death, however, my service is done to the Kingdom if you are reading this and are stirred and you do more than just read this, you decide, I want to "DO THIS." So, let's talk about what this is, build up some expectation and then you do it.

And one last thing, if you feel like the time you live in is too bad or too evil or it has been too long since GOD has done this kind of thing and surely HE doesn't move this way anymore, do NOT assume this. Remember, it was over 400 years since the last real prophet of Israel at the time lived and wrote words. His name was Malachi. And for 400 years, GOD was silent. As a matter of fact, you can read in the Gospels that there was no "general" revelation in those days so that when Zachariah, John the Baptist's father saw an angel of the LORD, he did not recognize HIM. And still yet, JESUS was born!!!!!!!!!! DO NOT GIVE UP! The darker your era, the brighter your little candle is going burn!!!!! GRRRR! I can show you through all of history how GOD moved like this. But, again, that is another book. For this one, I need to get to the point about the fullness of the Manifest Presence of GOD and HIS Kingdom.

So, as you can see in the chapter on the Kingdom of GOD, there are certain signs of what will take place in the fullness of the Kingdom of GOD in heaven in that day at the end and beginning of things.

Well, this Manifestation of the fullness of the Kingdom is simply that. It is more than the Holy Spirit. He, the Father and the Son and the entire rule and reign in a moment of overlap are breaking into our reality. When men see it they are awakened. For those who are believers that are in some backslidden state, they are "revived." So, when this happening takes place in a church or a community of faith, it is like the whole place and group have an "aha moment." All of a sudden, GOD has shown or manifested HIMSELF, HIS POWER and HIS FULLNESS.

So, we should be praying for something specific in the church. We are not just praying for a manifestation of GOD's Presence, but for GOD to "open people's eyes." HE is the GOD that opens and closes eyes. So, let's pray the right thing. Stop right now and pray, "Father, open my eyes right now. Let me see YOU manifested in the fullness of YOUR Kingdom." Isn't this the same thing as what Jesus prayed when HE said, "YOUR Kingdom come, YOUR will be done, on earth JUST AS IT IS IN HEAVEN."

And what happens is just like the two disciples on the road to Emmaus, they see and are moved overwhelmed and changed by the interaction. Just like the upper room, people go from fearful petitioners to powerful preachers. We need to pray for revelation to come for the Spirit of revelation to come on the church again.

When the Spirit comes on the church this way, it understands how far it has gone from its first love and it repents for its selfishness, its consumerism, its lack of passion and its being asleep in the light. Once repentance comes, the church is revived.

When this spreads through the whole Body of the church the effect is unmistakable. The affect is "love" plain and simple. People put others above themselves, they change the way they think and act and everything they do around "love." Jesus even said that people would know we are HIS followers by our love for one another.

If a church says it is in revival and yet no one prays for each other no one is passionate for Jesus and in love with HIM first and they don't love one another, it is not truth. The affect of true revival is not excitement for religious stuff; it is love.

GOD IS LOVE.

When this love of GOD spills out the doors and into the larger community, city or nation, the effect is people who have never done church or anything religious are changed as well when they come into intersection with the power of GOD through an awakened and alive, loving, gifted Body of Christ. This causes awakening. Listen, a revived church that goes out and does outreach is NOT awakening in a city. Awakening in a city happens as the Manifest Presence of GOD begins to spill out as well. Remember the descriptions I gave above? This is something that flows into the streets as GOD interacts with people. Really, the church then simply catches up with what GOD is already doing and the outcome is masses converted.

As in the Awakenings that took place in Argentina, you may find businessman like Carlos Annacondia who goes and rents entire sports stadiums to allow the Presence into the city. And when the message of the Gospel is preached, hundreds of thousands come under the power of GOD and are saved, delivered, healed and more as GOD manifests HIS power in ways that are unexplainable such as when people were given fillings in their teeth who could not afford a dentist and the fillings were something akin to dentin.

Explain this I cannot. This is real. This is more real than our real world. And my belief is that GOD wants to do this kind of thing in every generation. I speak this with authority because I have seen it and moved in it myself. I have seen whole regions awakened by the power of GOD such as in Kenya. If you want to read about those stories you can. They are in the book, A Warrior's Tale.

So, what do we do with this? I am going to give you the advice I learned when I was in college before we saw a small awakening take place on campuses from 1996 through 1997. We prayed. We did not pray little baby prayers. We prayed expectant, real prayers with real requests. We made plans by prayer for events. We prayed for those plans to spearhead more events and more happenings. We encouraged unity in all Christian groups and for their leaders to pray together. We supported our brothers in the faith. We staged times of outside open air worship that were spontaneous and crowds worshiped and prayed together.

AND THEN FIRE FELL!

So, what can you do right now? You can do what they did at Asbury College in 1970. They began to pray together at this small college in Wilmore Kentucky. Just 3 people prayed for 30 minutes a day and then they got together weekly and discussed what GOD was doing and prayed as a group. After 30 days, they broke up and each got a group of 3 started that they prayed with the same way. They did this over and over as more and more students began to pray for GOD to come. One night in a large group all the groups prayed and the Holy Spirit revealed that HE would fall on the next day's campus morning devotional meeting. And HE did. Revival fell and they went into day and night meetings that canceled school across the campus for days and weeks. So many repented and confessed sin publicly that it became a media phenomenon hitting the news stations in the area and then the US. The students on their own began going campus to campus sharing the story of what had happened and wherever they went, the Kingdom of GOD broke into that place with its Furious Love and revival and awakening happened. How do I know? Well, I have read accounts, I have heard the people sharing the stories and I know someone that was in one of the groups.

And I saw GOD do something similar at the University of North Carolina at Chapel Hill under the lead of me and three other friends!

So, you try it. Use that model. Ask GOD to do something crazy like for everyone in your school to come to know Jesus. And get two others to agree with you. Begin to pray Scripture into it. Weep for your friends. Keep a list of your top five you are praying for GOD to save and deliver. And then don't let go till it happens.

How much is one soul worth? Is it worth praying every day even if nothing happens for 13 years?

I say and even more years. That's how long it took for my Granny to come to Jesus and leave the cult she was in. And standing over her coffin I got to preach the Gospel per her request to our entire family for the first time they'd all heard it. It's gonna be worth it.

Here are some names of people to read about later: Evan Roberts, the Welsh Revival, Jonathan Edwards, Charles Finney, Peter Cartwright, John Wesley, George Whitfield, William Seymour, John "Praying" Hyde, the Great Awakening, The Second Great Awakening, The Jesus People, John Wimber, William Branham, D. L. Moody, Billy Sunday, Gypsy Smith, Charles Parham, A. A. Allen, Smith Wigglesworth, Lord Radstock, Count Zinzendorf, Francis Asbury, John G Lake, Andrew Murray, Kathryn Kuhlman, George Mueller, Praying Payson of Portland Oregon, Alexander Dowie, Aimee Semple McPherson and The Jeffries Brothers. (There are so many more I could add. However, this is a great place to start).

Some of these people had real issues and were still used by GOD. Learn from them and do what they did right. Also learn from what they did wrong and DON'T do that!

As Andrew Murray wrote: "Live in the bold and holy confidence that God is able to bless His Church through you ... God is really only waiting for prayer in order to give the blessing"

Brownsville Assembly of GOD had been quiet on the gifts and had been praying simply for 5 years having replaced their Sunday evening services with a service focused on crying out for GOD to move in revival and their youth had been ever increasing in fervor and prayer for months and months, desperate for GOD to move when the Presence of GOD fell on the church on Father's Day, Sunday, 1995.

"And you will seek Me and find Me, when you search for Me with all your heart." Jeremiah 29: 13

Gaining Momentum
The Warrior Prayer
Being Watchful
1. How do I pray for people?
2. Who do I pray for and how do I know?
3. What do I do and what do I ask?
4. Can any believer pray for other people?
5. When can I pray for people?
6. Pray with me now, "Father, please help me to come out of my comfort zone and to learn what YOU desire for me and through me. Help me to join YOU in ministering to other people. I want to learn, become ready and join YOU daily. Please lead me and never leave me alone and guide me Holy Spirit in everything I do so that I don't hurt anyone and they are drawn more to Jesus. In Jesus' name, Amen."

12 THE WARRIOR PRAYER

I call this section the warrior prayer because every time I walk into a room, I have declared war on everything of Satan's kingdom that exists there. My walking around the planet as a warrior for GOD is an aggressive act. I wake up in the morning with an "as you go" (Matthew 10:7-10) attitude and model. That being the case, I am always at war and I am always taking ground for the Kingdom. My going out into the world is an act of aggression against the kingdom of Hell as the Kingdom of Heaven inside of me (by the grace of GOD) is pushing through this current reality and administering heaven's rule and reign to every person who is around.

As I am going about my day to day activities, I am always asking GOD, "What are you doing?" I am always staying sensitive to what HIS timeline is and what HE is up to at the moment. I can do this all day long whether at work, church, home, the gym or in public running errands. Ministry to me is much less about moments in a church building or planned outreaches and more about day to day conversation and involvement with what "Poppa" (My term for the Father in heaven) is doing. I just want to be about my Father's business. I learned years ago from Henry Blackaby that GOD is always at work (John 5:19) and it is not important whether I feel able to do something since HE is the one doing it and I like the Son (Jesus) am only joining HIM in what HE is already doing. Some people are sad right now because there are so few real believers "doing the stuff" as John Wimber used to say (which doing the stuff means, the Kingdom activities such as healings, miracles and everything listed in Luke 4. I will share about that later in the Kingdom section). I am not sad. The darker the time, the smaller the light necessary to make a difference. The larger the vacuum, the more clearly the Voice of GOD can be heard. I walk out the doors and instead of seeing the "vacuum," of this world, I see THE GRAND INVITATION of Poppa. Right here, right now, we can make the biggest difference with the smallest effort. This is a day of David's versus Goliath's. It is a day of Jericho walls falling. It is exciting to join GOD in what HE is doing. And we don't have to try hard to find where HE is working. If the day is that dark and the times are that tough, then all we have to do is walk outside. HE IS WORKING EVERYWHERE!!!!! The whole world is a theme park for the Kids of the Kingdom and that is us. Jump in and ride!

People will be blown away by the smallest things let alone a Red Sea parting!

So, with that said, let's give you a great tool for the toolbox in being prepared for praying for people and this is not just for praying for the sick.

You can adapt this prayer to pray for anything. Just always be sensitive to the Holy Spirit as you do it and HE will lead you in how to adapt to the person's need. (We will cover intimacy and sensitivity to the Holy Spirit in a later chapter too).

So, the 5 step healing model is the model I use to pray for the sick. It is my favorite and I use it here in order to honor one of my heroes of the faith as well as to say that it is tried and tested and I have found it to work for many years now. If you want to read stories of how it worked, you can read another book I am writing called, "A Warrior's Tale." This model was developed by John Wimber to teach people to pray. It parallels the way Jesus taught his disciples to pray and how he prayed himself.

When learning to pray for people, it's important to try it out in a place where you feel safe and you know that it's OK to get it wrong, make mistakes and feel foolish. As long as the person you are praying for feels loved and cared for, they'll be alright. My encouragement is to do this in a small group setting such as a Sunday School class, small group, cell group, house church and fathers should teach their kids to do this in their families.

I always ask students I am teaching, "when we pray, who heals?" And everyone always says, "GOD does!" Then I always say this and I am saying it to you right now. If it is GOD's job to heal and our job to obey, then we just obey and pray the way Jesus told us and then whether someone is healed immediately or not, it does not matter. That's GOD's problem. And if someone is not healed immediately, I don't get down or sad and I don't put the other person down. I simply say, well, that was good, let's do this again. And I tell them that I am with them for the long haul. I will pray for them every time they come till something happens. "We are going to keep knocking on this door until it is opened up to us…"

"Ask and keep on asking, seek and keep on seeking, knock and keep on knocking…" -Jesus

"Our job is to obey, God's job is to heal, so we can't fail!!" John Wimber

Before engaging in prayer at any moment, already ask Holy Spirit to come and speak to you, lead you and guide you. I actually do this moment by moment in life like I've already said as I move around my day and I ask, "What are YOU doing, LORD? What's going on? Keep me posted…" Inviting Holy Spirit to come is the key. We are not out there working "for" GOD. We are joining GOD where HE is already working. I don't want to take the hammer out of the Carpenter's hand and tell HIM to watch what I can do. I want to hold HIS nails and hand HIM his chisel or hold the board. We need to know our role as a helper or as Wimber used to say that we are the Holy Spirit's midwife. We are there to help the process, not to direct it.

STEP 1 | THE INTERVIEW

Before you start praying for someone, especially in public, if you don't know the person, introduce yourself and find out their name (and remember it!) We care about people and we are not simply trying to get them to do what we want, we are demonstrating the same love Jesus had for people that HE showed when HE washed the disciples' feet. We are not here to show them how great we are, we are being obedient to GOD's directive and we are doing what we are led to do by our Great King. So, submit and serve. Remember, it is always our greatest honor to be used by the Father and it is always our honor to see HIM move. And when we serve others, we see Jesus in their faces. So, if you are seeking Jesus, do something to another "as unto Jesus" and you are doing it to HIM. (Matthew 25). So, with that attitude, continue on.

The purpose of the interview is to answer the question 'Where does it hurt' or 'What would you like me to pray for?'

When Jesus prayed for Blind Bartimaeus he asked what seemed like an obvious question 'What do you want me to do for you' Mk 10:46-52.

While they are replying you need to listen on two levels – the natural and the supernatural. It's not a medical interview and you don't need all the gory details. (as a matter of fact, these details often get in the way. Sometimes, Holy Spirit has led me to stop the person before they are done and begin to pray in faith where I have seen at least one person healed immediately after this happened).

As they talk it gives you time to listen to what God is saying to you about that person even beyond what they are saying.

Many times what God wants to do has nothing to do with the physical healing they were asking for! Wimber quotes 'it's more important to know what kind of person has the bug than what kind of bug has the person' It's more important to have details about the person and their relationship with God than technical medical details.

The goal is to leave the person feeling more loved by God than before they were prayed for. So, take time with the person. Begin to allow yourself to see the person with GOD's eyes instead of your own. Open up and listen and see.

STEP 2 | DIAGNOSIS

Diagnosis is about identifying the root of the person's problem. The root of the problem may or may not have to do with something physical. Please note here that we believe that people have levels of healing that often overlap. There is physical need which is very real and often we can see it with our eyes. There are mental needs. Sometimes people have truly psychological issues that can actually physically affect them and there are true psychological issues they may face. There are spiritual needs. This is an overlooked area, but sometimes we are facing something that is demonic. We do not think everything is a demon. However, often I have found that there are a mix of things going on inside of a person at any given moment and they all overlap and are interconnected. So, you may find someone that has a physical issue demonstrated with a true medical condition and upon further sharing, you find they have a history of pain or abuse that is interconnected with that issue which is psychologically affecting them sometimes with psychosis and on top of that there may be a demonic connection through judgments and unforgiveness that has allowed Satan's kingdom legal access to boot.

What do you do? Well, this is where you are asking God for words of knowledge, visions, Bible verses, insights and more to help you decide the type of prayer that is needed.

So, to help answer the question: Why do they have this condition?

There are a number of reasons why people may need help, let's break down what was said above

DIFFERENT CAUSES FOR CONDITIONS:
1 - natural causes – disease, accident
2 - sin – committed by them or to them
3 - emotional hurts causing physical or other pain
4 - relationship problems – lack of forgiveness
5 - supernatural – may be demonic

They may be telling you one thing and the Holy Spirit sharing with you something else that is the root of the problem!

Ask questions like…

EXAMPLE: "Is there a situation in the past where someone has hurt you and it's hard to forgive them?

Lack of forgiveness and bitterness and resentment can be the cause of physical illness and until they forgive a person they are holding unforgiveness for, their physical healing may not take place.

As a matter of fact, healing can often come directly after GOD reveals to them the unforgiveness and they confess it. James 5 says that this kind of confession is key to someone actually being healed. Go look it up. We are told to lay hands on the sick and they will recover and we are told that we are to confess our sins to each other so that we will be healed. This is really key!!!!!!

As they are talking to you, keep asking Holy Spirit for help – praying in tongues (inside your head) can help you to open up channels so that you can hear from GOD. John Wimber calls it putting up your spiritual antennae.

As you pray, always keep your eyes open! It is key that we watch what is going on with the person so we can see what GOD may be doing. We need to ask questions as we see people respond such as when we see someone's hand begin to shake, we can ask, "What are you feeling in your hands right now? Are you feeling GOD take your hand? Tell HIM to hold your hand as you go through this…" or something like that.

If someone begins to cry and we see tears come, we can know to ask questions like, "What do you sense GOD is doing inside you right now? What do you feel?"

And then as they share, we are able to pray for them and pray into that actual interaction. We are here to spend time with the person and soak them in prayer. We are not in a hurry. When GOD comes, it is sacred time and we will spend all the time in the world to pray. I have literally prayed for people with this method when over a thousand people came forward for prayer in an outdoor meeting and not stopped praying for people until the last person was prayed for at 3am or later after using van headlights to light the area into the night. We take our time. Its not all the time you get to join GOD in this activity so hallow it and honor HIM and the person you are praying for. These are precious moments.

Also, encourage the person not to hurry what GOD is doing. Ask them stay and wait and rest and relax and receive. Encourage them letting them know as GOD begins to move upon them that this is a special thing and that HE is not in a hurry and the longer they take, the more they are soaking in the very Presence of Heaven and that is a great thing. And just because they feel "done" doesn't mean HE is done at the moment. Remember that. Soak!

STEP 3 | PRAYER SELECTION

So, now we have to take a moment and decide what to pray. We need to ask ourselves questions like, "What kind of prayer shall I pray to help this person?"

This follows on from what Holy Spirit has revealed in the diagnosis.

So, start by asking the Holy Spirit to come and to minister to the person. This helps them become receptive, especially if they can tangibly feel His presence. And it isn't a style thing. We are not just doing it to help the person, we are literally inviting Holy Spirit to come and steal the show. This is not for you. No gift is for the edification of the person, including Healings. These gifts are for the edification of the whole Body of Christ and for the elevation of Jesus Christ and you aren't HIM!!!!!

Seriously, if you are tired of seeing man's outcomes in ministry, start asking GOD to show you HIS ministry and tell HIM you are tired of yours!

So, at this point you may want to share what God has told you which could include a vision, a word of knowledge, Bible verse, or it may be appropriate to hold back and share later. Just be sensitive and do exactly what the Spirit has led.

There are two main areas that need prayer regularly which are the Body and Past Hurts.

1 - Body

A - Lay hands on the person appropriately. (We usually place our hands on the back or shoulder. We do not encourage anyone to place their hands on any other part of the body, especially if the person is the opposite sex).

B - Ask for God to heal the area of the body that is affected.

C - God may lead you to:

D - Make a command of faith as in Acts 3:6 'In the name of Jesus Christ of Nazareth, rise up and walk'

E - Make a pronouncement of faith Jesus said 'You may go, your son will live' John 4:50

The key here again is to remember that even if you make the command or pronouncement and nothing happens immediately, don't panic. Wait on GOD in that moment and just see if something begins to happen slowly. It is not up to you to heal. It is up to you to be obedient to the command of Jesus and pray for those that are sick.

2. Past hurts

Often people need to extend forgiveness to others so that God will forgive them and they can receive His forgiveness. They may not always be prepared to do so, if not, just bless them and move on. Tell them to allow Holy Spirit to work on them on this issue over time and to remain open. There is no rush!!!!!

There may also be a great deal of anger and this needs dealing with and forgiveness sought for.

A word on the demonic – if it's really a demon you'll know. Just remember that we have been given the authority of Jesus and they cannot harm us. We can break their power and command them to leave just as Jesus did. Often what people think are demons manifesting is just a person's hurt coming out. If you meet and you're unsure either dial down and tell them to come back at another time or seek help.

As you are dealing with hurt, you may need to stop everything instead of jumping right into the healing prayer and getting these folks "fixed" and join the Spirit as HE intimately does internal, personal surgery with the person.

If you find that things come from a background of past hurt, then do the following before moving into the final two steps of the healing model.

So, for this kind of thing, I like to use the Cross model for forgiveness. It looks like this:

1 - Reveal

We ask Holy Spirit to reveal whatever unforgiveness may be related to the sickness or the "pattern area" of the person's life that we are praying for. (A pattern is something that happens over and over again that the person subconsciously falls into. For example, a person that keeps getting into bad relationships that are abusive. And the revelation is likely that their parent or guardian was an abuser as a child. Thus, there is a pattern of seeking abuse). He may show a memory or simply reveal what connects to the sickness or pattern.

"LORD, reveal to me patterns and the roots of where my condition has come from..."

2 - Recognize

We then embrace what we are seeing. This is tough for people. Sometimes we don't want to deal with past hurt. I encourage them at this point to stop and ask Holy Spirit to turn all associated memories of the hurt into something that is like a movie they watch and that HE disconnects them from the pain associated and the shame and that HE reveals what HE sees in them.

"I embrace what you are showing me LORD..."

3 - Repent

They must repent of the unforgiveness. This is tough for folks that have been mistreated or abused. They feel like it is their right to hold that unforgiveness and pain. I tell them at these points that we have NO rights after we accept Jesus Christ as LORD and that we are now owned by a new owner that has all right to tell us to stop clinging to "our perceived rights." We are now entitled to only one thing and that is to serve Jesus Christ our King. Also, I share with them that when we allow someone to make us hate them, in essence they still win. They are owning our ability to get past the issue. George Washington Carver is quoted as saying, "I endeavor to allow no man to so own me as to make me hate him."

When we give up unforgiveness, the person or people that have hurt us are no longer in the driver's seat. We are free. And the key is that the Bible says that we should let no bitter root take hold in us from judgment because it will grow and bear fruit of judgment. And GOD is not mocked. What a man sows, he will reap. So, if we sow into our hearts anger, bitterness and judgment, we will reap fruit of those things in our lives.

So, as Holy Spirit reveals where we have allowed ourselves to judge and hold hate, shame and pain, we actually must repent to GOD for holding this sin in our hearts.

So, we pray, "Father, please forgive me for judging _____ (insert the person's name who offended). Please release them of my judgment. I forgive them right now. I lay this down at the cross. It is not mine to bear. Jesus has already taken this from me. I will not carry it anymore. I only want HIS cross."

As this happens, that bitter root of judgment begins to whither and dies. The person may find that they need to tell the person if they are living that they are sorry for holding judgment against them. Tell them to finish the prayer first and then encourage them to do so. It is awesome to see how GOD can change relationships and futures this way. HE is a redeeming GOD and HE often releases an abuser of judgment when an abused says they forgive them. It is amazing. It doesn't always play out that way, but I have seen it happen.

4 - Render Dead
So, we pray that the Holy Spirit renders it dead. "Holy Spirit, kill the seed of judgment and render it dead. Free me from bitterness…"

At this point, the soul is being cleaned out. However, the Bible says we cannot stop by just cleaning the house. Jesus says that once the demonic is shown the door, we must refill with the Hoy Spirit, or that enemy can come back with 70x the attack.

5 - Resurrect Christlikeness
So, here we pray for GOD to put in roots of the Kingdom from the seed of the good news of the Gospel. If the person does not already know Jesus Christ as LORD, then this is the point where they MUST RECEIVE HIM!!!!! If they don't, the after affect is a nightmare as the enemy comes back and finds a cleaned out house.

And if they already are a believer or after they receive Christ's gift through the cross, we then pray, "Father, in Jesus' name, we ask that you resurrect Christlikeness in the place where this judgment and pain once lived. In Jesus' name, take the Gospel of peace and sow the seed of it in my heart and refill me or fill me for the first time with freedom and joy that comes with your Holy Spirit. Come Holy Spirit and fill me up! I never want to be empty again…"

And once this takes place, this is something that is repeatable. The person can do this over and over for the rest of their days if needed as GOD reveals more and more things they need to confess. This is not a one time thing. The accuser loves to come back and remind us of failure or sin or pain, so, we have to rise up as warriors at this point and take every thought captive and fight back. We fight back by running to our knees and confessing and getting into Holy Spirit's Presence and allowing HIM to refill us. And don't be afraid to call a brother or sister and keep coming back for more together. So, tell the person you are praying for that this is a possibility.

Now, onto our prayer engagement. This is the best part!

STEP 4 | PRAYER ENGAGEMENT

When you invite the Holy Spirit to come to meet with the person, it's likely that there will be physical signs of his presence. Do not grandstand these and do not react with shock. Just be ready and available.

These signs do not need to be present for God to work and to heal, and even if they are present it doesn't mean that God will heal, but it does mean that the person is very aware of and often reassured by God's presence. Sometimes I have found that people demonstrate what seems to be these signs but it's actually their desire or what they think we want to see. The most true I have ever seen physical manifestation of the Holy Spirit's nearness on someone has been in people that have never seen or heard of it. When they respond, they often are afraid and I have to assure them it is alright.

I use the literal illustration of an electrical socket. I tell folks, "if you stick your finger into that electrical socket in the wall over there, what is going to happen?" They always say, "I will get shocked." To which I reply, "The Person who is coming into this room right now and interacting with you is more powerful that that. Do you expect to not respond to HIM coming into the room and interacting with you? Just rest. HE is not here to hurt you. HE is here to heal you and you are just waking up inside and for the first time becoming aware of the One who made you..."

Know that the Holy Spirit is more interested in the internal that the external. Often nothing happens and people get healed. So, don't work toward a person manifesting GOD's encounter. Just celebrate when they do encounter GOD and are healed.

Always ask people what is happening. You won't disturb what God is doing and it may lead to further prayer. Or, you may be really encouraged by what they say.

When do you stop?
-When they indicate that it's over
-When you believe that God has told you to stop?
-When you run out of things to pray or when nothing is happening.

However, just because nothing is happening doesn't mean it isn't. Let the person know that we are not always aware of what GOD is doing and to know that sometimes we have seen people healed AFTER leaving a meeting or an interaction. I once had a lady drive all the way home before she knew she was completely healed. She didn't notice! And it was a huge growth that was on the outside of her neck. She just didn't feel anything and it disappeared which really bothered my personal theology on where it went.

Now, if you are stopping, you can indicate this to the person by removing your hand, speaking to them. However, speak softly. They can stay in a moment and not hurry. Just because you are done doesn't mean GOD is. And be sure to communicate that. It is always important to fully communicate with people as they are going through the prayer encounter. And it's not always wise to move away if they're engaged with God, check with them. Make sure that they stay and soak even if you are done.

STEP 5 | POST PRAYER DIRECTION

After you are done praying, it is important to give post-prayer direction. Jesus did this when he told certain people to "go and sin no more…" or when HE said, "go and sin no more lest anything worse come upon you…"

So, if they were immediately healed, what should they do to keep their healing? If they are still contending for healing and are in process, we press on. (I mean, sometimes we have to pray more than once before someone is healed. And sometimes it takes prayer and fasting for a deliverance to take place. This was what Jesus said. Remember, Jesus prayed for a blind man twice before he was fully healed. We are not scared of someone not being healed. We keep on praying over and over. We are only careful not to be disobedient).

John 5:14 To a man that he had just healed Jesus said ' stop sinning or something worse may happen to you' or 'Go and sin no more'

Encourage them to spend time with God, stay involved with their church, or get involved with small groups and to get someone to walk with everyday that will keep them accountable. If you know the person and they are in your community, you disciple them this way. If not, get them to someone. Don't just leave them out there to be destroyed by the enemy. Get them into relationship.

If physical healing takes place tell them to check with their doctor and certainly not to discontinue medication no matter how well they feel, it needs to be confirmed by a medical professional. We are not doctors nor are we psychiatrists.

And then there is the question of, "What if they're not healed?"

Just reassure them that God loves them and encourage them to keep on asking and assure them that God doesn't react with 'I wish they'd leave me alone.'

He encourages us to ask and keep on asking. -Matthew 7:7

Treat people as you would like to be treated. Protect their dignity. Again, we can't heal, only God can. We are only his instruments, if He doesn't do, it's his responsibility and he's big enough to carry it.

SUMMARY

Remember this model is not a formula. Use it as a guide when you're not sure what to do! Do not turn it into the only way, but add it to the toolbox of your memory and you will be able to flow in and out of it as needed. So, here is the quick easy to read version you may want to copy into a Bible or stick in your wallet.

STEP 1 | INTERVIEW

Before starting, invite Holy Spirit to come and speak to you.
Where does it hurt or what would you like me to pray for?
Introduce yourself
Natural level – what can you see?
Supernatural – ask God for Words of Knowledge, discernment, visions, words
It's not a medical interview- get the facts
Move to the next stage when ready – you know the cause, God tells you do

STEP 2 | DIAGNOSIS
Why do they have this condition?
Natural causes – disease, accident
Sin – committed by them or against them
Emotional hurts causing physical or other pain
Relationship problems – lack of forgiveness
Supernatural – may be demonic
Keep asking for God's help – useful to pray in tongues
Ask them questions if appropriate.

STEP 3 | PRAYER SELECTION
What kind of prayer shall I pray to help this person?
Ask the Holy Spirit to come and minister to the person
Body – lay on hands and ask for God to heal

Keep praying in the Spirit
Command of faith Acts 3:6
Pronouncement – of faith John 4:50
Demonic – rebuke(break their power) bind them(contain) expel (get rid)
Cross Prayer as needed:
-Reveal | -Recognize | -Repent | -Render Dead | -Resurrect Christlikeness

STEP 4 | PRAYER ENGAGEMENT
How are you doing?
Watch for the effects – keep your eyes open! Phenomenological signs (warmth,
tingling, shaking etc)
Ask questions – find out what God is doing
Stop when – they think it's all over, the Spirit tells you it's over, you've run out of things to pray, when it's going nowhere
Remove your hands, talk to them to indicate you are stopping

STEP 5 | POST PRAYER DIRECTION
What should they do to keep their healing? 'Stop sinning' John 5:14
Read their Bibles, spend time with God
Get involved or keep involved in the local church
Check with their doctor
And if they're not healed...
Reassure them that God loves them and encourage them to keep on asking and get more prayer!

Planning for Longevity
The Warrior's Comrades
Being Watchful
1. Why does it matter who I am around?
2. Why do I need other people to grow in Christ?
3. How do I go about having a mentor?
4. How do I have an accountability partner that will coach me as I coach them?
5. What is the point?
6. Pray with me, "Father, give me the grace and the humility to lower my defenses and let another person deep into my life. Forgive me for holding others out. Bring wonderful people into my life that I can grow with and help me to learn to open myself up so we can grow more like YOU. In Jesus' name, Amen."

13 THE WARRIOR'S COMRADES

The warrior needs to realize that to wage this war we need others. There is no safe way to fight unless someone is against your back, fighting anything you may face from behind as well as others that at times surround you when you are down. We need each other plain and simple. I have a high regard for knowing two things in my life:

1 - I know where I end and GOD begins. In other words, I am very well aware of my weaknesses in a good, healthy way.

2 - I know when to call in help and support. I am a very durable person and have bounced back from many a threat, but in ministry most lately, I learned a valuable lesson. One person as the point person alone on the pedestal is easier to destroy that a multitude of people that lead. I learned that I am a sitting target, but if I blend in with a community of pioneers and warriors, it is much less easy to directly attack me and it is more likely the the whole of us can survive the minor wounds we receive together verses what happens when you take all the wounding.

And you know, the more we have people that come together joined in GOD's love and vision, the more fun the whole thing is. I would rather any day worship loud and proud, dancing and singing with a crowd of passionate lovers of Jesus than being by myself on stage to sing alone. So, we need to have great comrades. We need great friends. We need to choose people to be around us and in our counsel who are deep in faith and are maturing with us in the lifestyle Jesus shows us in the Gospels especially found in Matthew 5-7 and John 13-17.

This crowd we are surrounding ourselves with are GODLY accountability and support. So, for the rest of this chapter, I want to discuss our need for mentors and coaches, 2x2 accountability partners, small group ministry and community, and accountability that is in your face and I will end with developing accountability and team ministry in our families.

DEVELOPING A CULTURE OF KINGDOM ACCOUNTABILITY AND DISCIPLESHIP

We need different forms of accountability, but it needs to start with a 2x2 relationship. I get this from the passage when Jesus sends out the disciples together in groups of 2 and they go out and "do" the Kingdom work. It's the starting point I will discuss below more.

When it comes to accountability, you can really dig down to the base of what it is by defining it as having other people from our communities of faith that we are partnered with and covenanted with to walk daily in growing more and more in the life of Jesus and by walking with them we are coached in becoming more like Jesus in our homes, work, school, community and church. This is in groups of 2x2 or "two's," between elders and young believers in mentoring like Paul and Timothy, and in small groups when the church got together in their homes and did communion together and shared about what the Apostles had taught about at Solomon's colonnade described in Acts. And my favorite, the comrades of the team GOD has given you already right there inside your own house!!!! YOUR FAMILY! GO HOME TEAM!

We must partner with people that GOD has drawn into our lives that are at the same place we are in life. And we are called to pier mentor each other as well as coach each other in becoming like Jesus. I say that we overtly state that are desire to walk this way with each other and then we do it. We need to even do this with our families. In my house, I have values and priorities we are after, a family mission and even a schedule we keep to protect our time. This has become even more challenging thus I have had to cut some things out in my life to make it work as the kids are getting older. But, folks, THEY ARE WORTH IT! MY DAUGHTERS and my son on the way are WORTH EVERY MINUTE and penny I pour into them. They are one of my greatest investments. I will never regret any moment I have used on them even down to the nights I have rocked and sung them to sleep. WORTH IT! I chose these kids. Even when a doctor wanted to abort my oldest before she was born, I chose her defect and all. WORTH IT! (Read more about that story in my other book).

It's amazing that in this time period, people have coaches for business and health but not for spiritual growth. We really do focus on the wrong things. Both of those are important, however, our spirit is even more important. Just because we grow in physical and business stature does not mean we are maturing in our inner man. I know a lot of successful men in business that has no depth in maturity and character. We really are living lives that are upside down right now.

MENTORS - PAUL & TIMOTHY

In the life of Paul and Timothy, we see that Paul gives directives for those that are walking together. The books of 1 Timothy and 2 Timothy demonstrates an elder who is down the road a bit further who is writing to the younger pastor and the younger is practicing "active listening" skills. (He is reading a letter that he obviously ingested and put into practice. He held the letter in high enough regard that it was preserved for us today to read and learn from as well). And this relationship has the key component of attempting to help the younger individual to unpack their potential, strengths, and learn to succinctly define and communicate their life mission. (As personally and non-programmatically as possible). There is a boundary as well that all of the rules with the prayer ministry team should be applied and "Paul" level folks in our church should be trained in Ministry Team training and Gifts training like we do for the ministry team. This is a safe, non-judging, non-fixing environment and is like a Kingdom "white-board" space. We exist to help folks unpack what GOD is already doing and to join the Holy Spirit in the process of recognizing gifts and releasing.

Timothy had to be open and transparent. Bring everything to the table. Come ready to talk. There will be listening ears and the time is for them. This is their space to BREATHE deeply. It is a listening space. The younger needs to come this way in this relationship. However, on a side note, both can learn from each other, so if you are functioning as a mentor like Paul, keep your ears open too. These young guys are smart!

PIER COACHING - 2x2 Accountability Groups

The 2x2 directives are pretty clear: This is a life-together thing. Those that are committing to a 2x2 relationship are going on their journey the way Jesus sent out the 72. So, there was a larger group that went in possibly in groups of 2. So, there is an aspect of large group following Jesus, and smaller groups that break into groups of 2 that are agile in ministry and "life as you go..." This is a great space for: "Confess your sins one to another…" like James 5 talks about.

It must be SAFE and OPEN. We have to have each others' backs. And we need to really want the best for each other. This is not something that we do as a competition thing. We are not competing; we are developing and completing each other. Real 2x2 partners are able to bring the best out in their brother or sister and it affects each person's family, church, work or school.

You Should Meet weekly: (This could either be inbuilt in small groups OR outside. These should be at the VERY LEAST a call on the phone checking in how people are and simply connecting through pre-agreed topics. These accountability topics should AT LEAST include some things I have here.

I utilize the Promise Keeper's Promises from Coach Bill MacCartney's movement in the 1990's as a basis. This is not the only way to do it, but it is a good basis. So, the promises then base my accountability questions I ask my partner. Once you have had this walk for a while, it becomes easier and you do not have to go through them in a legalistic way. Also, I have found that over the years, my accountability partner or "2x2" has a way of sensing what I am going through and I often do the same for him so even before he has something, I am already on it and we are in each other's face in a good way. When someone does this in your life, it really changes the way you live.

(See the end of this chapter for the actual 7 Promises of a Promise Keeper and my accountability questions I adapted from them).

These 2x2 groups are GENDER SPECIFIC and are not to be spouses.

PRACTICE OF THE PRESENCE
As a whole as well as in these groups we need to be driving each other into seeking the Father, HIS will, HIS ways and HIS characteristics, we need to be going after a simple Jesus lifestyle daily as well as going through a book like Brother Lawrence's "The Practice of the Presence of GOD." or another devotional that causes us to go deeper in truly experiencing HIM. I also like Oswald Chambers' book, "My Utmost for HIS Highest" and Henry Blackaby's "Experiencing GOD Day by Day" Devotional.

PRAYER INSIDE THE CHURCH
There should many groups given during the week in our community, month and year to focus each other in on prayer. There are different angles for prayer as well. We need to have some prayer that is intercession and petition which we are great at, however, for the development of relationships and community, we need prayer groups that are focused on encouragement, protection and blessing. These groups get together NOT for fellowship and not for intercession that is deep for some foreign need. They are simply focused on arm in arm directly linking to speak prophetically over each other, for deep soaking of the Presence, for ministry of protection and even healing. This is a space for "…a cord of 3 strands is hard to break…" We are not focused on deep accountability here, but on linking arms and making sure that we are all covering each other. These groups could be once a month or once a week and could simply be a time where we speak over each other one word encouragements, or one sentence prophetic protection and blessing prayers. It is a launching space. This could be woven into a small group. Small groups could have a 4th week breakout week where they focus on this. These could be grouped based on life-experiences.

HERE ARE A FEW DIFFERENT CONCEPTS FOR LIFE-

EXPERIENCE BASED GROUPS

You could have a Joseph / Daniel type of group for those with influence.
or a group for mothers.
A group for dads
A group for high schoolers or even from a specific school later. (It could be a campus group).

You can do these inside a church or outside. We need these. We do not have to have something that is perfect. In high school, I started a group that prayed in a huddle and we did meetings when we met around the flag pole at the school and prayed for salvation of our classmates and then went out and shared with them. I have preached at that flag pole before as school buses unloaded and shared the Gospel and my testimony. You can do anything. Just look for another person and then invite another. At UNC I started alone. Just me in my dorm on my knees. Then one other and I and then another. Prayer is possible in any space at any time and in tons of different ways.

THE SMALL GROUP EFFECT | EXPANSION

And beyond all of this, I want to see small groups expand into the workplace as well as into the school campuses where we can either have a Bible study OR we can join and affect an existing campus ministry or start a new one. The sky is the limit.

All of this should be done in a spirit of relationship and not as a program, however, there must needs be a commitment required. We cannot allow people to simply bounce. This stuff is for life. Just like G-hoon Kim (my accountability partner in life) and I have lived this out over the years, this is what we must do now in this season in order to survive. We cannot be either a Holy huddle or an Individual success.
The baby is dependent.
The teen is independent.
The mature are interdependent.

We are not successful as a Body unless the entire Body makes it to the wedding feast.

JUDGING THE FRUIT IN THE BODY

People say all the time that we are not to judge. And this is a half truth. We are not to judge the world around us. That is Jesus' problem. However, we are to judge the church and our own fruit. The truth is that it is easier to hide under our beds and pretend like nothing is happening, but it is not the case. The church is inundated with people that look like church people, sing like church people, act like church people (for the most part), talk like church people and for all anyone can tell are church people.

But something stinks.

The truth can be easily seen by simply looking at the fruit. If we were actual fruit inspectors, then like the book says earlier, we could not only see whether or not someone is mature or not, we can see if they are a true believer in the church or if they are simply a deceived church goer.

I would venture a guess to say that right now in America, over 75% to 80% of people that go to church are not true believers and do not know Jesus Christ and even worse than that, Jesus doesn't really know them.

Have you ever read the passage where Jesus said, "Depart from me you worker of iniquity, I never knew you?" What kind of people were they? There is another passage that says that when the sheep and goats are divided, Jesus says that there were people in the group that were hell-bound that did even miracles and preached in HIS name.

Hello!

So, what does this mean? It means that we can deceive ourselves into believing we know Jesus based on the good things we do rather than time spent in relationship with a real person. This is scary!!!!!

Maybe that's why the Apostle Paul said we should work out our salvation with fear and trembling.

What if the key is NOT whether we know or assert to knowing about Jesus and it is really whether or not HE knows us.

If I were you, I would read on right here.

This is where it is ever so important to have brothers and sisters in our lives that will tell us when we are "off." As a matter of fact, it's also why I have all my life found people that know Jesus and who have lived longer in the faith with good fruit of the Spirit to walk with who call me on the carpet and speak truth into me. We need accountability partners, we need mentors, we need friends.

If this walk with Jesus is as dangerous as it really is, then let's get serious about it. And truthfully, if we are acquiring people to coach us in our doing businesses and in becoming better professionals or to develop us in some skill set, how much more should we acquire coaches in our life with Holy Spirit?

We need to have folks around us that will say, "Hey _____ (fill in your name), you are missing some key fruit right there…" And they should name the fruit. Again, remember, fruit is something that comes from being in relationship with the vine. It is not something that we can do in ourselves. So, when they point out the fact that we are missing this key fruit, we stop and run back into intimacy and talk with Holy Spirit, repenting for our being fleshy and immature and asking HIM for a refill of Baptism of fire in our guts so that outflow of HIS power happens again.

And be careful who you pick to walk with you. Do not pick an accountability partner that is behind you. Pick one that is beside you. Don't pick one of the opposite sex you are attracted to, pick one that is the same and you have no attraction for. Do not pick a mentor that does not have the fruit. Pick an old faithful believer that has lived a good 40 or more years in the faith and that demonstrates love, joy, peace, patience, kindness, gentleness, goodness, faithfulness and self-control.

Let's get serious about this and let's buy into criticism that is good. Take note, learn. Get excited. GOD is proving HIS love for us in HIS willingness to waste HIS time on chastening us. Don't see GOD's critique as a putdown. He is not your earthly parent. See it as a love note. See the excitement of the blessing of that interaction.

And write it down!

THE 7 PROMISES
(from the men's movement mentioned before).
PROMISE 1
A Promise Keeper is committed to honoring Jesus Christ through worship, prayer and obedience to God's Word in the power of the Holy Spirit.

PROMISE 2
A Promise Keeper is committed to pursuing vital relationships with a few other men, understanding that he needs brothers to help him keep his promises.

PROMISE 3
A Promise Keeper is committed to practicing spiritual, moral, ethical, and sexual purity.

PROMISE 4
A Promise Keeper is committed to building strong marriages and families through love, protection and biblical values.

PROMISE 5
A Promise Keeper is committed to supporting the mission of his church by honoring and praying for his pastor, and by actively giving his time and resources.

PROMISE 6
A Promise Keeper is committed to reaching beyond any racial and denominational barriers to demonstrate the power of biblical unity.

PROMISE 7
A Promise Keeper is committed to influencing his world, being obedient to the Great Commandment

SAMPLE ACCOUNTABILITY QUESTIONS
Question 1
How has your worship life been this week? How was church? Did you go? Did you help serve? How is your prayer life? Were you obedient to God's Word in the power of the Holy Spirit this week?

Question 2
How is your accountability time? Have you spent time connecting to your 2x2, your small group, your mentor? Are you mentoring someone? How is that going?

Question 3
How are you doing practicing spiritual, moral, ethical, and sexual purity this week? How has your heart life been? Are you overcoming lust? Anything you want prayer on here?

Question 4
How is your family time going? Are you spending time with your kids and spouse? Date night? Outings and special time with kids? Have you been building your family altar and Bible Study time? What are you doing to grow your spouse in faith?

Question 5
How is your giving to church going? Are you praying for your pastor and getting his back? Can we pray anything for your pastor?

Question 6
What have you done this week to develop unity?

Question 7
Have you shared your faith this week and invited someone into the faith or church?

DEVELOPING KINGDOM FAMILY
After reading the above promises of a promise keeper and some of the accountability questions I wrote above that I have made based on the promises, did you notice the part about developing your family?

Did you realize just like it is not the public school's sole responsibility to develop your child and educate them, it is the same with the church. We cannot outsource the development of our children or we will regret it. The BIBLE is clear on the fact that we are called to teach our kids. The BIBLE says that if we train our children up in the ways of the LORD, they will not turn from them?

What are those ways and how do we teach them?

Let's look at what the BIBLE says about training our children in Deuteronomy 6

These are the commands, decrees and laws the Lord your God directed me to teach you to observe in the land that you are crossing the Jordan to possess, 2 so that you, your children and their children after them may fear the Lord your God as long as you live by keeping all his decrees and commands that I give you, and so that you may enjoy long life. 3 Hear, Israel, and be careful to obey so that it may go well with you and that you may increase greatly in a land flowing with milk and honey, just as the Lord, the God of your ancestors, promised you.
4 Hear, O Israel: The Lord our God, the Lord is one.[a] 5 Love the Lord your God with all your heart and with all your soul and with all your strength. 6 These commandments that I give you today are to be on your hearts. 7 Impress them on your children. Talk about them when you sit at home and when you walk along the road, when you lie down and when you get up. 8 Tie them as symbols on your hands and bind them on your foreheads. 9 Write them on the doorframes of your houses and on your gates.
10 When the Lord your God brings you into the land he swore to your fathers, to

THE WARRIOR'S MANUAL

Abraham, Isaac and Jacob, to give you—a land with large, flourishing cities you did not build, 11 houses filled with all kinds of good things you did not provide, wells you did not dig, and vineyards and olive groves you did not plant—then when you eat and are satisfied, 12 be careful that you do not forget the Lord, who brought you out of Egypt, out of the land of slavery.

13 Fear the Lord your God, serve him only and take your oaths in his name. 14 Do not follow other gods, the gods of the peoples around you; 15 for the Lord your God, who is among you, is a jealous God and his anger will burn against you, and he will destroy you from the face of the land. 16 Do not put the Lord your God to the test as you did at Massah. 17 Be sure to keep the commands of the Lord your God and the stipulations and decrees he has given you. 18 Do what is right and good in the Lord's sight, so that it may go well with you and you may go in and take over the good land the Lord promised on oath to your ancestors, 19 thrusting out all your enemies before you, as the Lord said.

20 In the future, when your son asks you, "What is the meaning of the stipulations, decrees and laws the Lord our God has commanded you?" 21 tell him: "We were slaves of Pharaoh in Egypt, but the Lord brought us out of Egypt with a mighty hand. 22 Before our eyes the Lord sent signs and wonders—great and terrible—on Egypt and Pharaoh and his whole household. 23 But he brought us out from there to bring us in and give us the land he promised on oath to our ancestors. 24 The Lord commanded us to obey all these decrees and to fear the Lord our God, so that we might always prosper and be kept alive, as is the case today. 25 And if we are careful to obey all this law before the Lord our God, as he has commanded us, that will be our righteousness."

Reread the passage above and answer the following questions.

What was supposed to be taught?
How was it to be taught?
Where was it to be taught?
When was it to be taught?
Who was to do the teaching?

Now, take a moment and write right here how you can apply this to your family. What can you do right now with this?

_____
_____
_____
_____

Sidenote: DO you realize whatever you wrote above that you sensed was what GOD was leading you to write as you read the passage, is HOLY SPIRIT talking to you as you were reading!!!!! Remember the chapter on "Hearing GOD." It talked about how to know it is Holy Spirit talking. And remember, it can be hard to understand if it is just you or HIM. Anything

"Good" is from HIM, Remember? So, do you realize that this little interaction is more important than a small passing thing. HE just spoke to you about your next step with your family. WOW! And if you do not have a family yet and you wrote something, HE just gave you vision for your family. This being the case, take a moment and rewrite whatever you wrote above and pray about it and expand it and write it in a journal or frame it and put it on the wall. That is precious. It's not every day that GOD gives us vision. Very cool!

Lastly, I want to point out that GOD desires to use you in the lives of your family both physical and spiritual. We are to take every opportunity like Jesus and teach with stories like HE did, object lessons like HE did and do it all the time. We need a style of life and culture about us that is always looking around for ways to reveal GOD's person, HIS will, HIS ways and HIS invitation to our kids. I do this all the time with my kids. We are always talking about the "why's" behind what we are doing and what I am seeing. I am always sharing with them how GOD is asking for us to join HIM and as often as it is safe, I am bringing my kids right into ministry with me.

I believe ministry is something we are all called to in our community as believers and children of GOD. I do not see the difference between a church building and my work place at the financial firm where I served as an IT Director or when I was on Corporate Sales or even working at a coffee shop.

We can do this everywhere. And I have a deep desire to engage our kids in the Kingdom life. Our family is a demonstration of the Kingdom of GOD. My life of love with Jesus is not hidden alone in my prayer closet. I take my kids with me and introduce them to Holy Spirit all the time. I work with them in how they hear. MY 6 year old and 3 year old are able to function already in much of this book and they put most of the adults in churches across America to shame in praying for people and sharing Jesus' love. I am often doing cleanup work in behind them as people are being totally affected by kids that know nothing else than that we are to "do" the works of Jesus and the Kingdom all the time and that we all have "superpowers" to help others called "gifts."

Right now in my life I am doing all the work I can with kids and youth in order to deepen them in faith and bring them in for the ride on this Kingdom thing. I bet the farm on them. If you want to hear the stories, then you will have to get the other book.

I want to make sure that everyone reading this book understands that my first ministry is to GOD and worshiping HIM and enjoying the life we have together. My second ministry is to my wife. My third, which is right up close, next is to my kids. The following is to minister in the church and then last on the list is business life and hobbies or recreation.

The thing that is burning in my gut right now is summed up in Malachi 4:5-6.
"5 Behold, I will send you Elijah the prophet
Before the coming of the great and dreadful day of the Lord.
6 And he will turn
The hearts of the fathers to the children,
And the hearts of the children to their fathers,
Lest I come and strike the earth with a curse."

I believe that Jesus is coming again whether sooner or later and I am writing this book and living daily in order to make sure that things are put in order and HIS steps are made clear. A long time ago I had a dream where I was a little kid running in front of a King on his horse and I was yelling excitedly, "HE is coming, HE is coming. THE KING IS COMING!!!! HE'S COMING!!!!!! HE'S COMING!!!!!! GET READY! HE IS FINALLY HERE!"

I am doing this with this book right now. And it is going to take intergenerational honor to return. Fathers and sons, mothers and daughters are going to have to turn back to each other as the Spirit of GOD brings unity in the family again. I believe that is why there is such an attack on the definition of family and what it stands for. I believe that is why even before that battle started, the enemy started attacking the foundations of the father-figure in the home, destroying his reputation, corrupting his activity and causing him to run from responsibility. Remember, "hiding" is something that never happened before Satan got two people to sin in the garden. And hiding is still a sign of sin. Fathers became abusers, disrupters, consumers, killers, haters, leavers and breakers. They did not keep their promises and more. It's time to change that!

Whether you are male or female, this is the call for you to keep your promises and to covenant with me that you will do whatever it takes to bring back the center of your family to Jesus Christ. If you are failing and your kids are running, you can turn now. Run back, repent, beg forgiveness and lead on your knees. If you are a dad, show your greatest gift to your kids with the love you have for your GOD and then second for their mother. If you are a father, don't frustrate your kids. Honor them, develop them, brag on them, build them up. You are their first concept of who the

Father is! Make it good!!!!

The design of family is not in question today. It was designed by GOD in order to demonstrate to a waiting BRIDE what heaven looks like.

Heaven is a picture of a BRIDE and a GROOM.
It is a picture of Fathers & sons.
It is a picture of a Husband & a Wife.
It is a picture of a Master & HIS Servants.
It's a picture of a King and HIS Subjects.
It's Sons and Daughters who have come home after a long wild party that went all wrong and a Father who says, welcome home. I want to change your clothes! I have missed you. Let me lift you from your brokenness.

Let me leave you with these couple thoughts:

"Teach all the time and with all manner of teaching the way Jesus did the parables."
"It is the father of the house's responsibility to be the primary caregiver to the shepherding of his kids just as the Father in heaven does with us."
"We are the high priests of GOD as a royal priesthood, a chosen generation..."

If you are joining me in this quest for fathers to turn their hearts back to their kids and wives and homes, pray today right where you are and give your family to GOD. Ask HIM to begin to reveal what HE wants for your family today.

Your kids and family are your greatest adventure! And the kids in your house are not GOD's workers of tomorrow but are the greatest teammates for you RIGHT NOW! They are your biggest fans. Do not lose sight of the gift GOD has given you in your family. "He who finds a wife has found a good thing." "Sons are arrows in your quiver." "Let the bosom of your wife of your youth fulfill you."

See the gift GOD has already given you. GOD, reveal what we have already in our families.

The Battle Cry
The Warrior's King & Country
Being Watchful
1. Who am I?
2. What is the Kingdom of GOD and what does it mean for today?
3. What is GOD really about?
4. Why do I feel like I am not from this planet sometimes? & How do I live between two worlds?
5. Pray with me, "Father, please open my eyes to what is really going on in this overlap of time between the cross' finished work and Heaven to come in fullness. Show me what is happening and teach me to join YOU. Reframe my reality morning by morning so I don't lived tied to emotions and the earth."

14 CHAPTER NAME

INTRODUCTION TO THE KINGDOM
Something you need to know is that bring the Kingdom into the room and we cause the room to align with the Kingdom we believe in whether it wants to or not. Our entering a room is an aggressive act against Hell's Kingdom. So, you are a warrior now.

This is not something we mean to do. This is a result of our being believer. When we are a believer, the Holy Spirit lives in us. And if we are abiding in HIS Presence, we carry our relationship into every room we walk into. Whether we mean to or not, we have just carried the Kingdom of heaven into the room. That means that the fullness of the divine rule and reign of GOD has just come in and everything around it that falls short of the fullness of GOD is faced with a standoff. It is not purposeful on our part, it is the result of our proximity to HIM.

With that said, it is time to know what the Kingdom you fight for actually is and how it works.

KNOWING WHO WE ARE IN CHRIST
People want to know who they are in Christ and I simply say this.

"You are the righteousness of Christ. You are no longer a sinner. You are adopted and grafted into the family and the vine of GOD. You are set apart, you are bought with a price. Inside you is the Hope of Glory, the law is written on your heart by the Holy Spirit. You were knit in your mother's womb and prepared for this before you were born. You are the apple of HIS eye. HE dances over you. HE loves you with an everlasting love. The Kingdom is within you and around you and available to the world through you. You only have to trust in HIM with all your heart and lean not on your own understanding, and in all your ways acknowledge HIM and HE WILL DIRECT YOUR PATHS!!!!!!!"

GRRRR!

I want to encourage you to wake up in the mornings for the next while and quote that chunk of Biblical truth to yourself. Here is why. It's ALL BIBLE! That chunk of what I wrote above is from the BIBLE and it is all true about you. So, repeat it like a creed until you believe it. IT IS TRUTH!

And beyond that, we need to know who GOD is better in order to know who we are. I have said this many times and I mean it. However, how do we learn about who GOD is? I believe we do this by:

1 - seeing GOD's activities that are being done through other people to us in Jesus' name.

2 - Reading the WORD of GOD and seeing what HE did in history.

3 - Talking with the Holy Spirit as HE reveals the WORD to us.

4 - Through daily interaction as we join HIM in what HE is doing.

THE FATHER'S HEART IN THIS TIME
Simply said, The Father wants to turn fathers and sons, mothers and daughters back toward each other. He wants the safe familial love back in families and the church. Malachi 4:5-6 says that this is going to prepare the way of the LORD. I actually believe that the Biblical view of family demonstrates the relationship of Sons and Daughters of GOD so that we can from an early age learn what GOD must be like. I believe that Satan has decimated the definition and standards of GOD's design for family in order to better destroy Kingdom understanding. I also believe that it was not the fault of those that the church wants to blame right now but the abusive and missing fathers of the world that birthed a generation of kids that wanted family redefined. Whatever the case or the cause, GOD is calling all Sons and Daughters to come back into unity and calling the family to be realigned into the Kingdom design for us to learn Kingdom together. You get your definition of THE HEAVENLY FATHER from the Father you have or don't have on the earth. And I have learned that I get my understanding of GOD's Father's Heart from being a father and having kids. I am not trying to humanize GOD. This is a Biblical thing. GOD designed it as a sign and a witness to HIMSELF. So, with that understanding we pray for GOD to reunify the generations that have been broken and to bring families back together and heal from abusive fathers the wounds that were done.

Come on kids. Come on fathers. It is time to reconnect and reflect GOD's heart. I can talk more about the father's heart in another book. For now, we must discuss the Kingdom.

THE OVERLAP OF KINGDOMS
The King and Country that a warrior believer is from is not defined by simply the place they were born. We are not simply citizens of an earth bound nation, although the Bible is very clear that we are to submit to the ones that GOD has placed over us as leaders and we are to pray for them.

This is actually a requirement as a believer. And as far as following the laws of our nations, we need to have a spirit inside of us that is a spirit of honor and we must as best we can observe the rules and laws of the land in which we live unless they overtly stand in contrast to the Bible itself.

We are blessed at this moment in time to live in a nation where we are able to observe all our faith practices and worship GOD the way HE desires. The ones that fought to found this country and bled and died did so not simply to create another country under the control of a church or religious group but to create safety for all religious groups from tyranny. So, at the time of this writing we live in a place where we are able to submit to all the laws of the land since those laws and rulers do not require us to break faith with GOD or break the 10 commandments and they do not require us to worship a false god or prophet. Some countries at the time of this writing actually do go against the truth of GOD's WORD and there are believers, some of whom I have met and worshiped with in the underground church that must break their nations' laws in order to worship GOD and follow HIS commands. However, we always encourage them to still pray for their nation and leaders and to pray for GOD to reveal HIMSELF and change them. Again, the heart is for honor and not dishonor, yet we honor GOD above all men.

This literally leads us into the tale of two Kingdoms. There are two kingdoms, two countries and two realities. The two realities we face are the present world and the world to come. And the world that is to come has two Kingdoms; The kingdom of Satan and the Kingdom of GOD. I use terms; the Kingdom of Heaven and the Kingdom of GOD interchangeably. We currently live between two countries, which are the country of our birth and nationality and the Kingdom of GOD, which is already at hand due to Jesus' coming.

So, let's set the stage.
When Jesus died on the cross, HE not only paid the price for sin and gave us access to salvation through HIS shed blood, but HE also by defeating Hell and the grave, HE took authority of the Earth back which had in the beginning been given to Adam (In Genesis GOD said that Adam was to have dominion over all the earth and he named it and oversaw it as GOD's ambassador), and was usurped from Adam when Satan deceived Adam into eating the fruit of the knowledge of good and evil. At that moment, what had been given to Adam as dominion authority was taken and the earth as well as man entered a fallen state as well as lost access to the garden and broke relationship with GOD the Creator.

Jesus dying on the cross paid the price that many eons of Passover lambs had paid for people to gain right standing with GOD. There had to be blood sacrifice in order to pay the price for sin in order for man to be right before GOD.

Once Jesus died and rose again, any believer could come back into right standing through the shed blood of the true only Passover lamb of the ages. When we ask Jesus to become LORD of our lives, we are simply asking for HIS divine dominion over our lives as LORD and GOD again. We are through HIS sacrifice brought back into right standing with GOD and we have been brought into HIS eternal life. When a person comes under Jesus' LORDSHIP, they are at that moment owned by a new KING, a new LORD, and they are under that new ruler's rule and reign. This reign supersedes the reign and rule of all other rulers. It does not usurp and it does not have an attitude of taking what it does not deserve.

This ruler deserves and earned the rule and reign that HE has now received from the new believer/convert.

Once this person believes in Jesus Christ for confessed LORDSHIP based on HIS death on the cross being the price for sin, repenting of their sins, forsaking their own way and believing Jesus rose from the dead again, they are immediately under the rule of two countries. The one in which they were born and the one in which they have just newly been born again into. The first country is the one of their human birth I have mentioned before and this new citizenship is of heaven. Therefore the rules of the Kingdom and the laws of the Kingdom as well as all of what the Kingdom is and does is available to this new believer.

So, we live in an overlap of two eras and two countries. The era that is passing away is of a fallen world where things are deteriorating and we physically see with our eyes. The era that is to come is the place Jesus is preparing for us in the future. He said, "I go to prepare a place for you in MY Father's House." This Era and Kingdom that is to come is the one that Jesus speaks about over and over in the Gospels.

So, imagine the timeline looks something like this:

Era of Fallen Man

Beginning_____

† (the cross)

_____End

Era of the Kingdom Reign of GOD

The top line represents the era we are currently in that is drawing to an end and will end as Revelation shows. The cross is the "t" in the middle. Under that, there is the timeline of the world that is coming next, the Kingdom of Heaven. This era begins at Jesus' coming and the cross and it is overlapping the end of the Fallen world era that we are living in.

See the overlap? We live in two eras. We live in the era that is ending and the era that is coming. We are still stuck in the law of the natural world we are in. However, we are now under the law of the Kingdom that is to come and the era that is already at hand. In other words, this new era's norms are breaking into the world we are in through our affiliation. We have just become access points through our submission to the Cross of Christ and now the entire rule and reign of GOD is coming through us into every relationship, location and action in our lives. All we have to do is submit to it. In other words, you have just become the greatest danger to the enemy. You are an access point of Heaven. You are an ambassador as Paul says. Heaven is breaking in and it is doing it through you. Are you starting to hear the cheers of the Saints who have gone before you and the Angels of Heaven? They are so glad you are here right here and right now. We could say just as Mordecai said to Esther, "Could it be that you were made for a time such as this?" The Spirit is saying, "YEAH!"

Jesus' coming was huge for the Kingdom of GOD and was an aggressive act against the other "kingdom" in this story, the kingdom of Satan.

Jesus said that when HE came and opened the scroll the first time we believe HE taught at the synagogue after HIS teaching there as a child, HE opened the scroll of Isaiah the Prophet which was speaking of HIM throughout and in Luke chapter 4, HE says, "…Today, this has come to pass right here in front of you…"

In other words, all of the things that were to come when the Kingdom of GOD was to come with Messiah's rule had already started in its fullness right there in front of them!!!!!

Jesus didn't stop there. HE actually listed what it looked like. What did it look like? Well, let's see:

Luke 4:16 He went to Nazareth, where he had been brought up, and on the Sabbath day he went into the synagogue, as was his custom. He stood up to read, 17 and the scroll of the prophet Isaiah was handed to him. Unrolling it, he found the place where it is written:

18 "The Spirit of the Lord is on me, because he has anointed me to proclaim good news to the poor. He has sent me to proclaim freedom for the prisoners and recovery of sight for the blind, to set the oppressed free, 19 to proclaim the year of the Lord's favor."

20 Then he rolled up the scroll, gave it back to the attendant and sat down. The eyes of everyone in the synagogue were fastened on him. 21 He began by saying to them, "Today this scripture is fulfilled in your hearing."

Now, this is Jesus' definition and this is Jesus' proclamation, not mine. In other words, we had all just entered an era of "Now and Not Yet…"

So, everything that had ever been for the day when the Kingdom of GOD would come and replace the current fallen earth and the current fallen Jerusalem had just broken into the current era and had begun to do what GOD the Father wanted right there and then!!!!!

And so many people have said that this stuff was for just then and there, but if you look at how Jesus taught all of us how to pray, you can see that this was not what HE believed! In other words, Jesus opened a door and HE never wanted it shut again. When the veil at the Temple ripped, everyone was to continually have access to GOD's Presence and not just by some special someone, every Tom, Dick and Harry could come into an interaction because GOD had sent HIS Son so HE could come and have relationship with HIS kids again and nothing would ever change that.

GOD's Furious love had broken through. The world from then on would have to simply deal with it!

Now what did HIS definition of the Kingdom include?

Good news to the poor.
Freedom for the prisoners
Recovery of sight for the blind,
To set the oppressed free,
To proclaim the year of the Lord's favor.

And actually, we can simply say that everything that is inside of what the Kingdom of Heaven is to be is inside of this definition. Every other story that Jesus tells is then not just for later, it is also for now to an extent if not totally.

This is EXCITING! We can now believe that we live not just tied down to this world's confines. As a matter of fact, the only thing that is holding us back is our own belief and our own imaginations. HE is able to do exceedingly abundantly above all we can ask or imagine! (That's straight out of the WORD! Look it up!)

Now, let's further define a kingdom as its rule and reign. It is not necessarily focused on land however both kingdoms are focused on land and property as it is in relation to human beings.

And all of the laws even the natural laws of this earth are no longer in control of us. We are under the supernatural laws of heaven. Does this mean we break man's laws or we do something to try and force GOD to prove HIS power? Well, what did Jesus do in the wilderness when tempted to do these very things? HE told Satan to get behind HIM and quoted Scripture that proved the very humility of the heart of Jesus through and through as Son of GOD.

Now, the kingdom of Satan is attempting to keep the entire world in bondage and desires for it to stay in a Fallen state. And the kingdom of Satan would love nothing more than to keep us all tied down to our sin and the natural laws of earth. He is more than happy to keep us in bondage till the end of days.

The Kingdom of GOD is the divine rule and reign of GOD and it takes place in the hearts of human beings. So, when the Kingdom of GOD takes over a person's heart it does this by a human repenting, asking Jesus to be LORD, confessing HIM and believing in HIS resurrection. At that moment, that person is no longer bound by natural law. They are released under the divine rule and reign of Heaven. GOD now says what happens and what doesn't in that person's life. The only limiting factor again is that person's "fear, doubt and disbelief…"

When the Bible says that anything is possible for him who believes and it says that nothing is impossible for GOD or that we could have faith that would speak to a mountain that would remove it and send it into the sea, it is serious. This is deep truth.

And it is an immediate reality. This is why I believe children become the best at doing the powerful things of the Kingdom after accepting Jesus Christ. They just don't have all the inhibitions of the world nor do they have the messed up world views that the world gives over time and pain.

So, GOD is interested in redeeming the world to HIMSELF by bringing every single human being into right relationship through the Cross and Jesus, HIS Son and HIS sacrifice.

GOD is interested in LOVE. HE is interested in relationships. The world is groaning in wait for the revelation of the Sons and Daughters of GOD, which means whatever they look like must be pretty awesome, it is so awesome that the fallen world knows that they will shift it into rightness with GOD again through their dominion. Bring it!

And if that is the case, then we can say that everything else that happens is just a side effect benefit of that amazing love conversation between the Father and HIS kids. Gifts, ministries, greatness or whatever else is just a side affect. I say this over and over and I think John Wimber said it first, but "we are not seeking HIS hand but HIS Face." When HIS Face comes, HIS hand comes with it. I don't want handouts from the Kingdom. I want the KING!

KINGDOM COLLISIONS

I believe awakenings, revivals and prophetic revelatory or words of Knowledge and words of Wisdom happenings are Kingdom collisions.

POWER ENCOUNTERS

John Wimber in his book, "Power Evangelism" (which is another book you should read if you can find it) called these power encounters. And after witnessing so many of these power encounters in my own life as I daily went about my business, I have come to the reality that when I walk into a room I am aggressing on the kingdom of Hell. My being there is a declaration of Heaven.

As a matter of fact, a power encounter happens when the Kingdom of GOD faces off with the kingdom of Hell and GOD begins through us and the Holy Spirit to do some serious work on a person's heart. I have found that often this is coupled with some kind of gift such as a word of knowledge or a word of wisdom. These things open up people's eyes to how real GOD is and they often stop right on the spot and say things such as, "Oh my goodness, GOD is real!!!!!"

GOD gets their attention and wakes them up with a little "aha." He shares something about their lives through a random stranger and they realize that GOD cares about them, GOD knows what they are going through and GOD has a plan for their lives. I have watched people have these encounters and realizations and so radically change that they are discipled in a simple single interaction more than in 10 years of discipleship classes at a church.

This stuff sticks!

So, imagine this. Do you think Satan is happy when this happens? No! HE has just lost a person he had under HIS control to the other kingdom. And like I said before, the Devil loves to be the center of attention. So, with that said, I tend to do the following immediately.

1 - I give the person follow-up steps: get in church. Get in the Bible. I tell them to read the Gospel of John first. I even give them Bibles and show them where it is. I tell them to get online and give them resources the can get not their computers. I give them music to listen to. I teach them how to watch their eyes and hearts and clean up their houses. You could give them this book.

2 - I teach them about the enemy and tell them to be aware of the way he attacks. I tell them to memorize Scripture and meditate on it and to recognize when a thought is from them, from the devil or from GOD.

3 - I pray for them and I teach them to pray immediately. I pray for myself and I am careful with life. Anytime I send people on a missions trip I tell them this. They need to come home and be careful. Satan attacks us personally the most after we do great things for GOD.

4 - I give GOD all the glory. DO NOT TOUCH WHAT IS NOT YOURS. CREDIT AND GLORY ARE GOD'S!!!!!!!!

5 - I personally disciple and baptize everyone I can. I have done baptisms in rivers, the ocean and even pools because people were changed and wanted to demonstrate their decision and their coming under Jesus' LORDSHIP the way HE said to do it first. Being obedient in the first things first is key.

6 - Tell them to SHARE ABOUT IT!!!! Immediately, they can begin to share what GOD has done for them and be witnesses as Matthew 28 said. If a demoniac can listen to Jesus for an afternoon after being delivered and then become a missionary to the ten cities, then everyone else can too.

Remember as you go forward, you are GOD's direct ambassador and you are strong in the LORD and in HIS mighty power. That when you feel weak, don't worry, HE is strong. HE is able to do more than you can dream of, so dream big.

And when you walk into a room, you are walking in with the Kingdom. Satan's minions see something that sparks fear deep into the heart of them. You are causing everything in the world around you to be drawn into alignment with the Kingdom of GOD which means that it is looking a little more like heaven when you walk by. So much so that the earth itself is rejoicing because it is being rightly aligned again with its maker. You are an access point for GOD the Father to walk through and it is so much so that the world around is almost mistaking you for HIM. And the laws of the fallen nature as well as the current era are literally bending into the alignment with the divine rule and reign of GOD so much that nothing is impossible if HE desires it. All you have to do is join HIM in what HE is already doing because HE is always at work around you and HE is going to do stuff that is going to lift Jesus up and show HIM off! So, say with me, "Come Holy Spirit, I want to join the Father in HIS work. I cannot do anything in myself. I want YOU to come and show up and show Jesus off! AMEN! GRRRRRRR!

LET ME REMIND YOU OF THIS SECTION FROM WARRIORS PRAYER FOR REFERENCE:

"...every time I walk into a room, I have declared war on everything of Satan's kingdom that exists there. My walking around the planet as a warrior for GOD is an aggressive act. I wake up in the morning with an "as you go" (Matthew 10:7-10) attitude and model. That being the case, I am always at war and I am always taking ground for the Kingdom. My going out into the world is an act of aggression against the kingdom of Hell as the Kingdom of Heaven inside of me (by the grace of GOD) is

pushing through this current reality and administering heaven's rule and reign to every person who is around.

As I am going about my day-to-day activities, I am always asking GOD, "What are you doing?" I am always staying sensitive to what HIS timeline is and what HE is up to at the moment. I can do this all day long whether at work, church, home, the gym or in public running errands. Ministry to me is much less about moments in a church building or planned outreaches and more about day-to-day conversation and involvement with what "Poppa" (My term for the Father in heaven) is doing. I just want to be about my Father's business. I learned years ago from Henry Blackaby that GOD is always at work (John 5:19) and it is not important whether I feel able to do something since HE is the one doing it and I like the Son (Jesus) am only joining HIM in what HE is already doing. Some people are sad right now because there are so few real believers "doing the stuff" as John Wimber used to say (which doing the stuff means, the Kingdom activities such as healings, miracles and everything listed in Luke 4). I am not sad. The darker the time, the smaller the light necessary to make a difference. The larger the vacuum, the more clearly the Voice of GOD can be heard. I walk out the doors and instead of seeing the "vacuum," of this world, I see THE GRAND INVITATION of Poppa. Right here, right now, we can make the biggest difference with the smallest effort. This is a day of David's versus Goliath's. It is a day of Jericho walls falling. It is exciting to join GOD in what HE is doing. And we don't have to try hard to find where HE is working. If the day is that dark and the times are that tough, then all we have to do is walk outside. HE IS WORKING EVERYWHERE!!!!! The whole world is a theme park for the Kids of the Kingdom and that is us. Jump in and ride!

People will be blown away by the smallest things let alone a Red Sea parting!"

RELEVANCE

There is something to be said for relevance here since there are so many concerned with how irrelevant the church has become. The discussion has become front and center. Churches are talking about how they are not growing and they are discussing how to fix this issue. Many are becoming focused on the performance of the church to get people into their buildings. I believe that this is a mistake. We do not need to perfect performance to become relevant or we bring in a crowd that is consuming a good or a service and we are moving inside the consumeristic culture around us. Instead, we need to ask ourselves what happened.

The Kingdom is always relevant.

There is nothing more relevant to a blind man than sight received. There is nothing more relevant to a deaf man than hearing.

There is nothing more relevant to a lame man than being able to walk.

There is nothing more relevant to a prisoner than freedom.

There is nothing more relevant to a lost, broken person than the Gospel of HOPE!

There is nothing more relevant to a mourner than joy coming in the morning.

There is nothing more relevant to a demonized person than being delivered.

There is nothing more relevant to a poor man than the fact that HE has met needs.

When GOD breaks in through a Word of Knowledge, a Word of Wisdom or a Prophecy in real daily life, I have yet to see someone say that it was not relevant immediately. EVERYONE IS AWAKENED in that moment. A one on one encounter with GOD in the larger world is the only relevance we should care about!!!!!!!!!!!

If the church is irrelevant in its culture it isn't because they are not following the movements and the culture shifts good enough. Movements are always moving. The anchor of the Gospel of Jesus Christ keeps us from being moved by movements or cultures and keeps us steady through the waves. Good or bad, movements don't move me. I have seen a ton of good and bad ones.

All it is saying is the Kingdom has departed from the believer's reality and daily lives. How do we become more relevant immediately? We must slow down and wait. We must listen. We must reorient. We must realign with the plumb line of GOD. Jesus said "wait" to the new church one time, didn't HE? Remember why? Read on to the next chapter to understand more about "why?"

There is so much more that can be said of the Kingdom here. Everything from Isaiah and the Gospels can go here demonstrating what the Kingdom is and what happens when the coming Kingdom in breaks into our current reality and GOD's Kingdom is established in a group of believers' hearts. It is culture shifting and it even changes the conversation of what is relevant from "what can I consume" to "what can I give."

People become healed, delivered and more and they are then empowered to go out and give it away and the relevant activity of the Kingdom in their lives spreads like a wild fire through a community as relevant, living, breathing testimony of the Good News sweeps through.

The power of GOD in real life meets people personally where their needs are. Instead of asking what we need to do to trick people into our buildings, let's start asking what it takes to bring the King and Kingdom into the midst of us and realize that when HE comes, relevance happens.

GOD is interested not in a glamorized representation of what we can do so that people are entertained. HE knows that this causes people not to grow into disciples, but into large consumers. When the big speaker leaves or the entertainment dulls or the culture shifts, the church empties.

When we focus on the King and HIS worship and knowing HIM personally, and we come together expectant, knowing HE keeps HIS promises, and we come in Jesus' name with two or more of us gathered, HE COMES!

So, today, in order to be relevant, we MUST discuss what Jesus said to HIS own disciples at the culture shifting moment of the New Testament Church as HE was leaving. The methods and model were truly changing and HE told everyone what they had to do.

They had to wait for encounter with Holy Spirit fire power…

And that is another chapter in the end of this book. We will look at why we must wait again until fire falls.

Right now, I hope I have stirred hunger at what GOD wants to do and you are beginning to realize that this intimacy with HOLY SPIRIT I keep talking about is leading somewhere which is leading to something so much more as you are becoming HIS best friend and are learning to be a life learner of HIS. I hope you have already been taking steps towards intimacy as this book has discussed, because I promise you, what I have learned about the power of GOD and encountering HIM, you are already on your way to an adventure.

Take some time here and ask Holy Spirit to stir you more and make you more hungry and expectant for things that are beyond you. Start to imagine in your head what can happen if GOD is breaking into your reality in a big way. Imagine what happens if heaviness of Manifest Presence begins to simply awaken the lost around you and without your doing anything people begin saying, "GOD is real…" as you walk by or imagine what happens if your shadow heals someone like in the New Testament. Take some time and dream. GOD is able to do exceedingly abundantly above all you can ask or imagine (HE CAN BLOW YOUR DREAMS AWAY). I mean seriously, don't you think HE would love to break in and blow HIS kids' doors off and kick the devil's kingdom's butt?

Planning Provision
The Warrior's Strength
Being Watchful
1. What is Fire Baptism?
2. Why do I need to wait for power?
3. How do I wait? And what will be the sign HE has come?
4. Is this filling a one-time thing?
5. Why would I need more Holy Spirit?
6. Pray with me, "Father, send fire baptism of YOUR Holy Spirit to pour over me, infill me and move me. I will not let go of YOU until I have more of YOUR Holy Spirit. Empower me for YOUR work. I will not go on alone. I will move until YOU move me. I long for YOUR Holy Spirit to burn inside me. I need unction and passion. In Jesus' name, Amen!"

15 THE WARRIOR'S STRENGTH

PREFACE: DO NOT BE AFRAID

I know people have abused these terms as well as the theology and Scripture behind them. However, again, please do me a favor and do not allow yourself to be afraid of what you read here. Simply realize that anyone that has abused the terms whether from a pulpit or personally, whether through manipulation or accident, it does not change that the Bible uses the terms and the Bible is true. We cannot allow anyone to control our believing in something that is in the Bible. So, do not let the abusers own this term. TAKE IT BACK! Let's learn by Holy Spirit the depth of the term and have it. Let's have it the right way!!!! FIGHT BACK FOLKS! Don't allow fear of looking weird stop you from having the fullness of the Kingdom at any level. Do not worry!!!! GOD wants what is best for you.

FIRE OR FLOOD?

Which is better? Fire or flood? I have been over and over this in my mind and I am going to have to say, "both" when it comes to Holy Spirit Fire Baptism. There have been many who have taken up this discussion and I have found few that I agree with on the topic completely, but just because it is something that is hard to understand or because some might be afraid of it does not give me pause.

We need a Fire Baptism again in this day. And we need the River of Life coming from the well of the Holy Spirit inside us to flood out the doors of the places we meet and pray and flash flood our cities again like that day in Acts when the Spirit came in an upper room and transformed a bunch of nervous seekers into powerhouses in the Kingdom.

I mean think about it, just a little over a month before, they had watched their leader killed, only to find 3 days later HIS body was missing. Afterwards, some of their companions had the insane idea that they had seen their leader again alive in some kind of new body. And then that same leader had scared them by showing up in their meeting and then appeared over 40 days all over the place teaching them and prepping them for what was next.

But what was next? HE has mentioned a Spirit, a comforter, a teacher, a guide and some kind of "power" but what did it all really mean? I do not think they could have ever had an idea what was getting ready to happen. Luke records it in the book of Acts in the first couple chapters. I am going to share some of this here.

Excerpt from Acts 1

After his suffering, he presented himself to them and gave many convincing proofs that he was alive. He appeared to them over a period of forty days and spoke about the kingdom of God. 4 On one occasion, while he was eating with them, he gave them this command: "Do not leave Jerusalem, but wait for the gift my Father promised, which you have heard me speak about. 5 For John baptized with water, but in a few days you will be baptized with the Holy Spirit."

Excerpt from Acts 2

When the day of Pentecost came, they were all together in one place. 2 Suddenly a sound like the blowing of a violent wind came from heaven and filled the whole house where they were sitting. 3 They saw what seemed to be tongues of fire that separated and came to rest on each of them. 4 All of them were filled with the Holy Spirit and began to speak in other tongues as the Spirit enabled them.

5 Now there were staying in Jerusalem God-fearing Jews from every nation under heaven. 6 When they heard this sound, a crowd came together in bewilderment, because each one heard their own language being spoken. 7 Utterly amazed, they asked: "Aren't all these who are speaking Galileans? 8 Then how is it that each of us hears them in our native language? 9 Parthians, Medes and Elamites; residents of Mesopotamia, Judea and Cappadocia, Pontus and Asia,[b] 10 Phrygia and Pamphylia, Egypt and the parts of Libya near Cyrene; visitors from Rome 11 (both Jews and converts to Judaism); Cretans and Arabs—we hear them declaring the wonders of God in our own tongues!" 12 Amazed and perplexed, they asked one another, "What does this mean?"

13 Some, however, made fun of them and said, "They have had too much wine."
Peter Addresses the Crowd

14 Then Peter stood up with the Eleven, raised his voice and addressed the crowd: "Fellow Jews and all of you who live in Jerusalem, let me explain this to you; listen carefully to what I say. 15 These people are not drunk, as you suppose. It's only nine in the morning! 16 No, this is what was spoken by the prophet Joel:

17 "'In the last days, God says,
   I will pour out my Spirit on all people.
Your sons and daughters will prophesy,
   your young men will see visions,
   your old men will dream dreams.
18 Even on my servants, both men and women,
   I will pour out my Spirit in those days,
   and they will prophesy.
19 I will show wonders in the heavens above
   and signs on the earth below,
   blood and fire and billows of smoke.
20 The sun will be turned to darkness
   and the moon to blood
   before the coming of the great and glorious day of the Lord.

21 *And everyone who calls*
   on the name of the Lord will be saved.'[c]
22 *"Fellow Israelites, listen to this: Jesus of Nazareth was a man accredited by God to you by miracles, wonders and signs, which God did among you through him, as you yourselves know. 23 This man was handed over to you by God's deliberate plan and foreknowledge; and you, with the help of wicked men, put him to death by nailing him to the cross. 24 But God raised him from the dead, freeing him from the agony of death, because it was impossible for death to keep its hold on him.*

HOLY SPIRIT'S FIRE BAPTISM

I want to spend some time pointing some things out from the text above.

1 - Jesus told them to wait till they were given power by the Holy Spirit.

2 - There was something about the act that made them seem as if they were drunk. What was it?

3 - Peter, who had earlier denied Christ became spokesman.

4 - They were immediately given gifts.

5 - They spoke with authority and not as someone who simply had head knowledge and training.

6 - They WERE waiting.

7 - There was true undeniable demonstration of the Spirit's activity in their being Baptized.

8 - What was the Baptism for? What were the gifts for?

9 - Who got all the glory?

First, Jesus told them to wait till they had been Baptized by Holy Spirit and HE would give them power. The power HE gave them was undeniable and it was able to reach thousands with the Message of the Gospel and in moments, they were added to the church. Not to mention, it was power that gave them the ability to walk outside and turn a normal day at the market into a church meeting. What if this happened at our local malls? It's the same difference. Think about it. And think about what it took to change the reality of everyone around. There must have been a heaviness and the

Manifest Presence of GOD that made everyone know they needed to stop in their tracks because this was more than a bunch of drunk guys, this was a powerful demonstration of GOD coming near.

Second, there was something about what was happening that made people around them think these possible crazed religious fanatics were drunk in the morning. What would have seemed so out of place that people would equate it with drunkenness? After having spent some time in the middle of this kind of Spirit phenomenon and after having this reaction in my own life, I can say this. I am an extreme introvert, but you would never know it if you walked with me in the Spirit. When the Spirit comes, I call it "getting a case of the i-can't-help-it's." The Holy Spirit can come in and take someone that does not get loud and boisterous and give them passion and drive and unction and in a moment, that person can become the greatest preacher anyone has ever seen and they can be literally driven to speak in open air meetings at the drop of a hat just because HE gave them the passion, drive and unction.

I cannot explain it well, but I have experienced it so very often. HE comes and I get brave!!!!!

As a matter of fact, let me put it like this. I believe the similarities that I have found between the actions of someone who is drunk and someone overwhelmed by the Baptizing fire and unction and outflow or overflow of Holy Spirit and the River of Life coming out of their belly as Jesus put it are interesting and deserve review.

1 - When HE comes, just like someone inebriated, inhibitions go down.

2 - When HE comes, just like someone inebriated, reality gets reframed.

3 - When HE comes, just like someone inebriated, love is easier to come to the surface.

4 - When HE comes, just like someone inebriated, it gets really easy to talk and listen.

5 - When HE comes just like someone inebriated, you can feel a little out of control and it can affect your mental acuity as well as your physical motor skills.

However, unlike being inebriated;
1 - When HE comes and we allow HIM, HE becomes more in control

and HE does NOT do foolishness for foolishness sake.

2 - When HE comes and we allow HIM, as our reality becomes reframed, we know much more how real HIS world and Kingdom are and how less important anything and everything in our world is. (I believe this is why Stephen as he was being stoned had the ability to still forgive and not even seem to feel it as he was dying). So, HIS interaction in this baptism of fire experience makes us acutely aware of HIM and HIS plans and WILL in a moment and detaches us from anything that could distract so much so that everything else can become a nuisance and we can understand what Jesus means when HE says that someone cannot follow HIM unless he hates his own family. (It isn't that you hate your family. It's that you become so attached to this new reality that your love is so high and reality so keen that anything else just doesn't make sense anymore. And if your family members are believers, then you all "get it" and are on the same wavelength anyways. So, they are cheering you on in this rather than trying to hold you back. WOW!)

3 - When HE comes, your inhibitions go down as your reality is reframed because you automatically have this amazing, constant abiding awareness and you cannot stop feeling, sensing and knowing what HE wants and you also become aware of how GREAT GOD IS and that reframes your image of yourself in a moment where you place HIM high again and in a moment you realize that as a son or daughter of GOD that you are so far from who HE is and yet HE calls you beloved child and in that realization, you just cannot care about all the junk that used to hold you down. It just doesn't matter. And inhibitions go out the window so much that you find yourself at a restaurant in one of these baptism moments and you cannot help it as the waitress at your table accepts Jesus just by hearing your talk at the table and you become so super charged that everyone in the back has to hear about it so without thinking, you walk in and speak words of knowledge over them and they receive it and no one in the restaurant stops you because of the heaviness of GOD's Manifest authority is there and afterwards, you walk out with your friends who have just been a part of people coming to know Jesus by live encounter with the Kingdom in a collision and you all look at each other and say, "What the heck just happened???? That is so not like us!!!!!" Don't think it cannot happen. I have not only seen it, I have done it. I have seen the fire of Baptism hit like that. I do not fake it when it is not there, but I love it when I get to join HIM in those moments. (Again, read my others books for fuller stories). Wouldn't that make it really easy for you to lose grip on what people call reality in this normal, fallen world? And people wonder why I am so crazy! Look at what I know HE can do!!!!!!!! I will not let go until HE does it

again. And thus this book. I believe you can cry out even right now before going on any further and pray and beg GOD for fire to fall on you and for you to have a revelation of HIS nearness and to be Baptized and empowered by Holy Spirit and HE WILL COME!!!! Ask now, pray it now. I want you to have it!!! HAVE IT! If you are one of my kids and you are reading this or one of my grandkids and I am not there with you, please bring me honor and ache for this and dig in and don't let go until you are filled with the Spirit afresh. I want this for you. It's the best gift I can give you besides sharing Jesus' story and you accepting HIM. Holy Spirit longs for you. The Father longs for you. Let HIM HAVE ALL OF YOU NOW! TELL HIM! Don't wait till the end of this book or the end of this chapter. Tell HIM NOW! I feel HIM burning all over me and stirring me as I write this. I believe HE is going to do this right now in you. Please be stirred. Hear my precious beloved calling you. HE longs for you more than you ever longed for HIM. HE desires you. HE chose and made you. HE has better plans for you than you can ever understand. Yield now. "I yield, LORD!"

4 - When HE comes, I can listen and talk better. The words come better. Like this book, the gift Holy Spirit has given me in writing it is that I can feel HIM and it is like HE is pouring over me and over me these 10 days I have written this text. It is a gift to know HIM this way and to listen and share. What an amazing honor. And as far as listening goes, I have found it so very hard to share the Gospel at times in America and then other times both here and in other countries, I have seen it become so easy. It's all about HIM. And since HE is the one that contends with men's hearts, we should be asking HIM on a daily basis to open up people's ears to hear and listen and for HIM to be there with us in that moment. I have found that the best times I have seen HIM move in power and more people come to know HIM has been after I have been in a long time of communion with HIM and then HE won't leave me alone and won't let me stay in communion in a closet, HE drives me to do something. And then, when I go, it's like the cushion of the relationship and HIS nearness is there with me softening the blows of the tough words of the Gospel and instead of people pushing it away, they are softened and wooed. It's all about HIM folks. And the baptism of fire and unction that comes with it makes outreach and ministry EASY! If ministry and outreach are hard, something is wrong. GO FIND HIM! GO GET FIRE!

5 - When HE comes, even though we lose a little control, when HE is in control, we may act a bit different than we are comfortable with, but HE does the work. I am so tired of working "for" GOD. I want to work "with" HIM and allow HIM to work "through" me. Notice the words I am using.

SO many times we are telling GOD in prayer, "GOD, I have this plan, bless it…" or we pray, "GOD, tell me what you want done and I will go out and do it for you…" Rather than praying the right prayers,

"GOD, what are YOU already doing and where can I join YOU?"

"GOD, can I do what YOU are doing?"

"Holy Spirit, come, please join me as I act on what YOU are directing me to. I will not leave this mountain alone. If you do not go with us, I will not leave!" -Moses (paraphrase)

It's that simple. GOD does not make us act foolish and leave us as foolish. HE may make it so that we cast off inhibitions and do something strange, but HE has stacked the deck in whatever Kingdom collision HE has planned and I can tell you this, HE can make something that looks totally crazy make sense in a matter of 30 seconds. HE can change things on a dime and often HE offends our very intellect as the Bible says in order to use us in ways that demonstrate HIS power more. Remember, GOD does not choose the wise and the rich and the ones that have. He chooses the foolish, the small and the weak. It's all about HIM getting glory. So, if you feel that you are not the right person for HIM to use and that you have nothing to offer, let me tell you, even if you do not believe me, I feel the same way often and HE cares little about your ability. HE cares much about your availability!!!!!

"I don't care if you stutter, Moses, what's in your hand? I can use that!" -GOD (paraphrase from burning bush)

Third, Holy Spirit used ones like Peter that had first denied HIM. This in itself is a sign that GOD was working in miracles!!!! Seriously, just a month before, this guy was lying and cowering and here he is the spokesman. Look what GOD can do in one baptizing moment!!!!!

Fourth, they were immediately given gifts. Now, some people want to contend and say that the only gift that someone baptized in the Spirit MUST have is the gift of speaking in tongues, but that is not Biblical and it was not my experience. The Bible never required this to be the first sign and Paul when discussing gifts even said that that gift, although he used it all the time was not to be considered the BIGGEST gift. He told people to eagerly desire all gifts but to ask for prophecy more than the rest. (Notice though that he did not say to ask to be a prophet, just desire the gift).

My personal experience, this was the case. I have now, years sense functioned in every gift, however, in the beginning, that was not the case and the first gifts I functioned in were words of knowledge and words of wisdom. However, I do believe that when the Spirit Baptizes and as we lay on hands, there are gifts released. And they are released and given to us by the Spirit's directing and they are for the edification of the entire Body of Christ!

Fifth, they spoke with authority and not as someone who simply had head knowledge and training. As a matter of fact in one part of Acts, they noted that the disciples were untrained men, but that they had been with Jesus and they marveled at the authority with which they spoke. (And they were only with HIM 3 years!) Isn't it amazing that some of our ministers have been to seminaries for years and more time than the disciples and yet they have no authority when they speak? Could it be they need a baptism of fire and encounters with Jesus' Spirit? Could it also possibly be that we are elevating some people who have no calling, no fruit, no stewardship, no purity, no disciples they've discipled and they are hirelings instead of pastors? I mean, maybe like the prophets of old talked about, we have wolves in among the sheep that are calling themselves the prophets or the preachers? I think so. I did not enter ministry because I thought it was a good idea. I wanted to do soccer or chemistry. The calling ruined me. I could not do anything else. Now, 20 years later, the proof is in the Presence, neither in my ability nor my ideas. I submit to an obedience that many men do not understand and I walk every single day under Proverbs 3:5-6. Authority comes from nearness to HIM. HE is the only one that can give authority. DO NOT TAKE A TITLE UNLESS YOU KNOW THE PERSON AND HE KNOWS YOU BACK! GRRRRRR! Hate me if you must. I preach the truth.

Sixth, they WERE waiting. Could it be our ministries and plans fail because we did not wait till HE sent us? Could it be we were moving on our own authority and in our own power? What is the truth? Have we waited on HIM? If we haven't, stop everything, drop this book and run off and begin to wait. Tell HIM that you will not move from this moment unless HE MOVES YOU! HE WILL! Then come back and read the rest. I will tell you why this is the case.

Seventh, there was true undeniable demonstration of the Spirit's activity in their being Baptized. If we are seeing only man-sized results, we are not seeing the power of GOD that comes after people have been baptized in fire! I am not saying anything more on this point. IT IS WHAT IT IS! And call it what it is. We have got to stop trying to fake ourselves out. People are leaving in droves because we are irrelevant and yet, Isaiah 61 and Luke 4 are

ALWAYS relevant to those that need to hear that message and when that takes place, everyone else will see the Oaks of Righteousness demonstration and then "enough said!"

And that is the truth! So, take a tally on the ministries around you and take the time and look at the effects and return over the long haul and make some educated decisions. If you are happy with the crappy outcomes, that's fine. I am not. I am not settling for halfway any longer. I WANT IT ALL! I WILL NOT REST UNTIL HEAVEN BREAKS THROUGH! And if Heaven does not break through in my lifetime, I will not stop asking, seeking and knocking. I am going home to break into it!

I guarantee that the Father will not be angry at me for this response. I know it has to make a dad so very happy HIS kid won't leave HIM alone. Oh if I am blessed enough that my children keep barging in the doors of my house even until I am old and grey and they always keep taking the place over. I love my house being LIVED IN!

Poppa, I am coming HOME daily!!!!!

Eighth, what was the Baptism for? What were the gifts for? Was it for them? NO! It was for Jesus to be lifted up and for men and women and children to come to know Jesus by encounter and come into relationship with GOD. GOD is interested in that one real goal and then for the Bride and Groom to have a wedding. It is that simple. So, all the gifts and everything else there is in the Kingdom is literally tied into that goal of preparing a Bride to be radiant for a wedding day. HIS SON deserves it after what HE did! SERIOUSLY! It's the least we can give the one that died for us.

And we know that on that day when the disciples were baptized, Jesus got all the glory!

Ninth, baptism of fire from Holy Spirit's coming had been eagerly sought. They knew they could not do it alone and it was an obedient act for them to do what Jesus told them. I mean seriously folks, if you notice you've been missing something in your faith walk and you are missing the fire and passion in your guts, don't let the fact that someone misused the term or they acted dumb after saying they had been baptized in fire stop you, press in and want it for yourself. Ask GOD for the real thing. If you cannot trust what others are doing in your day, do not judge what the Bible says as wrong due to some Americanized revivalist or TV preacher and how they act. YOU GET IT FOR YOU! Don't let them hold you back. The devil will use every argument he can to offend or scare you, but that's just it. He knows that if you are not empowered and in relationship, he has you where he wants you. Do you really want him to control your destiny? Then, fight back. Take the term back. Be baptized in fire and do the relationship right! Do it for you! Do it for Jesus! DO NOT LET GO TILL YOU HAVE THE REAL, AUTHENTIC, POWERFUL, BAPTISM OF FIRE!!!!! You will know it is what it is because of what I described above.

And we know later in the text in Acts that thousands heard them miraculously in their own languages meaning it had been translated in their ears. And thousands were added to their number in a day, which is a pretty dramatic response, by any measure in any culture in any time.

IS BAPTISM OF THE HOLY SPIRIT A ONE-TIME THING?

I don't think so. You know, through Acts, we see how there was a "first" time that people experienced the Baptism of the Holy Spirit, yet at the same time, we see where GOD did it again. Where they got together again and everyone was baptized in fire and the place where they met was shaken, or they met with another group and it came there on them all. I began to wonder if it was a one-time thing or if it is something I can keep running back to. I like the idea that I keep running back to HIM and HE keeps pouring back into me. Almost like as I minister, I am poured out and I run back into relationship time with Holy Spirit and HE refills me. We used to joke that church was like a "filling station" (this is a term we used to call gas stations).

And with that said, I want to share a verse here with you…

Ephesians 5:18
Do not get drunk on wine, which leads to debauchery. Instead, be filled with the Spirit,

Let's take a moment and go to the Greek on something. The words and language used for this passage is not a "one time" filling. It is a continual activity of being filled. It could better read, "Be you being filled." It's like we are to live lives that are not just "filled" and stamped "done." We are to have a lifestyle of going back and being refilled. We could say then, "Be filled and refilled and refilled and refilled and more…"

This is a really cool thing. Why?

It illustrates what I am saying here about being baptized and/or filled with the Spirit. GOD desires for us to have only one substance we are addicted to and it isn't wine. HE desires us addicted to the Spirit. Could it be also said that the vine/branch relationship is a little codependent? HECK YES!

We spoke before about how we are not to be codependent with other humans. However, this is exactly the relationship I have with the Holy Spirit. HE needs us to be HIS hands and feet and WE NEED HIM TO SURVIVE AND THRIVE! Once someone told me I was codependent on GOD and I just agreed with them. And said that it was much worse than that! Someone else told me that the Bible was my crutch and I said, "NO! It's not my crutch, it's my entire wheelchair!" SO LET IT BE!

May we find ourselves utterly without the ability to go through a year, a month, a week, a day, or even an hour or moment without just reaching out to touch HIS hand. May we be so blessed to be so addicted to HIS nearness. I am NOT talking about these people who walk around the planet with their head in the clouds and their feet off the ground. I am not talking about these people that are so heavenly minded that they are not any earthly good. NO!

I am talking about the people that are so heavenly utilized that they are so much good to the communities and world around them, they are so connected with what the Father is doing around them and they are so able to be used in a moment's notice by the Spirit on little covert, missions (Jesus said to do your good works in secret) that they are truly detached from the attack of the world or its attractions and yet so available that they are constantly doing the relevant needed Isaiah 61 activities of Jesus' calling just as HE did it and they are being so poured out that they know they cannot continue in their humanness without the powerful baptizing flood of the Spirit and the daily renewing of their minds in the Scripture. BRING IT! May we be such people! This is where I attempt to live every day and if you read my other books you can see I DO IT! It's not because I am so good at it. I am simply an obedient, humble servant and if I can, then you all the more. You don't have to be more gifted and come from better stock than I do. I was just a farm boy. YOU CAND DO THIS! If HE can use me, a spotted, blemished donkey, then HE CAN TOTALLY USE YOU!

You can make your own decision as to whether it is a one time thing or not, but I have to tell you, I am going to keep going back. It seems to be my experience that I MUST HAVE MORE in order to keep living every day for HIM. It's like the branch saying to the vine, "keep that nutrition coming… I have fruit to bear…"

Here are some other thoughts:

1 - How can we know when we need another refill?

I simply know I need a refill when the fruit are not exhibited in me. Go back to the chapter on maturity and you can see what those fruit are. But, when the fruit are lacking and I have hardened, I run back to relationship. I run back to the closet.

2 - What must it feel kind of like?

It must feel a lot like being drunk. And I can tell you from experience, it is like no kind of high you can ever get from anything else. Imagine something happening that is real in this world and yet you know is otherworldly. It is exhilarating. And at the same time, HE leaves you feeling better about yourself even when HE corrects you. And that is nothing like drinking or doing drugs, right?

3 - Then, what are some of the results that affect the symptoms of needing to drink wine for release?

I won't rehash this, but it is discussed more above, I just want to say that if you have an alcohol problem, what better way to deal with it than replace it? There are folks out there that say not to replace addiction with addiction and I agree. Even religion can become an evil addiction. So, let me say here. This is NOT religion. It is relationship. If you find that in HIM, wow! You are set.

Someone that gets touched by the Holy Spirit of GOD should immediately think to himself or herself, "I have to figure out how to have this again?" The thing is that the person we are interacting with is better than anything we have ever experienced or tasted before and if you are in any way a person that is addicted to something, HE can satiate that desire in such a way that the addiction is replaced with an immediate need for more of HIM. HE is addictive. Jesus is more than addictive. HE is attractive. HE is someone that once you truly know, you will sell all you have and buy that field!!!!!!!!

JUST TO GO A BIT DEEPER:

There is precedence in the Bible for people having encounters with GOD that are powerful. Acts church was shaken every time they prayed together. GOD's Presence was manifest often. It was an expectation.

Being Baptized in Fire is in the Bible. It is defined by people being overwhelmed by the fullness of GOD. "I will give you a river flowing and overflowing out of you..." If we don't have that demonstration in our lives, we need to seek it. Also, if we notice we are having to work hard to have "fruit of the Spirit," that is not a commentary on how bad we are. It is showing we need to go get into an Encounter with Holy Spirit. Fruit is an outflow. If outreach becomes work and salvations are not happening, is this our work to be done? No. Holy Spirit convicts and saves. So, we need to get in communion and then it will be an outflow as we are refilled with fire from our communion. In communion, Holy Spirit and GOD's reality becomes more real to us than our external reality and we become enraptured by HIS desires and what HE is doing.

It does not have to be followed by a specific sign or specific gift. It will always be proven by the walk of the one who had the encounter after said encounter. If it shows the life of Jesus and the fruit of the Spirit afterwards and lifts Jesus high, then that is a sign of it's happening.

The encounter is something more than a mental assertion. This is not an intellectual thing. Actually, it offends intellect. And once an intellectual gets past the offense, it EMPOWERS ALL THE teaching and information you have in your intellect. It makes it all "aha."

There are elements that are demonstrated through Scripture before people are baptized in fire and as they are flooded with the River of Life from their inmost beings:

1- It is always both preceded and followed by hunger and drawing of the individual.

2- There must be seeking involved.

3- There is always a first encounter so if you cannot point back to the moment, then you have not had a first encounter. Begin to seek more today.

4- There is always the element of revelation of GOD, "aha!" That awareness of the nearness and realness of GOD blows off inhibitions so much that people look drunk. Nothing matters more than the revelation at that moment!

5- When we encounter GOD, no matter how amazing we think we are, we always realize how far we still fall short and there are always elements of repentance.

6- The encounter causes refill and refocus. Sometimes people after an encounter find they have been retooled. (They have new gifts, vision or more).

7- There is always empowerment. People walk away from an encounter with Holy Spirit of Fire Baptism and they are empowered to share the Gospel. As a matter of fact, that kind of becomes the easiest thing since HE is so real to you, all you want to do is to get other people to try this too. It is exciting.

Remember, encounter took some scared disciples and turned them into amazing Preachers that saw thousands added to the church through the simple Gospel in moments. The fact that evangelism happened so easily in the very place where just weeks before, Jesus was murdered and the converts were people that had just witnessed the whole thing a little over a month before and the fact that many were not necessarily believers of Jewish religion but were there from other countries drawn in by Herod's huge Roman transit and trade center, was the sign that something powerful had taken place.

Let's look at more times the power of GOD came in Manifest Presence and people were led to salvation and/ Baptized with fire...

DL Moody was told by two of his parishioners who were amazing intercessors that they want him to be baptized in fire. He could not understand how they would think he was not already so baptized since there were people being saved and added to the church. And they just pressed in and said they knew and wanted to see what would happen through him when he was. After he had encountered GOD in Holy Spirit baptism, He was never the same and he went through a whole new level. His ministry saw a whole new power of GOD and salvations increased massively.

Charles Finney had a face to face encounter with Jesus in the back room at his law office and was immediately empowered and baptized.

John Wesley at Aldersgate felt waves of liquid love strangely warm and flow over him as the Holy Spirit baptized him and made him aware of his need to be converted through what the Moravians described as a more personal relationship with GOD.

Peter Cartwright was met by Jesus in a cave after feeling he would never be saved and he was empowered.

GROANING INWARDLY

I would love to spend tons of time on this, however, I cannot. I am coming to the end of this writing and I myself am an intercessor and I am often aching inside for the souls of people. In the Bible, there are some passages that mention being stirred in the depths of the belly and groaning. Jesus had this experience before he raised Lazarus. He had compassion, wept and groaned deeply within HIS being.

I want to invite us into asking GOD to inwardly stir us into praying till we, our churches, our families and our communities are baptized in Fired and Manifest Presence of GOD comes. I want us to ask GOD for the gifts of the heaviness of the garden and that we would feel with Jesus the weight of lost souls. That this would stir us to beg for whatever empowerment we need to reach the lost. I ask us to beg GOD for the gift of repentance and intercession. GOD, give us the gift of tears.

INTERCEDING AND PETITIONING TILL IT HAPPENS (an upper room wait).

We don't pretend we have something we don't. We are very aware of the lack in the church and ourselves and we wait on the One that comes to endue with power.

In Matthew it says, "Ask and keep on asking, seek and keep on seeking, knock and keep on knocking…" and we will find, receive and the door will be opened. We must KEEP ON doing it till it happens. This shows the fruit of faithfulness when we won't give up!

"How much more will YOUR Father in Heaven give the Holy Spirit to those who ask…" It's in the Bible, so why not press in and remind HIM of it. Jesus said that if we asked, the Father for more of the Holy Spirit in HIS name, so, let's hold HIM to it. And James says that we have not because we ask not. DO NOT "have not…" HAVE!

Lastly, remember the story of "The persistent widow and the unjust judge" that Jesus told. The judge was bad (And GOD is good). And yet, her coming back and driving this judge crazy got the answer. LET'S KEEP PRESSING IN!!!!!! Also remember the story of Daniel who had been seeking an answer and when the angel came, he said he had been detained by the Prince of Persia which was a demonic principality! You hear that? Sometimes our answer is on the way whether by the Spirit or an angel and we keep on keeping on till there is breakthrough. I mean heck, are you a wuss or a warrior? RIGHT? THEN WAR! KNOCK! ASK! SEEK! And don't let go.

GOD keeps HIS promises! Elisha was told he would have a double portion and he did exactly a double amount of Elijah's miracles till the day he died… minus one. And then during a raid, some men through a dead body in Elisha's tomb in order to escape the attack and the body touched Elisha's bones and came back to life and ran past them! AND THERE THE PROMISE WAS KEPT! DOUBLE!

Just because it isn't done in your lifetime doesn't mean GOD won't keep HIS promise. SO PRESS HIM FOR IT! HE WILL! If HE wrote it, HE meant it!

GRRRRR!

Come Holy Spirit, send fire baptism again so that Rivers of living water will flow out of the churches again and through the streets! AMEN!

Taking Ground
The Warrior's Heart
Being Watchful
1. Why do I need to care about the poor?
2. Why can I not do it alone?
3. Why does social justice need Jesus to work?
4. Who is social justice for?
5. Who benefits the most?
6. Pray with me, "Father, please soften my heart for the poor, the broken, the needy, the orphan, the widow, the prostitute, the destitute and all those that are to be YOUR Oaks of Righteousness. Please help me to have compassion and empathize with their pain, but not stop there, bring me into YOUR action that YOU are already desiring & where YOU are working. In Jesus' name, Amen."

16 THE WARRIOR'S HEART

KINGDOM JUSTICE
Passion that leads to Compassion that leads to Action!

Something GOD revealed to Me personally very early on in my time doing inner city missions work is that, "The poor do not need us, they need Jesus. We need the poor so we can see Jesus."

When I got that down pat in my heart, I could begin to serve the broken, the widow, the orphan, the outcast, the addict, the prostitute, the poor and the needy.

This revelation has ruined me for my old way of life. Now, ministry for me has become an upside down thing where the greatest is not the one that lords over all others, the greatest in the Kingdom are the ones that serve the lowest in the world, the best with no reward in mind, just ONE SMILING FACE standing at the gate at the end of the story, proud of HIS faithful servant.

DOING JUSTICE
Isaiah 61

The Spirit of the Sovereign Lord is on me, because the Lord has anointed me to proclaim good news to the poor. He has sent me to bind up the brokenhearted, to proclaim freedom for the captives and release from darkness for the prisoners, 2 to proclaim the year of the Lord's favor and the day of vengeance of our God, to comfort all who mourn, 3 and provide for those who grieve in Zion— to bestow on them a crown of beauty instead of ashes, the oil of joy instead of mourning, and a garment of praise instead of a spirit of despair.

They will be called oaks of righteousness, a planting of the Lord for the display of his splendor. 4 They will rebuild the ancient ruins and restore the places long devastated; they will renew the ruined cities that have been devastated for generations. 5 Strangers will shepherd your flocks; foreigners will work your fields and vineyards.

6 And you will be called priests of the Lord, you will be named ministers of our God. You will feed on the wealth of nations, and in their riches you will boast. 7 Instead of your shame you will receive a double portion, and instead of disgrace you will rejoice in your inheritance. And so you will inherit a double portion in your land, and everlasting joy will be yours.

8 "For I, the Lord, love justice; I hate robbery and wrongdoing. In my faithfulness I will reward my people and make an everlasting covenant with them. 9 Their descendants will be known among the nations and their offspring among the peoples. All who see them will acknowledge that they are a people the Lord has blessed." 10 I delight greatly in the Lord; my soul rejoices in my God. For he has clothed me with garments of salvation and arrayed me in a robe of his righteousness, as a bridegroom adorns his head like a priest, and as a bride adorns herself with her jewels.

11 For as the soil makes the sprout come up and a garden causes seeds to grow, so the Sovereign Lord will make righteousness and praise spring up before all nations.

Isaiah 61 is the definition of what "JUSTICE" looks like in the Kingdom. GOD's design for the salvation of the broken and using those very same broken in the redemption of the ancient ruins and destroyed cities is an amazing concept that we in this day would do anything to see. There are groups out there pouring money into the proposition that this scenario could be possible and instead of anchoring their work in GOD and HIS Kingdom, they are approaching it through literacy, social welfare programs, better education, money for the poor to receive medical attention and so much more. However, their efforts have been found to be futile for over 60 years now. Government and the designs of man are not the answer. ONLY GOD can do this work. Isaiah is HIS design.

Justice is such a hot topic that I am careful as I approach it. People want to do social justice all the time but doing justice because we want to and not from outflow of love relationship with Holy Spirit is dangerous.

Any group out there that is simply doing Justice on their own without the name of Jesus being lifted up whether they are a church or not is simply doing social work.

Doing work inside of men's plans with men's resources and men's ability will result with man-sized results.

This has been the problem for the last 70 or so years as the church has been leaving the social sector open to be taken care of solely by the government.

However, compassion done, led by GOD, joining GOD's plans, with GOD's ability, in Jesus' name, and by GOD's resources will render GOD-sized results!!!!!!!!!

In the verse, we see that "they" will rebuild the ancient ruins? Who will rebuild the ancient ruins of our cities and the places long since devastated? The "they" that are mentioned here are the people that are oppressed, poor, bound and sick that were mentioned in the first of Isaiah 61. The poor, the broken, the disadvantaged, and the sick who are freed, healed, delivered and blessed will be the "Oaks of righteousness." What if the answer to the ruined cities being reborn is in the very broken and poor of that city? What if we are hurting the whole redemption of things because we are leaving GOD out of the equation and we do not see what HE sees in them and what HE can do through HIS transformative power? What if?

If I'm wrong, who cares, what does it hurt. But what if I'm right?

The fact that our activity leads to nothing but a donor or benefactor mentality rather than empowering the disadvantaged and seeing them rise up and changed as Isaiah's prophecy shows, will be the prophetic result of Jesus' being lifted up and the Kingdom being demonstrated is why all of our social justice work is not working and why so many are simply "stuck."

Do you want to see the ancient ruins rebuilt? Do you want to see the broken and disadvantaged become oaks of righteousness?

Then maybe we need to change our approach!!!!!!!!!
Let's look at what the Bible says GOD desires from us in this area!

Micah 6:8
He has shown you, O man, what is good;
And what does the Lord require of you
But to do justly,
To love mercy,
And to walk humbly with your God?

WE CANNOT DO JUSTICE WITHOUT:
1 - First being justified (this creates compassion inside of us. We then "love mercy").
What does this mean? This means you must have received grace from GOD before you are able to understand that no good work is even able to come from you without the Holy Spirit doing it through you. (See Ephesians 2:8-9).

Then you will be able to "extend" the grace of GOD. We are unable to give away what we have never received.

This creates huge inward humility as you realize the only thing that separates you from the lowest of the lows in our world or anyone we deem unlovely is simply the grace of GOD intervening and you become so thankful in that that you want everyone to enjoy the encounter with grace you just had. Being forgiven much as I've said before in this book releases love! And look at the woman at the well. Once she encountered Jesus and had that full on power encounter and had received grace as Jesus revealed her sins completely and still embraced her, she had to tell everyone.

It's not that we lower the bar once we receive grace. We cannot do that. It's that what is inside our heart is so full of love and compassion and we are so able to identify with the broken that if it were possible to lower the bar, we would try.

It's a heart thing. We want everyone to encounter and meet this man that told us everything we ever did and still loves us!!!!!!

And let me tell you, the verse doesn't say to "love justice." That would make us hard. We "do" justice and we "love" mercy!

2 - Second being just. (You cannot do Justice work unless you are just in your heart toward your own brother and sister).

I have said this a million times and I am saying it again. The first best way to put the porn and sex industry out of business which is putting children in slavery worldwide every day is for us to be first in stopping the consumption. If you are one that does not defraud your sister by lusting after her and consuming her shameful moments and exploiting her, then you are one less person that they receive financing from.

Seriously, just like everything in a free market society and a consumer driven world, if money stops pouring into it, it will stop being sold.

So, be a person that says first, "I will make a covenant with my eyes not to look lustfully." It's what Job did.

And you have removed one more person from the financing vehicle. If you say to yourself, "It's ok, I am not paying anyone money" and yet you are giving something views on a website, then you lie to yourself. Those clicks and those views are money in the bank for those people.

By the time this book is read there may be some other means to get pornographic material spread. Whatever it is and whatever the means, if you have already settled in your heart that you will not succumb to the temptation to look and that you will begin to see every person as not an object, but a child that our Heavenly Father loves, then you will begin to tear down this monster.

Don't even try to tear down the monster of injustice if you have not begun to fight it in yourself first.

The same is true with poverty and the hungry. If you treat food and money wrongly and you want to go out and help them or if you defraud the poor and make jest of them, don't go out and show them your petty empathy. They don't need it!!!!!!!

And let me tell you, the broken, the poor and the abused can see through you. If you are not genuine and you are not real, they are going to read you like a book and besides them, GOD knows your heart and if you are out for anything besides love for Jesus and doing everything in love in HIS name, there is no reward!!!!!!! You must "BE" just before you "do" justice!

3 - third walking in proximity to GOD

This is the most important part. As I've said before and as Micah says clearly here. GOD desires all of the above from us and the last thing is that we are unable to do it on our own or out from proximity to HIM. HE does not want us to slave for HIM. HE desires partners that want to join HIM in what HE is already doing. (John 5:19 again). Since HE is already at work, this changes our approach. Instead of looking at our cities and finding our places to fix things, why don't we pray over our cities and ask GOD to reveal where HE is already working and to show us HOW to join HIM. Don't worry about how to know when to act. HIS revelation IS HIS invitation to join. So, when HE shows you and you go "aha" inside, pray, get some friends to minister with you and jump in!

Some things I want to mention as we go forward as I frame the "Justice" conversation.

WE DO WHAT WE DO FOR JESUS

1- Matthew 25:31-46
*31 "When the Son of Man comes in His glory, and all the holy angels with Him, then He will sit on the throne of His glory. 32 All the nations will be gathered before Him, and He will separate them one from another, as a shepherd divides his sheep from the goats. 33 And He will set the sheep on His right hand, but the goats on the left. 34 Then the King will say to those on His right hand, 'Come, you blessed of My Father, inherit the kingdom prepared for you from the foundation of the world: 35 for I was hungry and you gave Me food; I was thirsty and you gave Me drink; I was a stranger and you took Me in; 36 I was naked and you clothed Me; I was sick and you visited Me; I was in prison and you came to Me.'
37 "Then the righteous will answer Him, saying, 'Lord, when did we see You hungry*

and feed You, or thirsty and give You drink? 38 When did we see You a stranger and take You in, or naked and clothe You? 39 Or when did we see You sick, or in prison, and come to You?' 40 And the King will answer and say to them, 'Assuredly, I say to you, inasmuch as you did it to one of the least of these My brethren, you did it to Me.'

41 'Then He will also say to those on the left hand, 'Depart from Me, you cursed, into the everlasting fire prepared for the devil and his angels: 42 for I was hungry and you gave Me no food; I was thirsty and you gave Me no drink; 43 I was a stranger and you did not take Me in, naked and you did not clothe Me, sick and in prison and you did not visit Me.'

44 'Then they also will answer Him, saying, 'Lord, when did we see You hungry or thirsty or a stranger or naked or sick or in prison, and did not minister to You?' 45 Then He will answer them, saying, 'Assuredly, I say to you, inasmuch as you did not do it to one of the least of these, you did not do it to Me.' 46 And these will go away into everlasting punishment, but the righteous into eternal life."

We see Jesus in their faces! Every single person we do kindness to with compassion in Jesus' name; we will see HIM in their faces. And when we see HIM at the end of days, HE will say "well done." You did this to me. It's kind of the same feeling I get when I see my own kids get along and share and do nice things for each other. It makes my heart happy. We make HIS heart happy when we care for the rest of HIS kids.

TO CHOOSE NOT TO ACT IS SIN AND IT IS ROOTED IN OUR COMPLACENCY & BEING OVERFED

2- Ezekiel 16:49
"Now this was the sin of your sister Sodom: She and her daughters were arrogant, overfed and unconcerned; they did not help the poor and needy."

What was the sin of Sodom and Gomorrah that got the two cities destroyed? Was it all of the impurity and the lurid acts they did? No, in GOD's own words to Ezekiel, HE said the issue that caused HIM to destroy the cities was that they were:

A - Arrogant
B - Overfed
C - Unconcerned
D - And they did not help the poor and needy

Does this sound like any other cities we may know? Arrogance is rampant in our churches. We have been given so much access to so many great preachers in our American churches that we are definitely overfed. The question of whether or not we are unconcerned need not be asked.

Our attitudes now are so full of snide, critical, condescending words and sarcasm that to say we were concerned for others would be an utter travesty. We are NOT concerned. Anyone can see we would rather throw money at people and programs than relationships that will link arms with brothers and sisters in real problems and dire need and bring them out with a long term, love filled, compassion that is active and leads into discipleship. This is messy Christianity and we don't mind sending someone else to do the dirty work, but we don't want to reach out into the crack houses and even to the beggar on the street.

It's time to stop easing our unconcerned consciences with what I call "Christmas Charity" and begin to every single day watch where GOD is working and begin to FEEL THEIR PAIN WITH THEM. A community and/or Body is only as strong as it's weakest member.

And they did not help the poor and needy. We have to ask ourselves two questions.

1 - Do I do everything I can to help fight inequality, poverty, and need in my neighborhood and larger community or city?

2 - With what I do, do I actually do things that really help? I remember watching people give some of the men I worked with in the inner-city just $5 as a tip for being kind to them when they came to visit our work in the inner city. The men were not supposed to accept money from people coming to the ministry, but they sometimes would and the person that got that $5 would be gone and back binging in drugs within the week. Lost to us. Does the quick payoff really help the person? Are we asking Holy Spirit what HE wants us to do? Are we joining the Father where HE is working? Or are we easing our consciences? Guess what? Easing your conscience doesn't count and it is NOT HELPING THE POOR AND NEEDY!

We are not their donors or benefactors. We are a family. And we are called to walk with our broken sisters and brothers as well as our hungry and needy ones because what were we really without Christ but poor, wretched, naked, blind as Revelation says about our filthy rags works before HIM?! We do this because of the Grace we have already received.

GOOD SENSE LENDING

3- *"He who gives to the poor, lends to the LORD…"*

Proverbs says a lot about the poor and one of my favorite verses says the above. And the kicker is that GOD is the one who pays back the giving lent to the poor. And GOD rewards better than anyone. Think about the returns the Kingdom gives that Jesus talks about. 30, 60 or 100 fold. I will take those returns. I have found through the era where GOD began to bless my investments that HE took my investments that I had few of and multiplied them by thousands when I had actually for years put most of mine and Lori's income into ministry, paying people's debts, paying for others' kids to go to school, starting businesses for other people, investing in micro-credit and doing outreach and missions as well as investing in Tapestry where we were the chief givers for over 7 years with me working my two jobs to get to "pay" to do ministry!!!!!! (Again, read my other book for these stories).

And in one brief less than a year time, GOD radically switched my fortunes and made what I had invested in make such large returns that I could literally become almost totally debt free, work to make the church debt free, sell my house and move to a nicer house and pay most of it off, and do missions as well as huge amounts of humanitarian work on my own dime!!!!! And even in what HE returned in those profits, I gave half of that to ministry and missions again. And guess what, I am not even the best at this. There are others that have done more. I am just telling you that I have lived this and seen it. Give to the poor as the LORD leads, join HIM in the giving and watch and see what HE does in your future! You will not regret it. Banks give a small percentage below 1% on their returns. Stocks are lucky to give 12% annual returns. GOD gives 1000% returns. WATCH AND SEE! I have lived it and am living it!!!!!!!

I want to say one more thing before I close my thoughts on this chapter and that is that GOD protects the orphans, widows and poor. He watches over them. HE does not just say that once or twice in the Bible, it is throughout the BIBLE. GOD says over and over again that HE protects these individuals and that HE takes care of them and that HE fights for them. So, with that said, we do not even have to ask "if" GOD is at work in our communities where there is need and poverty. We need to begin to ask "HOW" we can join HIM. Frame the question right!

BLOOD-N-FIRE ATLANTA

When it comes to compassion and justice work, I learned everything I know from a group of people at a place in inner city Atlanta called, Blood-n-Fire Ministries. It had been launched by one of my mentors, Johnny Crist and was founded, planted and led by David VanCronkhite and his wife,

Janice. Some folks there I owe much of my formation in Kingdom work on the streets include Ned Hill and his wife Susan, David and Val Kula, Vincent and Erin Houben, Jim and Pia Arrendale, Charles Davis, JB and Charles Keel.

There are many others as well as many more stories, but those are going to be recorded in another book of mine called, "A Warriors Tale." So, what I want to say here is that this chapter is dedicated to them.

I do not take credit for this part of this chapter. David never wrote a book, however, if it were to be written, I believe it would have looked a lot like this. So, below is his outline we used to train people in what we did at BNF. Read it and be stirred. I want my kids to know where their Poppy's DNA and guts to serve came from!!!!! The last 12 years of ministry is learning based on this foundation and the above things GOD revealed to me in this season would have never come without the foundation of these teachings as well as what I learned from Jackie Pullinger, Bob Lupton, Steve Sjogren, Mark McCoy and John Wimber as I heard them speak as well at Blood-n-Fire. (Thank you Pastor David).

FROM MY NOTES FROM DVC's SPEAKING:
POINT: Compassion starts with seeing! It is fulfilled with an action

How important is "seeing"? Here is what Helen Keller thought about "seeing":
"Miss Keller can you imagine anything worse than being blind all your life?"
She replied: "Yes, I can. It would be far worse to have sight all your life and not be able to see!

Can you see? But, more importantly, can you see what Jesus saw? Just what did He see? How was He able to see?

1. He saw!
2. He had compassion on the multitudes!

He had compassion! Where did He get it?

His Father - The ultimate in love and compassion! (It's all throughout His Book!)

EX 3:9-10 - *"I have indeed seen the oppression of my people. I have heard their groans and have come down to set them free!"*

We too, must see, identify with the people; hear, take action and be prepared to "deliver".

PS 10:7-18 - *You hear, O Lord, the desire of the afflicted; you encourage them, and you listen to their cry, defending the fatherless and the oppressed, in order that man, who is of the earth, may terrify no more.*

Compassion is best defined as pity for the suffering or distress of another with a desire to help. Biblical compassion is not measured by how I feel but what I do in response to how I feel.

BIBLICAL COMPASSION ALWAYS LEADS TO ACTION

Compassion causes a yearning deep in the bowels over the afflictions of another; grief or pain awakened by the misfortunes or sorrows of others. For Jesus, He saw the misery of the people and wanted to give the Father's mercy. His greatest compassion was that for souls among the destitute and weary; the oppressed and harassed; the hopeless and outcast; the poor (The banquet table of Luke 14:15-24)

And when He saw that the "church" and the religious leaders were putting burdens on the people His compassion heightened to the point that "He wept".

EXTRA: And His first instruction to His disciples was to pray for the workers of the harvest...There is a great harvest; don't pray for for the harvest (it is already His), but rather pray for the workers of the harvest. Pray:

1. Is 6:8: Here am I! Send me!

2. Then send other workers to go with me because He who wins souls is wise. Prov 11:30

Therefore, it is very clear that compassion is not passive; not an emotion; not a feeling. Compassion is an action rising out of the pity for the suffering or distress of another.

Jesus had eyes that could see like no man. He had eyes that saw with the compassion of His Father for His people. Jesus could see the internal as well as the external suffering of a harassed and helpless people. And it caused Him to weep over entire cities. A weeping that came from deep within. It was as an eruption much like the fire building in the heart of Jeremiah to preach the Gospel (Jer 20:12)

And it was out of this compassion that Jesus did His works of healing, deliverance and raising the dead.

Compassion starts with seeing and results in "going" and reaching out or touching in some manner!

CLOSING THOUGHTS ON COMPASSION

Don't Pastor David VanCronkhite's words above just burn in your gut? Are you not stirred?
Well if you are now, which I pray that you are, I am adding the following tips that can help as you begin to do ministry in an area you may have not worked before. So, take these thoughts and be prepared. This work is messy, it is not easy, it is dangerous (read my other book) and it can cost you your very life. Actually, it will cost you everything. So, be ready up front. And do not let the BAD stop you. Read one book by Jackie Pullinger called, "Chasing the Dragon" and another on Compassion by Henri Nouwenn. With that said, here are my quick tips.

SOME TIPS FOR GROWING IN MINISTERING THROUGH COMPASSION:

1- Never minister alone.
2- Don't be stupid.
3- Pray with your eyes open!
4- Prayer walking before activity is always a great start.
5- Research the area. Use news, web, etc. Then pray over what you find.
6- Learn names and remember them.
7- Picking up trash, giving away groceries, smiling, praying for people's needs, and just showing kindness wherever possible are inexpensive ways to start as GOD leads.
8- Lift Jesus up from the beginning. Pray before you go, as you go and when you return.
9- Begin with worship and listen to where the Spirit leads and ask HIM for a first step or a first place to join HIM.
10- You are not the great hope. You come to serve. It's your honor to get the opportunity to join GOD in serving the community.
11- Listen, don't tell.
12- Learn and go as a student.
13- Be aware of your surroundings.
14- Engage the kids. Back yard Bible clubs work well and show all that

you care and demonstrate your love as well. Play with the kids in a meaningful and safe way. Throw a football. Kick a soccer ball. Be there and have fun with them.

15- You can always give, you don't always give what they ask for.

16- Girls need to be careful allowing men to hug them. Cover themselves and half hug with authority.

17- You are not the savior. NEVER FORGET THIS!

18- Ask Holy Spirit for compassion.

19- Remember that they do not need you, they need Jesus. You need them to see Jesus!

20- It is a command that we take care of the poor, however, Jesus said the poor we will always have with us and it is a greater command to love HIM first!!!!!! We minister first to HIM and washing HIS FEET! Do not do this work without staying intimate and abiding in the Presence of GOD.

CLOSING THOUGHTS ON COMPASSION

At any rate, we can always give. Even though we may not always give what people ask. After having a few life years of living with homeless and seeing them become successful, I know it isn't always cut and dry and not always easy to just use a template when dealing with people.

So, let's take a long walk with her. I know you already have and I am so proud of you for doing it. Christianity and the life of Jesus is messy. I love making room for the messy and we as a community need to learn to have the capacity for failure and messiness and the parental capacity to Father them out of it. That is not enabling. It's empowering.

"The stiff and wooden quality of our religious lives is a result of a lack of Holy desire." -A W Tozer   Jackie Pullinger's book, "Chasing the Dragon" is great to read for perspective as well as Bob Lupton's "Theirs is the Kingdom."

"Let's not become hardened just because they steal our TV." -David VanCronkhite

We have capacity. I will never forget John Bryant "JB" who was murdered doing Kingdom work. His life was not taken by a kid stealing his stuff. It was already given to Jesus many years before. No one can take what was already "given."

THANK YOU'S

I want to say a few thank you's. Thank you to Lori for being there through it all. Thank you to my kids for being used by GOD in teaching me what I needed to share. Thank you to my mom for your support these last years. Thank you to Johnny Crist for giving me a shot. Thank you Daniel (G-hoon) Kim for being my "2x2" and a true comrade all these years since college. You and I have walked this stuff. Thank you to Holy Spirit for talking inside my head. Thank you to Tapestry for being the testing ground. Thank you to all the ministries I've been in for the lessons learned. Thank you Temple Baptist Church for allowing me to see Revival up close and personal for the first time in my life. Thank you Blood-n-Fire Ministries for "the Streets" and the chances to walk with the greats of our time, to Alan Smith for finding me again, and to Gospelway Baptist for pouring life back into me! Thank you to Patrick and Su for pastoring the church I discipled them in. What an honor!

Thank you to YOU, Jesus for YOUR sacrifice on the cross. I have no words for what YOU mean to me.

APPENDIX

Timeline of GOD's Activity

I am adding something I did years ago when Dr. Henry Blackaby told me to study the history of revivals. I did study revivals and the great men and women of GOD. I have and am attempting to do what they did right and not do what they did wrong. And to this day, I am always joining the Father where HE is working and not becoming a mediocre preacher. I have fire because HE has me!

So, this timeline of movements of GOD is here for my kids. Just in case their stories are hard to find, if you find this book, you can see one long history of GOD's movements through our times. And don't trust just anything that gives dates and stories. I wrote these accounts down from eyewitness accounts and first hand biographies and autobiographies, some of which I have collected that are not registered anywhere and some never knew they were in print.

Get the fire in your belly and never let it go! GRRRRR!

Lightning Struck

A History Of Christian Revivals

"If I shut up the heavens so that there is no rain, or if I command the locust to devour the land, or if I send pestilence among My people, and My people who are called by My name humble themselves and pray, and seek My face and turn from their wicked ways, then I will hear from heaven, will forgive their sin, and will heal their land."

- 2 Chr. 7:13-14

DUSTIN HEDRICK

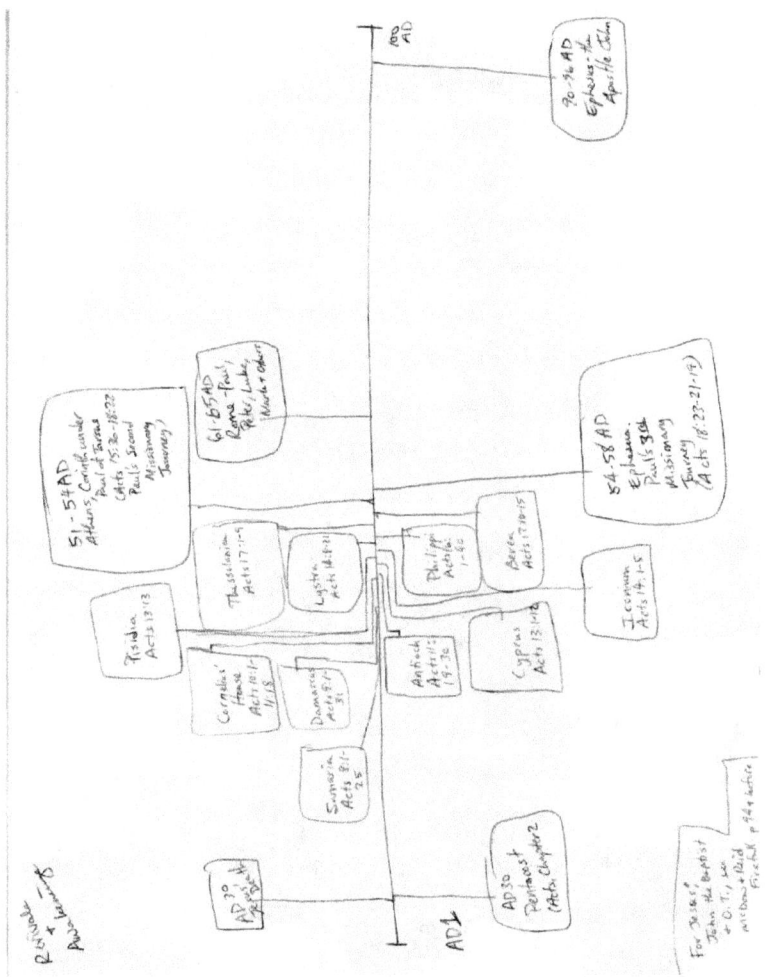

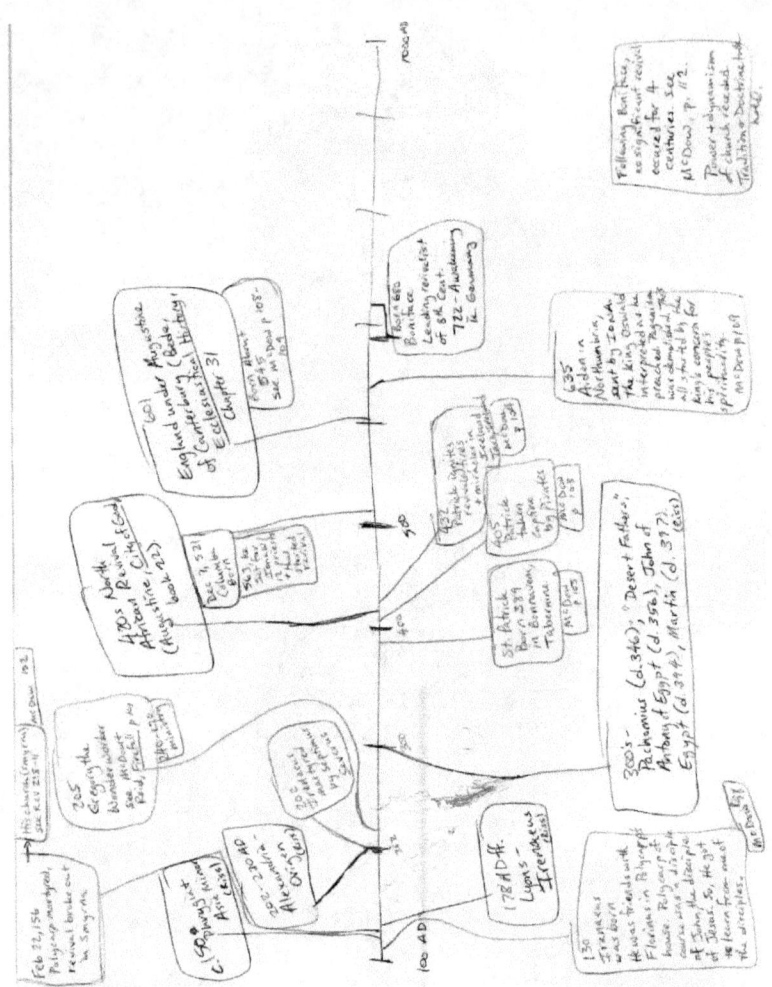

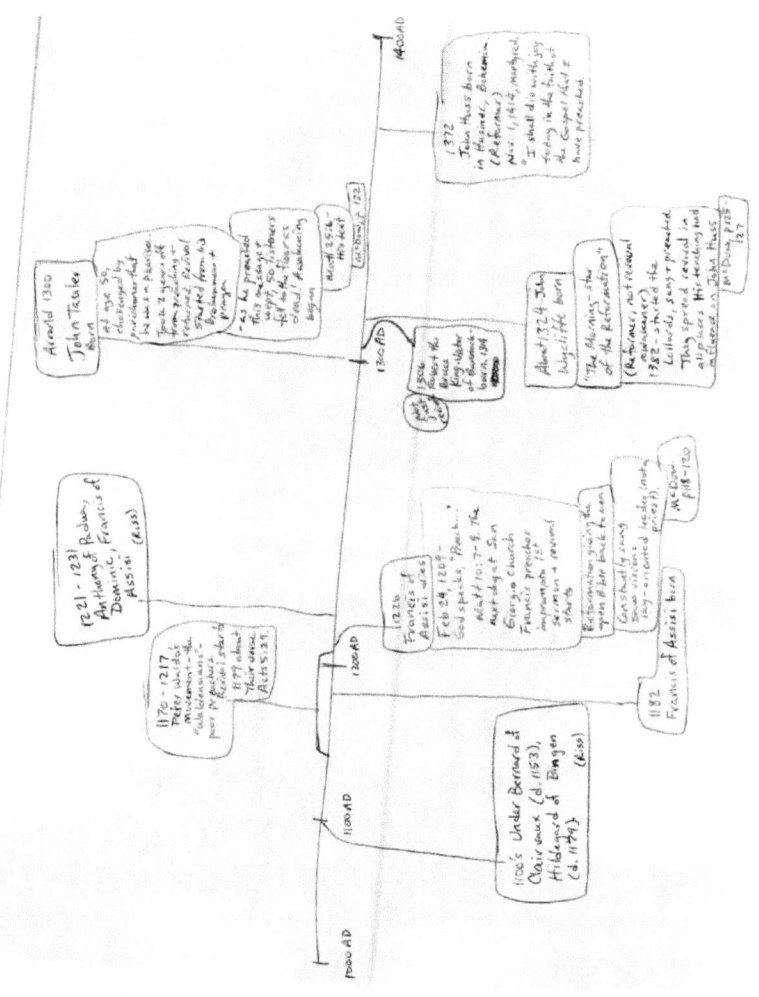

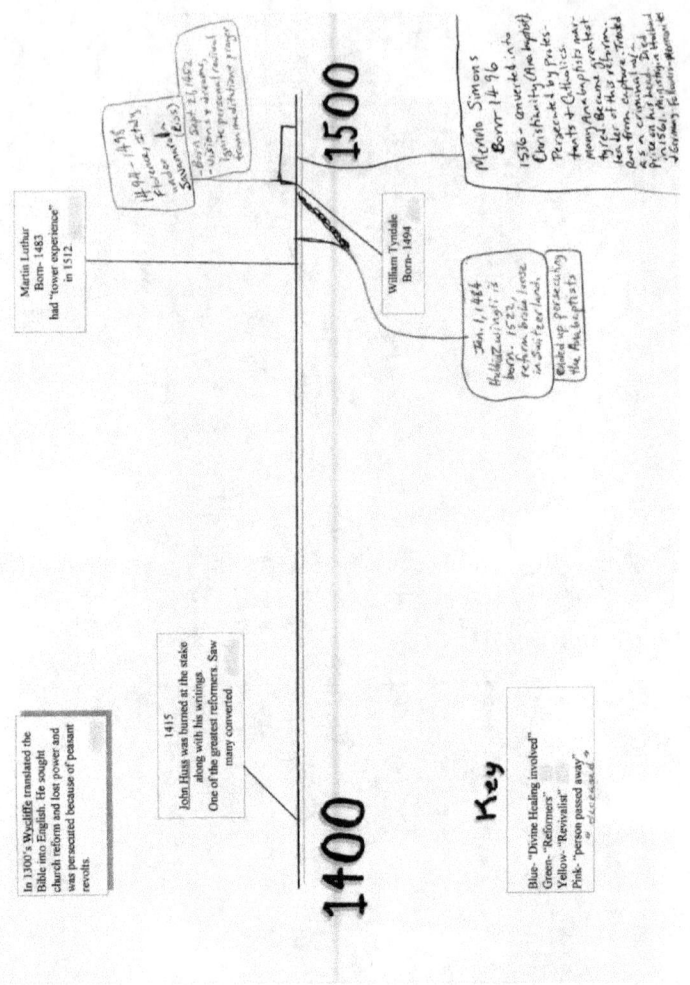

THE WARRIOR'S MANUAL

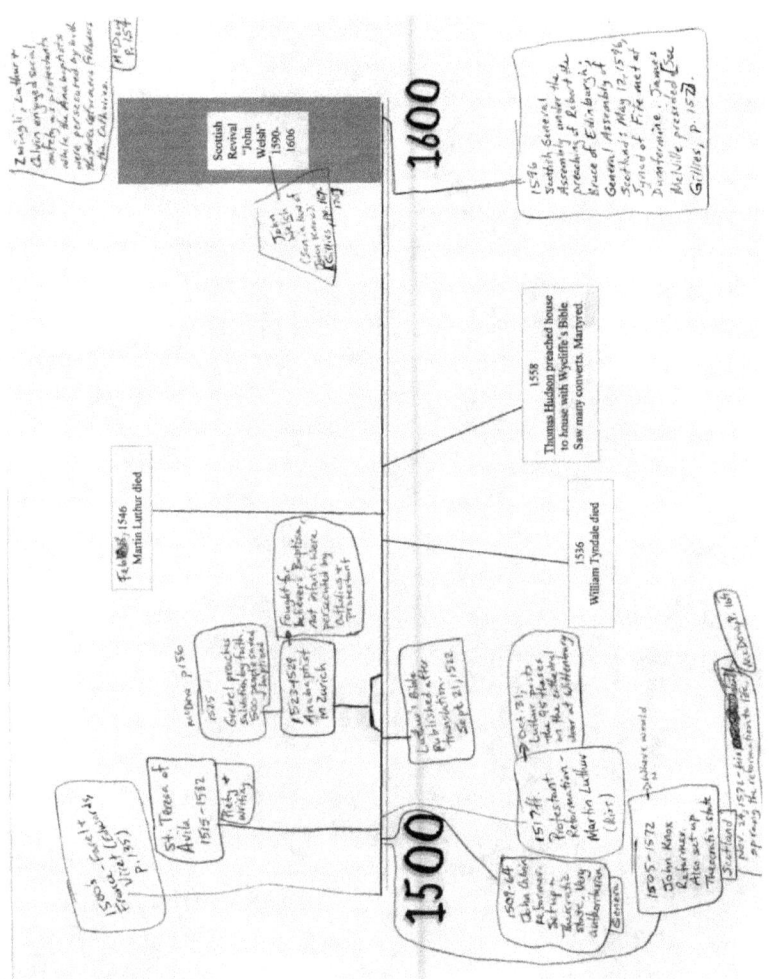

253

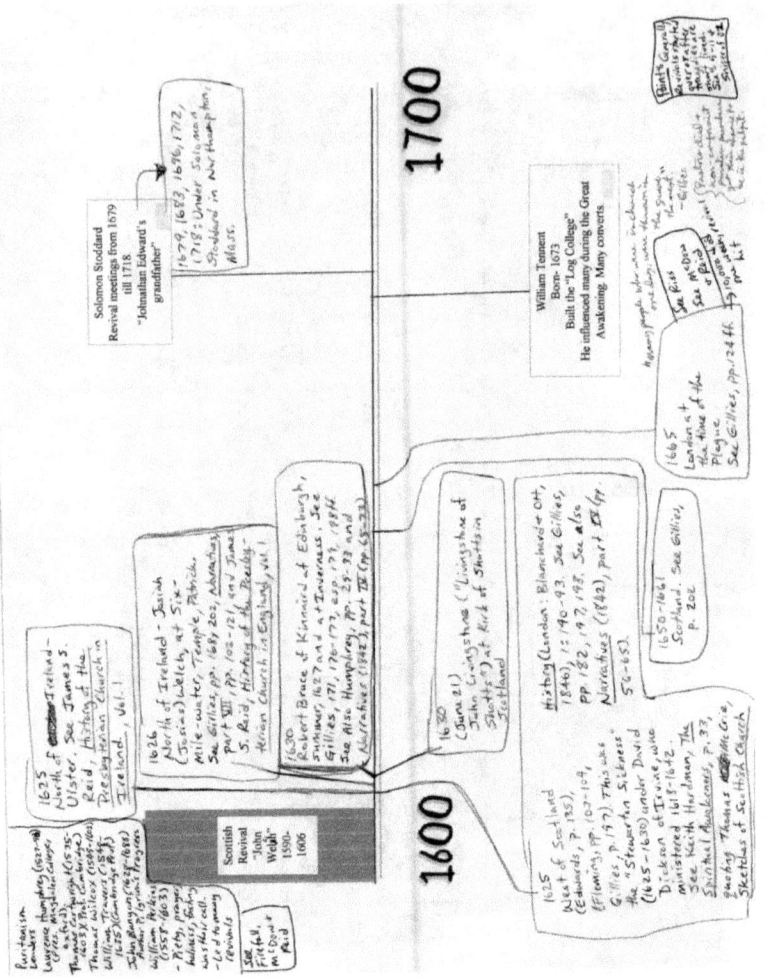

THE WARRIOR'S MANUAL

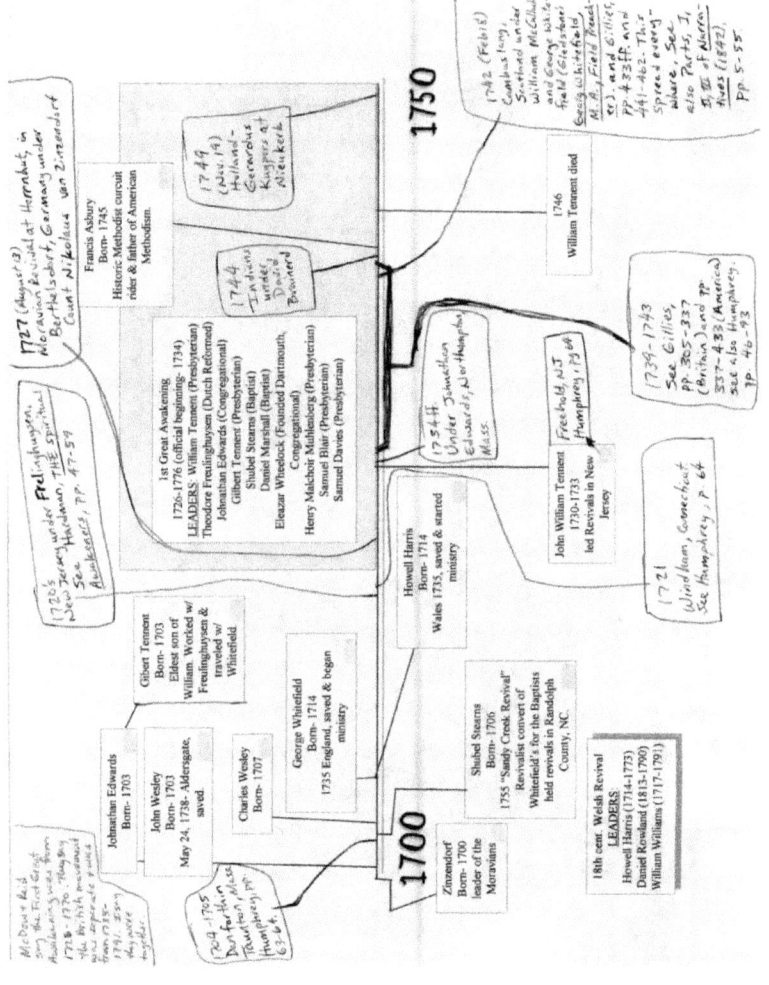

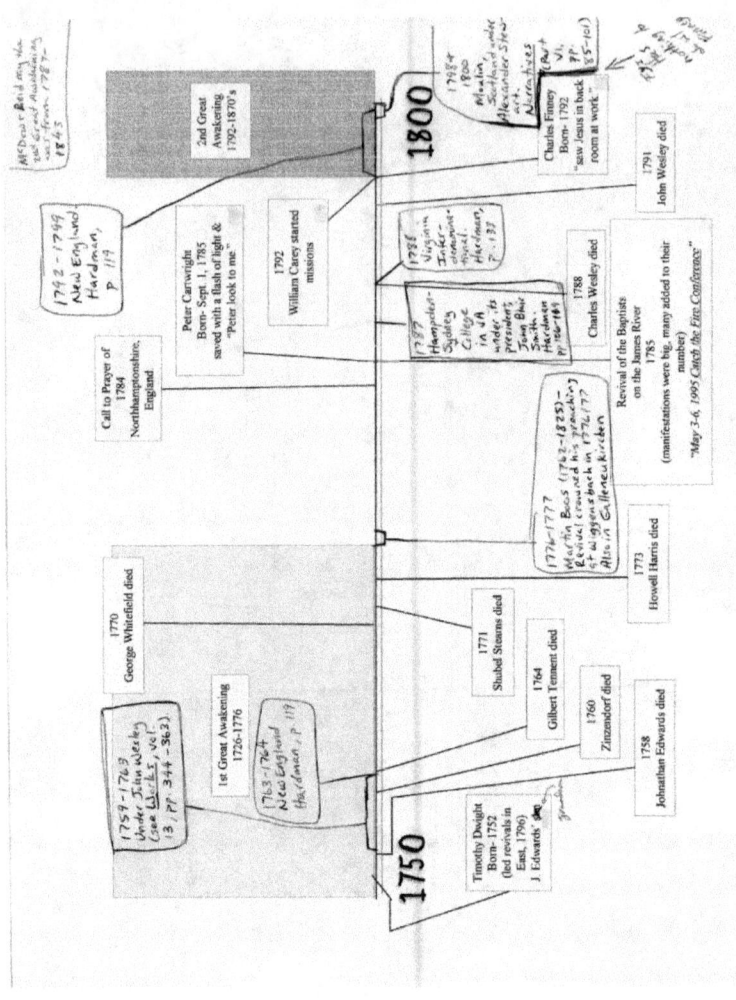

THE WARRIOR'S MANUAL

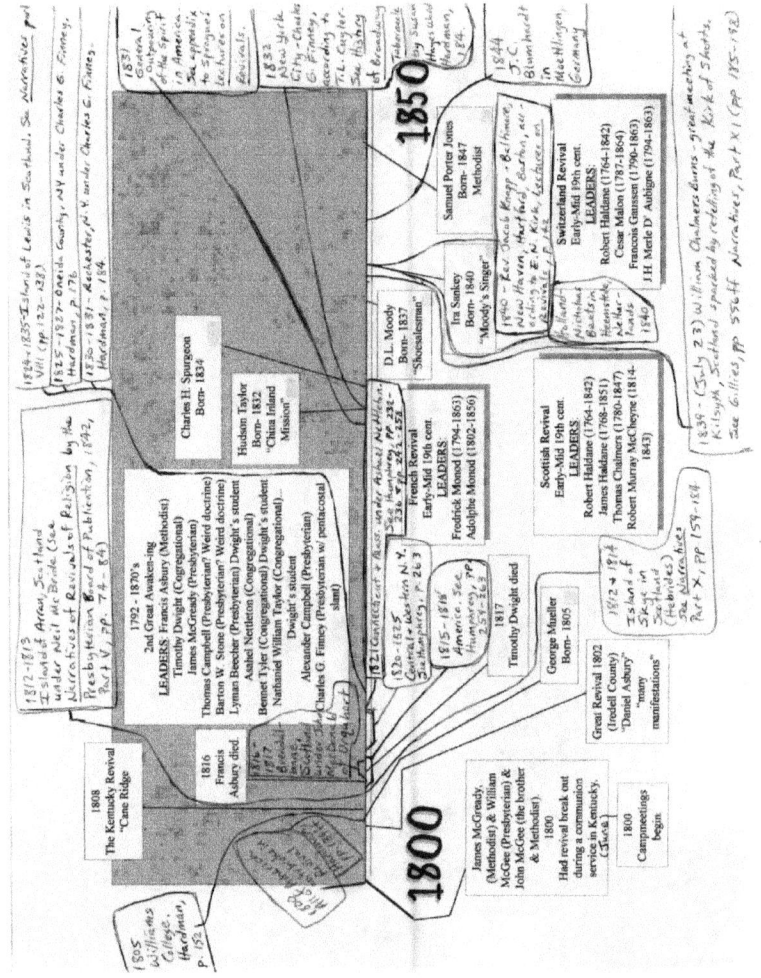

257

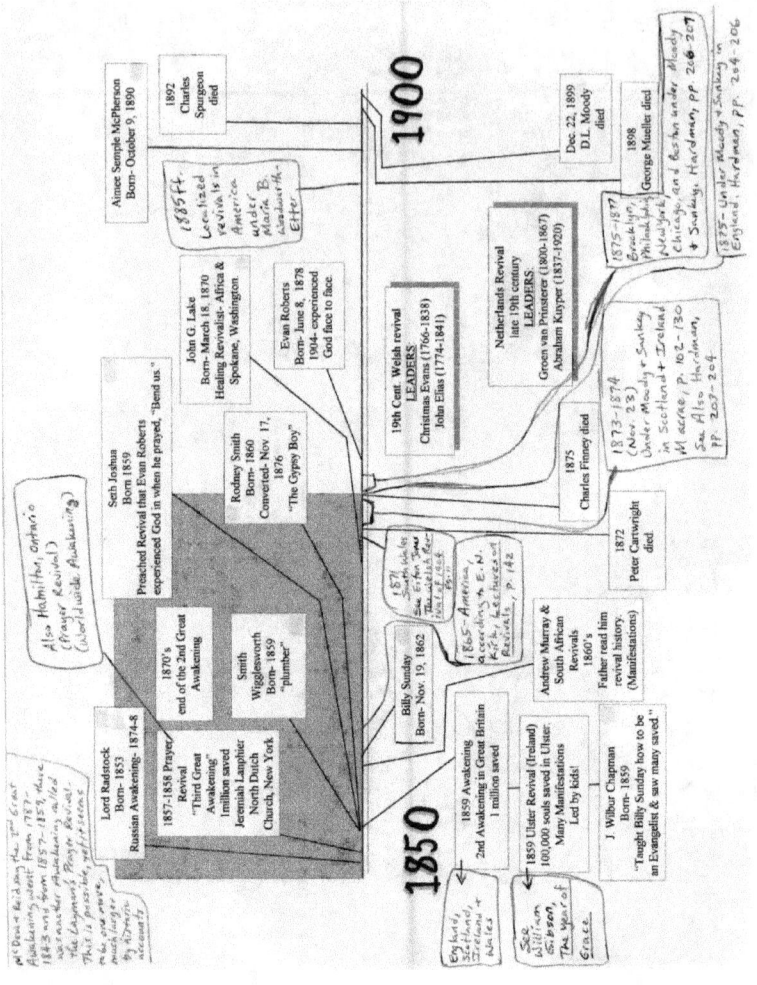

THE WARRIOR'S MANUAL

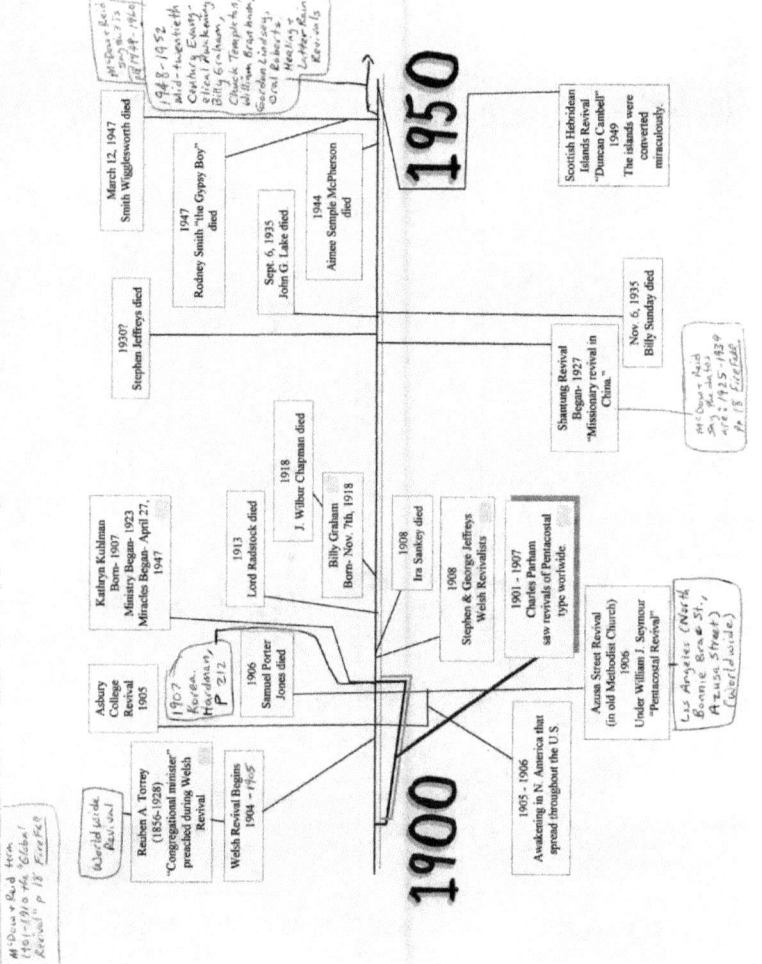

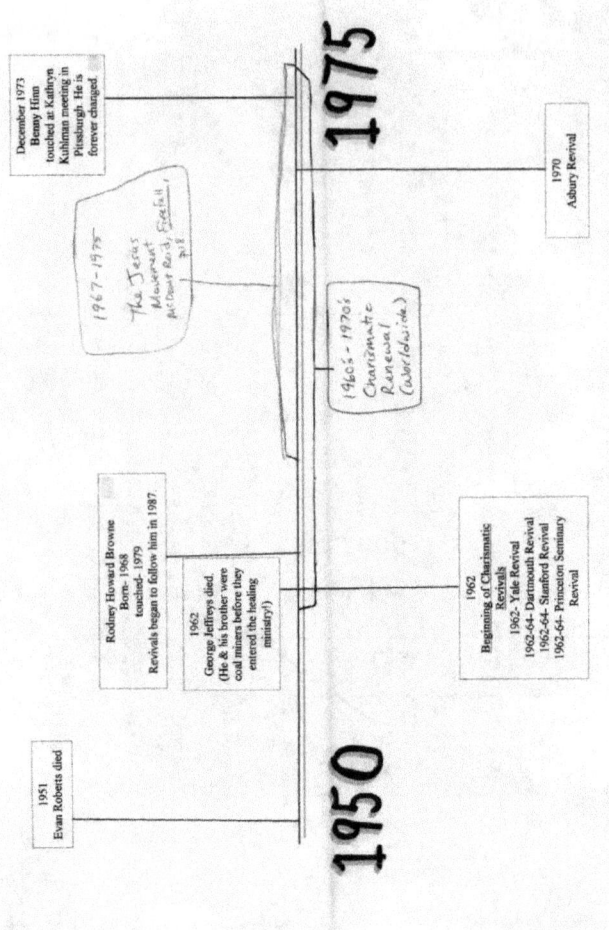

THE WARRIOR'S MANUAL

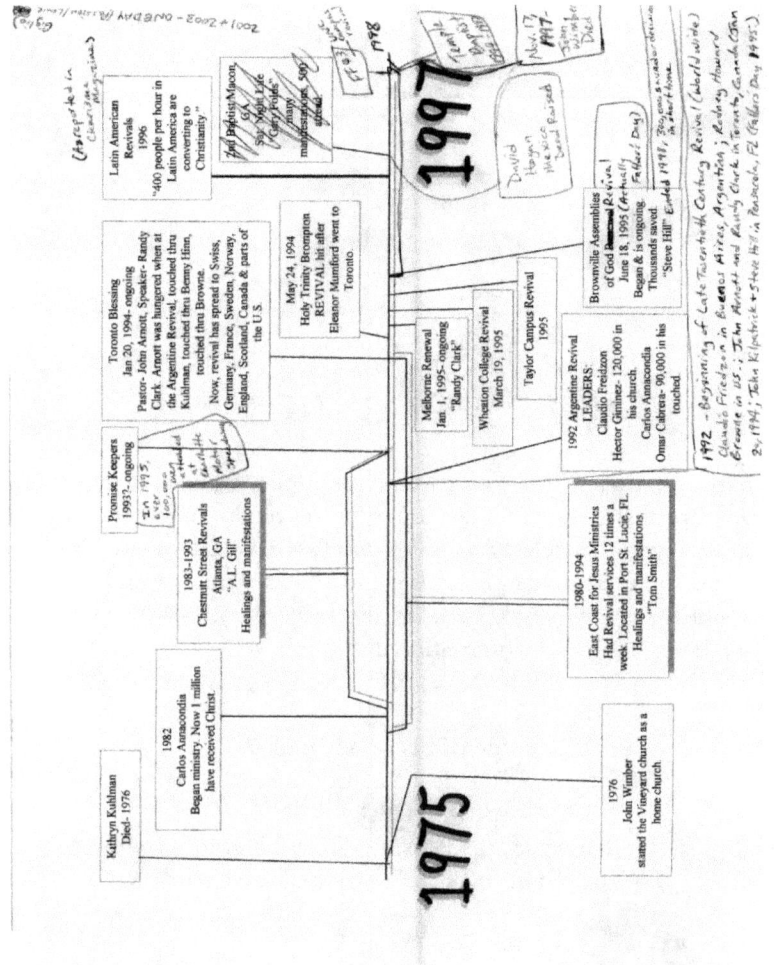

ABOUT THE AUTHOR

A husband, a father, 20 year minister, church planter, pastor, inner-city missionary, evangelist, artist, IT Developer, entrepreneur, micro-enterprise developer and world traveler. And most of all, a devoted lover of Jesus Christ. He has founded four non-profits and coached many more church plants, business startups, entrepreneurs and leaders both nationally and internationally.

See some of his other books:
The Forest Fire
GOD Spells Love, "T-I-M-E"
Whoever Has Ears, Let Them Here
So You Want to Be A Warrior of the Cross

www.dustinhedrick.com

Go Through the Overflowing Life Site:
www.overflowing.life

The adventure continues . . .

Go Deeper with more resources here:

http://www.dustinhedrick.com

Stay in touch with the author via:

Facebook: https://www.facebook.com/dustinhedrick

Twitter: http://twitter.com/dustin_hedrick

Instagram: http://instagram.com/dustin_hedrick

Youtube: https://goo.gl/6VtVZr

Soundcloud: http://soundcloud.com/dustinhedrick

Also, we welcome you to join us on our family Vlog, "Fascinated With Jesus." We as a family are living the Kingdom Family values every day.

FWJ: http://www.fascinatedwithjesus.tv

Facebook: https://goo.gl/20vixT

Twitter: https://twitter.com/jesusfascinated

Instagram: https://instagram.com/jesusfascinated/

www.ingramcontent.com/pod-product-compliance
Lightning Source LLC
LaVergne TN
LVHW051545070426
835507LV00021B/2416